Also by Agnes de Mille

SPEAK TO ME, DANCE WITH ME
DANCE IN AMERICA
RUSSIAN JOURNALS
LIZZIE BORDEN: A DANCE OF DEATH
THE BOOK OF THE DANCE
TO A YOUNG DANCER
AND PROMENADE HOME
DANCE TO THE PIPER

Where the Wings Grow

AGNES DE MILLE

Where the Wings Grow

DOUBLEDAY & COMPANY, INC., GARDEN CITY, NEW YORK
1978

Lines of lyrics from "We'll to the Woods No More," by A. E. Housman, from *The Collected Poems of A. E. Housman,* Copyright 1922
by Holt, Rinehart and Winston. Copyright 1950 by Barclays Bank Ltd.
Reprinted by permission of Holt, Rinehart and Winston, Publishers.

Library of Congress Cataloging in Publication Data
De Mille, Agnes.
Where the wings grow.

1. De Mille, Agnes.   2. Choreographers—United States
—Biography.   I. Title.
GV1785.D36A39   792.8'2'0924
ISBN: 0-385-12106-7
Library of Congress Catalog Card Number 76-18339

To Dr. Fred Plum
Dr. George Gorham
and to Walter Prude

Acknowledgments

I am deeply indebted to Dr. James Morley, head of East Asian studies at Columbia University, for historical facts and information about Japan; to Fuki Wooyenaka Uramatsu for information about her country and her father and for her kindness in reading the script in its various stages; to Jane George Werner and Mary Beatrice Badger Grove, to George Braga, to Edward Seeley of Forestburg, Sullivan County, for pictures, memorabilia, and memories; to Beatrice (Little Bea) Atkinson Wharton who, until her death, was enormously effective and generous; to Jonathan Prude for criticism and practical advice; to Mary Green, who steadfastly transcribed my dreadful left-handed manuscript and gave me hope; to Pauline Forbes, whose devoted labor in carrying and handling the manuscript and running messenger to the Xerox machine surpassed patience; and, above all, to Kate Medina, who believed in the book from the day she first read the rough notes and persevered through difficult and tedious times, undaunted, to shape the story. Her excellent guidance has been a life line, as has her unfailing cheer.

List of Illustrations

Elizabeth de Mille Pitman and her mother, Aunt Bettie.

Aunt Bettie in her wedding dress.

Ruth, our cook.

Mamie Harlow, our nurse.

following page 144

My sixth birthday party with bows and wreaths.

Maggie Ming in dress-up as bride.

Mother, Grandmother (Bibi) de Mille's English sister, J. I. C. Clarke, Aunt Bettie, Auntie Clarke, listening to J.I.C.'s poetry.

Sho-Foo-Den.

Caroline.

following page 192

Captain Ebenezer Hitch and Mary Fields Hitch, at the time of their marriage.

Caroline Hitch at eighteen.

Mama in her white French house cap.

Marie Morelle Septima Hitch George, as I knew her.

Jo, Jr.; Jokichi Takamine; Eben.

Jane, Caroline, Marie, Beatrice George.

Lady Caroline with Dr. Takamine and Jo.

Lady Caroline.

"Little Bea"—Beatrice Margaret Atkinson.

"Stand up," said Martha Graham to a pupil
(John Butler), hitting him on the back.
"Keep your shoulders straight. Never forget—
this is where the wings grow."

Chapter 1

❧ It used to take six hours to get there, three trains and a ferry across the Hudson, and past Tuxedo, Harriman, Middletown, and Hartwood; fashionable places to which neither we nor anyone we knew had ever been invited. The entire family with bags, boxes, and baskets, the domestic staff with enormous packages of supplies to last the summer, the children lugging games and dolls; the trunks followed. The trip was long and boring for the children and exasperating for the grown-ups. And there were waits at the way stations, and we arrived dirty from the wood-burning locomotive, since every time the engine puffed the soot came through the windows. When the train whistle shrieked in the wilderness, flocks of birds started up and whirled away over the endless wooded hills.

At St. Joseph station a wagon waited drawn by two large stamping farmhorses with Frank Felter sitting high in the driver's seat. Next day he would come back and fetch the trunks. He drove down the rocky mountain roads through the spring dusk, the three miles to our house.

"May flies are in fine shape," said Father to God and the landscape. "The fish will be biting." And to Frank, "Has Fred started to roll the tennis courts?"

"Too wet." Frank squirted tobacco juice obliquely so as to miss our laps. I admired Frank. "A skunk died in the George cellar."

"That means sulfur candles," said Mother and sighed. "When did you find out?"

There was a long pause during which the horses clopped and swished their tails. "Made sure yesterday. But I had a hunch it died in November."

"How did you know it was there?"

Frank laughed.

"Well, why didn't you get him out sooner?"

"Why should I? Nobody wanted the cellar this winter. We'll get him out tomorrow. He's easier now than last month."

"I'll help," I offered brightly. "It'll be interesting."

"No," said Father.

"She couldn't use sulfur candles," said my little sister flatly. "We've never had them before." She put her thumb in her mouth and went to sleep.

I sat high up in front with Frank Felter and stared at the horses' magnificent rumps lifting and sinking before me. Suddenly a tail rose and a giant defecation tumbled down.

"Oh, look!" I cried in admiration, so round, so richly colored, so glossy, so steaming, so much better than I could do. "Look, he's done it!"

"Yes, dear," said Mother, "the pretty curled ferns! It will be a lovely summer."

"Ah, the innocent babe," sighed Mamie, our nurse, and creaked in her starch and stays.

"Naughty," said my baby sister waking up. She understood nothing but sensed that older sister had somehow lost caste for one glorious moment. The tail went down, the rump rocked rhythmically; the patient maned heads nodded; thin iron-rimmed wheels slithered and squeaked on the stony road and all the forest rustled as it prepared for our summer. We were going into our green home and I would be free and wild for the months and weeks and days before me, days uncounted.

Father understood. He felt like an animal, he said. He wanted to get his muzzle on the ground and dig with his claws. He smelled with his skin. Mother loved the color and revivifying odors but wildness really meant windows to shut and drawers to clean out. Wet feet meant colds which she, not Father, tended.

At our house Mamie and Ruth remarked about the damp and threw open windows, lit the wood stove and fiddled loudly with dampers and pot lids and started to get supper.

There was audible feminine horror at the discovery of small winter tragedies—the mouse that couldn't get out of the sugar bowl, the mouse that had succumbed to too much soap, the porcupine that couldn't get out of the guest room (I wept when I saw how the trapped creature had gnawed at the window frame), the starlings that had made a nest in the stove pipe and cried most piteously for minutes when we lit the kindling. My horrified attention was diverted by Mother's triple salutation when she found an entire live nest of baby shrews in her stockings, pale, pink, and palpitating; and then Father's hearty "Good Lord, Anne, here's the chocolate I thought Nettie had stolen!" And, indeed, there it was, lined neatly behind the drawers and forgotten by the chipmunks who had planned a well-stocked winter. I thought of them, hungry and disappointed, pressing their tiny inadequate skulls to their lean ribs in frozen holes.

There was always a peculiar smell to the closets, the Merriewold smell. The clothes smelled of damp, stale and woodsy, and of mouse, very odd. Mother used lavender everywhere.

Then I discovered there were stairs. I, who had spent eight

months in a New York flat, went up and down and up and down again until Mother put her hands to her head and begged me to "sit still, dearie, just for a few minutes."

And then I discovered that the front door led directly to outside and the earth. In and out and in and stamp on the ground where there was new grass and violet leaves, and out of the parlor and put your feet on the earth without waiting for Mamie or the elevator or the doorman, go out alone and stamp directly on the ground! And do it again. And begin again and again. "Well, at least she'll sleep," said Mother.

And then the first whip-poor-will called.

"Anne," said Father, slipping his arm around her waist, "we're home again. We're in our forest."

That Mother and Father were in love I knew as I knew that the woods were green and budding. They walked hand in hand; I remember them picking lilies of the valley as the first birds called, and the look he bent upon her, and the blue dazzle of her return gaze. The whole forest quickened for me. The world thrilled. Everything was beginning and the good, free summer lay ahead. The three-tone call of the wood thrush became their personal whistle—their signal to one another when they wanted to summon each other in the garden or in the forest. (A woman's voice calling was a kind of household musical signature. Each mother and aunt had her own little cadence which punctuated from time to time, like bird notes, the comfortable kitchen and household noises.) And every spring when I hear the thrush my heart shakes. Mother and Father loved absolutely. This was the meaning of the place, of Merriewold; this green secret; this expectancy.

I awakened with the first birds and lay in the cocoon of my mosquito netting. And then came the beginning domestic sounds, the creaking of the iron roller as Fred Felter rolled the tennis court under my window, the slamming of the kitchen screen door. If it had stormed in the night the nursery floor would be wet with rain, and the maple trees glistening, and there beneath me, crouching, would be Fred painting the tennis court lines freshly with white paint. He did this every day.

We had a large breakfast with cereal (cream of wheat bearable, oatmeal not and never mind about iron and bones). And then fresh strawberries or huckleberries (gathered by all of us in sunbonnets and with tin pails tied around our necks) and peaches and milk from the neighborhood cows. And then—out! To mud-pies and my imaginary pals, Gockle, who waited for me in the bracken, or Dickie, who waited at his rock.

And then at eleven the walk to the lake and swimming with water-wings or Mother's hand under my chin. All the ladies wore serge suits and black stockings and canvas shoes and they smelled of wet cloth and lake water. We dressed in primitive houses with the lake water lapping at the boat bottoms, and the light reflections rippling up the walls, the arrowroot and iris and jewel-weed in the marshy margins under the gangplanks, and also snakes. Sometimes the snakes came into the boat locks. And always the dragonflies and daddy longlegs. And the smell of lake water and wet pine planks and old bathing dresses pervaded. We all dressed naked before one another until thirteen and then the older girls hid themselves, and it was sort of sad. The grown-ups went through damp intricate rituals of drying and dressing under clinging serge. But the body was sacred and our mothers and aunts were altogether pure and they had to care for our young sensibilities which a glimpse of their bare flesh might alter. Body hair was particularly risky.

On the big maple tree by the dam there was a rope on which six generations of children have swung and dropped into the deep water. Whenever it frayed past repair, somebody has replaced it and we have always had a swinging rope. I learned to my delight that in October, after all the summer visitors had left, the sisters from St. Joseph's used to trespass in order to swing on the rope. And there they were with habits and wimples flying. One or two got deliciously dunked.

Father seldom went swimming. In the mornings he wrote plays in a small house in the woods and no one for any reason whatever might go near him, nor play in the vicinity, nor shout. At one o'clock Mother rang a bell for lunch.

When it rained and we couldn't go swimming there was fudge in the kitchen, and licking the pots, and taffy pulling, which was very hard and fun, and Parcheesi, and sitting and looking at the bound *Harper's,* Howard Pyle's knights and Edwin Abbey's "Shakespeare Scenes," and Elizabeth Shippen Green's pictures of children like us, doing all the things we did, but cleaner. We looked at them sitting in the bay window while the rain drummed on the tin roof. And after the rain there were rubber boots and finding red salamanders, or walking barefoot in the wet grass, or walking barefoot in the mud, a highly sensual experience. When it rained the mothers did absolutely nothing but amuse us. We demanded that because they were responsible.

If the ladies did not go swimming on good days they gathered on a porch and read aloud or, not infrequently, listened to J. I. C. Clarke read his poems. These poems were not only very bad but also very long, requiring the heart of the morning to get through. As he thundered, the ladies thought of their domestic concerns, and hand-hemmed pure linen napkins, hand-initialed tea-cloths on embroidery hoops, with Japanese floss so fine and delicately shaded that it was kept in linen cases like pastel crayons, and split for the finest stitches of a single thread in the cloth. Mother was adept at this. She made the fine-boned lace collars that covered her throat, the lace coverings of every piece of silk that touched her flesh at wrist or neck, the frills and jabots, the bands, and belts; the lace ruffles on petticoats, with beading of ribbons running in and out (and after every washing and starching fresh ribbons had to be threaded through with a special bodkin—I loved to help at this).

Her work box was a tool chest of formidable effectiveness. She wore her mother's gold thimble. She was a master cutter and embroiderer and a witch with a sewing machine. Her skill was a matter of emotional importance. She considered it a breach of motherhood to buy anything for us not homemade except, possibly, shoes. It seemed a weakening of allure to put garments between her body and her dress that she had not stitched exquisitely with anticipation.*

The ladies sipped lemonade and chattered for hours, lightly, musically, and quietly. They did not have to raise their voices as there were no sounds at all in the surroundings to be shouted over (no planes, for instance, no cars). You could hear, through a closed window, feet walking on dirt. Today throats are rasped by cigarette smoke and by shouting over traffic and radio. All the mechanical wonders which lighten women's work or enliven their leisure are noisy, from the Waring mixer and vacuum cleaner to air conditioning and TV. As a result voices have grown in volume and deteriorated in quality. The deeper and more masculine timbre has become acceptable, the bell-like soprano almost obsolete. My mother was bell-toned.

When I think of our mothers it is sitting in the leaf shadows, embroidering. They were dressed mostly in white or pale pastels. The ladies cooed and sipped as they chattered. They did not gossip. Gossip was for behind locked bedroom doors and never,

* Mother's dresses for me are now in the Museum of the City of New York, and her trousseau is in the Fashion Institute.

never before the young, who were called "little pitchers." And it was never, never about their husbands. Disloyalty to one's husband was considered lower than disloyalty to one's country— almost as low as disloyalty to one's sex—and loyalty to one's sex meant never, under any circumstances, making love to someone else's husband or destroying another woman's reputation, which was her livelihood as well as her chance for happiness.

My mother's favorite household motto was, "Control yourself." My uncle, Cecil de Mille, always claimed that no lady could become an actress because the restraints she had submitted to prevented her from any visible emotional release. The one factor overlooked in this pronouncement is talent.

A lady used first names only for friends and for the people she cared about, and she felt no lack of friendliness in preserving formalities. The terms of address had for her importance. No shop girl ever called her "darling," no servant "dearie," no man, whoever he might be, "doll," saving only her legal master.

The ladies of Merriewold all seemed to me to be friends, because they were so much finer than we children who hated one another and were mean. But if ever one of the grown-ups slipped, if one of them broke "the code," the ladies were merciless. No expiation, no remorse could buy back forgiveness. This hard attitude was less a matter of morals than the necessity of preserving the economic structure, scab labor being tolerated here no more than in other quarters. This is one of the reasons they were so hard about the child, Laura Graves, who put up her hair at fourteen and used lipstick. It was thought she was a border-line case. She was young and she was pretty, but she was "not quite fine," and this went for her mother, too.

After the reading sessions the ladies walked home under broiderie anglaise parasols and had lunch with their children and

husbands. Lunch was the big meal of the day and hot with lots of garden vegetables and Mother's wonderful spices and condiments. All meals were cooked on wood-burning stoves, even in August.

After naps we played in the woods or watched tennis or had birthday parties. We never went swimming in the afternoons because the house servants went swimming then and we weren't allowed in with them. There were no negroes, none at all. All the house servants were Irish Catholics, but naturally we weren't allowed to swim with them.

Once a week the butcher went around with his wagon, the meat packed in ice and a hanging scale on the back; twice a week the vegetable dealer came. You could tell the date within a week by what was for sale. I would leave off my interesting pursuits of stringing phlox blossoms on long grasses and run to watch. We could hear the creaking of wheels down the road and the clopping of horses' hooves, but the vendor also had a bell to announce his arrival at our path. The vegetables were kept under green nets. There were lots and lots of flies and sticky flypaper, blackdotted, hanging from the roof of the wagon. There were lots of flies in every kitchen, and the fly strips hung over the sinks and over the tables. We used fly swatters a lot, too, but strike and bat as much as we might, we made small inroads. Plenty of people still died of malaria and typhoid.

Meat didn't keep long. (The housekeepers had to plan exactly.) All produce was stored in our icebox, square and zinclined, the ice (cut from the lake in midwinter and packed in sawdust all summer) was taken from our particular icehouse (each domicile had one) by Fred Felter and hosed down before he chipped it to size and inserted it in the icebox.

Milk came every night in great closed tin pails. It was not pasteurized but we knew the cows personally.

The summer kitchen was a very interesting place, the hub of the domestic factory. There two busy people spent every day in neat cottons working hard at our most interesting preoccupation, which was, of course, eating. There were side benefits such as pots to lick and sugary spoons. There were bottles of the most astonishing oils and odors. There were tiny bottles put immediately out of our reach, marked with skull and crossbones, but there anyway, a terrible reminder of mortality in our gingham mornings.

There was always something to watch in the kitchen. Mayonnaise and whipped cream were made up as needed, and mayonnaise required an hour of beating and a strong arm. Ice cream was turned by hand in a home freezer packed round with the salt and cracked ice (cracked and chipped in a burlap bag with a pick and mallet by Fred Felter). Because food spoiled easily, and there were no preservatives; it was a choice of virgin fresh or botulism. In very truth, our lives were in Mother's hands.

And then at regular intervals during the summer Mother took over after early breakfast. There was a great industry in jam; strawberries early on and then plums, peaches, huckleberries and in the autumn the bag of purple grapes grown on our own arbor and dripping into a pan while the late bees buzzed. The tables were all covered with clean newspapers, and there, set in rows, were dozens of boiled Mason jars, dozens of boiled lids and rubber bands, hot, prophylactic, not to be touched, a pot of boiling paraffin, and then the mounds and mounds of berries picked by all of us (not Father, he was the thinker), our berries picked over and cleaned and boiled in sugar in bigger pots than are used in any private kitchen today. Mother applied the paraffin and screwed on the lids over the rubbers and wrote the labels and the lot was set on the back porch to cool and we had to tiptoe around. Mother was dewed with sweat and her hair stood in

golden squiggles. The day's jam was not considered work. It was a handy chore which she was proud to add to Father's table.

His handiness was the fresh trout he sometimes brought home after a day's solo outing on the Neversink, or the photos he developed, which were excellent.

Some other neighbors were more handy. Uncle John Moody, the financier (Moody's Investors Service), used to build all sorts of additions to his house and little hideaways from his family. These were hobbies. The jam, brandied fruit, cake, ice cream were not hobbies. They were not work either, not like what the men did. It was not paid for. Mother was supposed to act as though it hadn't happened or happened automatically in the inferior regions and not to be spoken of. It was uninteresting. On Father's approach she put it aside and rushed to make herself look lovely and leisurely; bath, violet water in her hair, fresh cotton lingerie, fresh voile dress, welcome neatness. When he tramped home, when he arrived through the woods after twelve hours of wading, damp, soiled, garlanded with dead trout, he rehearsed every cast and he kept stressing how interesting the new flies were. Father allowed as how the next day he would probably write some jolly good scenes down in the forest in his little writing house. And above all he stressed how healthy he felt. Mother blushed and put on her flounciest nightgown with the pink ribbons running through the eyelet embroidery and brushed her hair long and long in the candlelight, and then they shut the door tight and if I said I wanted a drink of water they were cross.

There was never any mistake about who Mother was and what her rights were.

Once on a walk someone said to Mamie, "I suppose you really are their mother? Their mother doesn't see them much?" Mamie simpered. But I, aged four, rose like a lion and put the matter straight. Mother was Mother. My devotion to Mamie did not touch this fact in any way.

Mother was indispensable in every situation in life, but sometimes I arranged for Father to be indispensable too. (I had to arrange this, with Mother there at every turn.) One spring I announced that I was not going to Merriewold with the family for the summer, but would spend the summer months with my great-grandmother Samuel. Mother was exasperated. "Don't you want the woods?" she begged. "No!" I snapped. "I want the striped awnings and city ice cream." Mother was baffled. I packed for the city. This went on for weeks.

Father stood over my crib dark and straight against the light. "Your mother tells me that you don't want to come to Merriewold."

"I want to stay with Gan," I murmured.

"Well, you're coming with us. It's decided."

"It doesn't matter what I say?"

"It doesn't matter a bit. Not one more word. It's settled; you're coming."

Oh peace, oh decision! Father had spoken. I was in his hands and safe.

Mother was decisive about other subjects. She knew about cold baths, fresh air, health foods, and bowel movements and about dosage. Cod liver oil, plain and undisguised, was administered by the tablespoonful every day in winter and castor oil every week, and oftener if I wanted to visit the family doctor, Dr. Mendelsohn, with whom I was infatuated. I took a full-sized tablespoon of castor oil without trimmings as a token of love because Mother said it would make him so happy.

The family medicine cabinet was of crucial service. In the woods there was no professional help. One midnight Auntie Black (she was not a real aunt, of course, just a good neighbor) came knocking at our door with the news that her little girl needed a doctor. Father dressed, walked the mile to Superintendant Moore's, borrowed a horse, and rode without light the six miles to Monticello. They arrived back with help just before dawn. That's how he was in those days; that's how all the neighbors were, and that's how isolated we were. But Auntie Black never forgot Father's kindness (nor his love for Mother—she didn't forget that either—"They used to walk the woods hand in hand. It was like a promise to all of us."). But mostly the mothers did without doctors and relied on their own knowledge and ingenuity. Grandma George once crammed an entire pound of country butter down a housemaid's throat and saved her from rat poison. Burns were also treated with butter. Purge was the rule and haste the condition, and no one lost her head or fainted until the crisis was over. And then she might lie down and remember how the finger hung by a thread or the face had turned blue in suffocation.

Insects caused not only bites but diseases and the diseases caused by insects or not were deadly. Malaria, typhoid, typhus, diphtheria, scarlet fever, whooping cough, no family escaped. Quarantine was a repeated condition. These were hardy women, even the ladies, and in their delicate and absolutely unnatural way they coped, and they coped with basic good sense, and they coped every day. They didn't talk about it to their men, however, not openly. They hoped to maintain the illusion that they were mysterious and very fine, "quite fine" as my mother would say. And they were. But in spite of their little stitches they lived very close to the bare earth. Anything physical was considered "low," unless it was chocolate ice cream. And yet they were involved with the physical more than we are because they had less to help them.

Garbage was disposed of according to taste. We had three pits.

One was for tin cans and bottles, not so very many; another for loose food, and the third for the accumulations from the out-houses, decanted twice weekly by Fred Felter with decent sprin-klings of lye and ashes. The flies hummed but not to much avail. Everything was cleanly buried under earth and ashes. Refuse in those days seemed to be no great problem. Some unfeeling families threw tin cans into the forest but, even so, the forest didn't die. It was large and we were few. The raccoons and the black bear helped clean up.

There were some few conveniences. Indoor plumbing, it is true, we had (some of the kitchen sinks had hand pumps and the grating of the handles was a happy morning sound) but no toi-lets, and the outhouses were reached through weather and were, of course, unheated and unlit, and pregnant women and the old and sick and very young had to make do. The alternate was chamber pots. Every bedroom had its crockery set and washstand, but not hot water, and accordingly the daily routine was time-consuming. Oil lamps were lovely but required constant care and were dangerous besides.

All the houses of Merriewold were built by journeymen car-penters and the plans, when there were any, were drawn on yel-low paper. The chimneys were stacked by the brick- or stone-layers and there were no engineers and no state examiners, no licenses or supervision and certainly no graduate architects. There were, also, no unions or requirements to meet, and in seventy-five years the roofs still hold without leaks and the chimneys still draw without smoke and the floors, except for occasional encoun-ters with carpenter ants or porcupine, are still true and unwarped. And in those weathers! Thirty degrees below and snow and ice for seven months, and in the summer endless rains.

We had lovely old-fashioned gardens and a quarter acre vege-table patch. Our paths were of tan bark, golden-red. In the great rotted black stumps of three-hundred-year-old oaks Mother planted nasturtiums. Everything grew, everything was jolly and robust, colorful and buzzing with bees.

The deer, very few, were shy and night or day came nowhere near the houses, so we could grow anything we liked without molestation, and since there had been a recent fire everything did grow, vegetables and flowers. The surrounding wall, three feet wide, was dry-stone and sturdily built with flat natural rocks on the top of which I could scamper followed haltingly by my baby sister, Margaret.

We had three natural pools of rock water, absolutely pure, and very cold. One was for prettiness with ferns and forget-me-nots, one was for drinking with a pump house and stained-glass windows, and one was for bathing. The men turned blue when they jumped in. I did not risk more than a hand. Nearby was Ann's Ledge, named for Mother; marvelous climbing rocks where I am certain black bears laired. I was forbidden to go there alone.

The drinking water tasted better than any water I have ever drunk in my life—alive, reassuring, rocky, delicious as the air which was new and fern-fresh. You took a breath and flew. It was the first time you had breathed. It cleared the head like snuff, colors deepened, hearing sharpened. The head was full of open responses.

And the silence: the glistening, rustling receptivity, with now and then the happening of a bird flute, a woodpecker's rhythmic threading, a snapped twig. It was life everywhere, and all one. You heard with your skin; you breathed light and shade; you participated; you were.

And you were free. Behind our house for three miles there was not a living habitation. Oddly enough, this condition still persists. And as before, there are no unfriendly strangers. None. The place is safe for children. And is still, years later. "How do I find Billy

Tobey?" asked my son once, aged three. "Straight down the road, turn left, and yell."

Supper was at six while Mother urged us on with the healthy parts we didn't particularly care for. And then by lamplight Mother or Father read. Father read *Uncle Remus* (Father was from North Carolina and could speak the dialect) or Kipling's *Just So Stories*. And then I sat on his lap in the growing dusk and listened to the whip-poor-wills, "the Wickie-Wees." Mother and Father sometimes went canoeing at sundown to watch the deer come down to drink, buck and does. And occasionally, if I promised not to speak or move, they sat me between them. Father paddled Indian style, without taking the paddle from the water, merely turning the blade. There was not even the sound of dripping or the noise of sucking and slapping rowboats make. We slid in the darkened waters. But, most often, they went alone just to be alone, and when I found myself left out I howled until I threw up. They paid not the slightest mind.

"Naughty girl," said Mother, "now it's time for bed. Kiss your father good night."

"I don't think so," said Father. "I'll kiss Miggie."

My little sister had been asleep all during my passion. She wasn't old enough yet to know how to be bad. I was led away bucketing with sobs, cast out. They were enough without me.

My relation with my sister Margaret varied. She was an intimate and she was my baby charge and I felt protective but not always. I couldn't stand her being pretty and helpless and meddling. I used to choke her, both hands around her throat. That stopped questions. Mother believed in Montessori and John Dewey, but she reverted to primitive discipline at this point.

"You won't stop doing this, will you?"

I smiled enigmatically. How could they stop me? Appeal to my chivalry? I had none.

"Now," said Mother practically, "I am going to choke you hard. And it will hurt." She put her dainty, little hands around my throat and pressed until my eyes started out.

Margaret regarded all this from the corner, and simpered wickedly. I didn't want to cry in front of her, but I did. It was really a surprising experience. It was, also, a salutary one.

Yet Margaret and I did everything together without really noticing one another, meals, bed, bedbugs (oh, that was a merry spring evening, with carbolic acid put into all the mattress tufts), berrying, wading, mud pies, swimming. Chickenpox, whooping cough, setting one another off in spasms. (I remember swinging on the specially stenciled curtains between the dining and living rooms and bringing them down and laughing and then both of us were sick all over the table and rug and Father was frighteningly cross. Then Mamie and Mother cleaned us up and put us to bed.)

Lacking brothers or other sisters, I suppose we were close. I know according to our ages we had the same interests, at first because she was little and droll, and later because she thought the things were funny that I thought were funny, and because being around all the time she spared me the trouble of explaining. But we must have had an intense sibling rivalry because I took a terrible revenge; I have forgotten her as a child. There are very few episodes I remember sharing. For her part she always believed Father and Mother loved me best, which wasn't true but nothing will ever dissuade her.

What did she think about, back then? I never asked her, and she never said. I don't think I introduced her to Gockle or Dickie.

Saturdays were different. It never rained on Saturdays. We had the club dances. Aunt Bettie de Mille Pitman, Father's young Southern aunt, played the piano. She sat at the upright (everyone had an upright) between two pendant oil lamps, and played "Too Much Mustard," "Alexander's Ragtime Band," the waltz from *The Merry Widow*. The grown-ups danced the fox trot, the two-step, the one-step, and quite frequently the waltz. The more fancy ones, one of them my mother, danced the Maxixe, as modeled by Irene and Vernon Castle. Private citizens never did the tango (except at home to the Victrola) which involved clutching and leg exposure. For the dances Mother wore a homemade and enchanting dress of Japanese silk and real lace which revealed her milky bosom. Her masses of red hair were caught up by gold combs.

Father rarely danced. He had cocktails (no woman ever drank), fifteen cents apiece, smoked cigars and talked to Bill and Boompty Clarke, who laughed very loud at his jokes. Their father J.I.C., the poet, with walrus mustache, sat on the porch with the ladies and was gallant. The little boys sat in all available wicker chairs with their feet straight out before them, saying nothing, looking sullen and not moving. The older ladies sat on wicker chairs on the porch and fanned and remarked how fast Laura Graves seemed. Laura Graves was inside in high heels dancing with Jo Takamine, and, they thought, making a spectacle of herself, with lipstick and bold eyes. She was only fourteen, eight years older than I, and actually she was still a child. It goes without saying that Laura was pretty. Laura flaunted her charms. She not only wore lipstick, but she also put her hair up. I echoed every grown-up condemnation, but I was crazy with envy.

"Mother, can I wear high-heeled shoes?"

"Certainly not," said Mother, "but I'll tie spools to your heels tomorrow and I'll let you wear my hat. That is, if you've had a good nap. Lipstick! Whatever is left for her? She'll be burned out at fifteen."

This sounded interesting. I looked forward to the spools as a step in the right direction.

The little girls raced and giggled and eavesdropped, for fortunately on the back, outside stairs Earl Hanse, who was rich and disreputable, spooned with the Inn's Irish waitresses. The little girls stood underneath and sniggered. I did precious little sniggering, as I was sent home early to lie in bed listening to the piano through the trees, to life going on without me. And then gradually the crickets took over and then, presumably sleep. But not just yet, the whip-poor-wills kept crying. There were rustlings in the bushes outside, bats swooped and clicked, little feet scampered over the roof in a frenzy of impatience. Sometimes there was even a hoot owl, and the great bullfrogs down at the lake, like plucked wet bowstrings, and the trains, the trains, one a night and desperately lonely, and the far, haunting cry of the whip-poor-will.

The whip-poor-will was no bird to me. Its cold whistling triad seemed the repeated cry of some lost creature warning off and warning off just where domestic day ended and the dark forebodings and enticements of the wild wood began. With the sudden initial shriek, comfort disappeared and people were exposed as before, as always, roofless to the wilderness. Behind that bird came the night.

Once when I was five, I waited after supper in my night clothes for Father to tell his bedtime story. A pale dissolved moon mounted softly in the waning east. I stood by the nursery window watching the trees press closer. Then came the voice from down there, where I had been told never to go alone. I ran and put my head under the pillow so I would not hear. But presently I felt Father's step on the stair.

He opened the door and looked in holding a lighted lamp in his hand, and I was safe.

"You came just in time," I whispered, "just in time."

"All right, all right," he said. "I'm here."

I fell asleep remembering the good tobacco odor of his neck and the human reassurance of his chin. But in the dreams I was haunted again. I kept dreaming that the forest was cut down and there was nothing but city streets.

Sunday was just like any other day except that we had ice cream, and in the early morning Frank Felter drove the station wagon from house to house collecting the Irish cooks and drove them the three miles to St. Joseph's Convent for mass. We were not Catholics except for Mamie and Ruth, but I liked mass and the organ music with one black-robed sister pushing on the organ bellows and another pulling on the bell rope. And the bell sounded clear and clanging in the roof. The bell we could hear miles away at vespers and matins, clear over the pine forest and over all the myriad sounds of the wilderness and all its millions of lives, living and moving and changing and making tiny, brief sounds, their manifold voices lying like a carpet of sound on the summer earth. Above all cut the voice of intelligence, The Bell, through and through and through and through the humming silence, and we knew no matter what we were doing, morning or night, that there were people over there on the hill, on their knees, praying.

Father was not rich, but we had two full-time servants, a cook and a nurse, who stayed with us the year round and made the summer trip. And we had Fred Felter in the summer. Ruth (I've forgotten her last name—she must have had one) was our cook. Ruth was a good cook, a decent family member, and she got ten dollars a week. She was just the cook. I didn't consider her important. Middle-aged, I believe actually about twenty-four. But in

Father's Kodak pictures of this big Irish girl she turns out (to my present adult eye) to be a raving, voluptuous beauty with one of the sweetest and most provocative mouths I've ever seen. Mary (Mamie) Harlowe was indeed older, Irish, loving, and with a face that was altogether good and motherly. She was the tent pin of our household. She got ten dollars a week, also, and she was trying to save so she could go back to the Old Country, and so that she could stay out of the poor house in her old age.

At one agonizing point Mother decided to get rid of Mamie, who had quaint and non-advanced ideas of child-raising, taking me to see the pretty flowers at all the neighborhood funerals; also, teaching me to speak as though I had been born in Dublin. At five I had a strong brogue and my family had difficulty understanding me.

I learned of the hideous departure from Mamie herself.

She sat on her bed wiping her tears.

"Ye'll not be forgettin' me, darlint, will ye now?"

I looked at her ashen-lipped.

"I must go away and leave ye, my own darlint babe, to the likes of strangers."

"Why?"

"They say I'm teaching ye to talk like the auld country."

"Holy Mother of God!" I sobbed. "Ye'll niver be doin' the likes o' that!"

And I collapsed on the starched shelf of her great, protecting bosom.

I was found later wedged behind a cupboard weeping into the wall. Mother pulled me out like an animal and took me to Father, who presumably could deal with female hysterics.

He held me on his lap and chuckled softly.

"It's not so serious, you know."

When will people learn that children's despair is absolute and desperate? I know Mother always knew that. Father didn't believe it, embarrassed as he was by any passion not his own. Children seem inarticulate and easily diverted. I may have got over Mamie. I never got over Father. I never forgave him for not realizing.

Mamie went off all right. They sent off her trunk and boxes, and blind with tears which she could not stem in her sopping handkerchief. She kissed me wetly good-bye. She was replaced by a French Mademoiselle, with black hair and a mole and very sloppy ways; also, a language not to my liking. Mother had taken Spartan means indeed to erase the brogue. Live frogs took care of all that. Mademoiselle lasted two and a half weeks. I had, in the meantime, mastered one Gallic word, "Non!"

Mamie returned. The Virgin had arranged it, she explained. She had been on her knees throughout the interim and had not unpacked her bags.

She tucked me in that night, and arranged the mosquito nets and kissed me and blew out the lamp. But Mother made sure to come in afterward and officially kiss us good night and hear our prayers in the Protestant form, with "the power and the glory" and all the Anglican trimmings.

Now, we were exotics, of course, in the Sullivan County landscape, but we were not transients. Like other pockets of similar people dotted all around the countryside, we were there and we intended to stay, and we loved the place and we cared, for it was our home too. Accordingly our cosmopolitanism and sophistication, in its turn, affected the country life. The country people learned to take us into their calculations and they learned to deal and live with us, although they were independent and very proud. They had once owned the whole terrain, whose children now in summer went without shoes and ran with the chickens and pigs in and out under the rotting and sagging porches.

Mrs. King was local and washed for a number of cottages. She came to us on Monday. She lived in a ramshackle house just this side of the St. Joseph station and she had an indeterminate number of children of various ages and various stages of disrepair; stockings with the knees out, boots without buttons, hair tied with string and the like. They were all uncombed and the place smelled from the old well-known smell of poverty which was, to be precise, stale urine. All the country houses smelled of this. (As a matter of historic fact, we are told that pre-revolutionary Versailles smelled the same, but I think this detail would not have occurred to us as recommendation for Mrs. King.) Mrs. King seemed to me old. I imagine she was in her late thirties. Her feet hurt and she shambled in her run-down high-button shoes. (She had, of course, one pair. In winter she put on her husband's old boots.) She had missing teeth and one entirely black. She walked at sun-up through the forest two and three-quarter miles to our houses and then after a cup of coffee (Mother was considerate) she got to work. Zinc tubs were set on trestles on the back porch, which she filled with steaming water boiled on our wood stove. Sleeves rolled to the armpits, she got to work with the washing boards and yellow Fels Naptha soap. (Fels was a Georgist so, as Henry George was Mother's father, of course we used Fels soap.) As the dew burned off the grass and the flower bushes, she tackled the entire week's wash, sheets and pillowcases from five to seven beds (depending on guests), table linen, children's fern-and-mud-smudged rompers, stockings galore, and the incredibly numerous underwear of the adult women, as well as my father's shirts. She did it all alone with her arms and back. And then she lifted the soaking lot out on the grass and hung them up on the lines (wet double-bed sheets are heavy), prodding up the sagging ropes with long forked sticks made for her by Fred Felter. It took all her force from the feet up to hoist these lines. They dried in the sun and air and then she took them into the house and, no matter what the temperature, she heated the heavy flatirons on the roaring wood stove, and sprinkled and ironed the lot. The folded linen and garments always smelled delicious because they were full of sun and a hint of wood smoke.

At the end of the day Mrs. King walked home. I remember her with a newspaper parcel often, no doubt something Mother had given her, cookies for the children perhaps. She walked back alone in the dark, while the whip-poor-wills whistled and little low animals crossed her path, silent as shadows. When she got home she had to start cooking supper for her brood, the only hot food they had had since the previous night. For the day's work she was paid two dollars.

Mrs. King smelled not only of poverty but occasionally of raw gin. I hope so.

Mrs. Soeles did the washing for the Other End. After Frank Felter moved from the park, she took over his house where she lived in unrelieved filth. Her husband was always drunk. Mrs. Soeles would have liked to have been drunk also but there was not enough money for both of them. It is generally conceded that Mrs. Soeles had the worst breath in Sullivan County and her teeth were black from ear to ear. She had thirteen children.

Fred Felter, our gardener, seemed to me old and scrawny. He was, by his pictures, in the mid-twenties, well set-up, sinewy and bony. He had an alert Adam's apple and his fingernails were broken and stained. He smelled of unwash. He chewed tobacco and his teeth and mouth corners were dark brown and oozing. His eyes were melting brown and quite sad. He could do anything. He painted the tennis courts, he hosed down the sawdust-packed ice, he changed the privies, he set the traps, he shot varmints, he gardened and he gutted animals and fish (I always watched fascinated, viscera charmed me). He could do anything except, of course, think. He drank far too much cheap liquor. He worked from seven in the morning until dark every day for fifteen dollars a week. He aged early. He never married.

His brother, Frank, was older and more stable. He had a wife and a considerable number of children played on his porch, or stood picking their noses in the doorways. Frank was a responsible man. He became our superintendent after the Moores left.

The Moores were the first superintendents of the Merriewold Inn and cluster of homes and they lived in the big field opposite the George house. Bertha Moore was a bosom friend of Beatrice George, Henry Jr.'s daughter. On the front porch was the seat of an old buggy with the springs coming through the rotting leather. I never went inside their house but looking from the doorway into the gloom I saw antlers on the wall and cut-glass on the round dining-room table.

Bertha Moore said that come November, when the trees were at last stripped and the real winds began, they more or less sewed themselves into several layers of garments which were not removed until spring. For the cold was Canadian; thirty degrees below occurred at least once a winter and there was no heat except the open wood-fires and the cook-oven or the Franklin pot-bellied, iron stove. The bedrooms were nearly fatal, even with heavy quilts and hot bricks for the feet, and the journey from the side of the bed to the kitchen was a dreadful one. But Mrs. Moore was kind, her son told me forty years later in his electrically heated living room, and permitted the children to dress, that is, put on their outer garments and shoes and stockings, by the cook-stove. And then, with a hot breakfast inside them and muffled to the eyes, they stumbled out in the cracking cold and walked the mile and a half to the one-room schoolhouse on Route 42. If there was a wind it was terrible and a good thirty minutes was taken on arrival in the unbending and loosening up their fingers so they could hold a pencil.

Down Route 42 and over into Forestburg there began to be an infiltration of Germans. These were mostly farmers but they grew very rich in landholdings. One of them later became a very good friend of mine, Lydia Pick, Sudeten Deutsch. The big, old-fashioned house that she and her husband had run, before his death, as a tavern and rooming house for hunters was struck by lightning and burned to the ground without a cent of insurance. Barefoot and alone she attempted to clean up the burnt timbers and rubble. Once I came upon her and friends sitting on old, springless chairs by the burnt-out stacks of the chimney places. The cinders, broken glass, and burnt wire crunched under her bare feet. She was supplying pitchers of beer to her friends and they were listening to Viennese waltzes on an old tin Morning-Glory gramophone.

"Gemütlich, no?" she said. "Nice?"

The country folks, the permanents, went on living. They gave birth, they died, but all quite privately like the animals. It was just that suddenly one of them wasn't around any more and sometimes that was inconvenient, but not often. Mostly they just continued.

We were aware of the animals all the time. In those forests they were as important as we were, and they'd been there first.

I thought of them often. I thought of them always. They were with us, a shadow, a lesser life. They didn't think. They didn't know. What strange existences the animals had, living beside us, around us, all the time with us, all the time dying, all the time starting to live, all the time in extremis, frightened, eating and digesting and spawning, seeking what comfort they might!

We found some of the remains of their duress, bones of deer, bits of fur, dry skeletal remnants. Mainly we didn't find them; the forest is very tidy. Fearful, trembling, their short lives were passed in the brief afternoon of physical contentment, so very short. They seemed happy enough but we didn't see their terrors. There was the final terror and they were finished.

The deer were shy, the raccoons were not. We could hear them scratching at the low kitchen window, their black masks pressed close to the glass, their claws tapping, their eyes brilliant. They were commanding garbage. If one handed it to them, their long nails daintily but definitely seized, but always they went away a bit fastidiously to feed. If they got into the house there was desolation, or if they prized the lids off the garbage pails the whole lawn became a smörgåsbord of orange rinds, coffee grounds, and eggshell. Their most astonishing characteristic was their silence. They were there gently without any announcement, up from under the porch. Not a leaf gave warning. They were just there. Some had four legs, many three, and one poor thing had only two; trappers had been at work.

The porcupines were silent also. They ate the buds off the hemlock branches and were terrible to dogs.

And the skunks were silent and of a plump, elegant beauty.

There were a few episodes. One night we heard a continuous knocking on the back porch and Mother and I crept down to see. A tiny skunk had got its head caught in a jam bottle and was desperately trying to free itself from its trap. Its dangerous end was, of course, exposed. Mother woke Father but he muttered that he could not think how to cope and that he was sleepy. We tried prying the bottle off with a broom handle. Impossible. The poor little thing ran away knocking and banging through the bushes to almost certain death. Mother put her arms around me. "We tried. Probably the bottle will break. We can pray for that. I'm sure it will." Mother was cheery, but I cried bitterly with helpless, horrified gasps. I heard the knocking dwindling away for almost twenty minutes.

In the spring the sunfish made nests, flat circles in the sand, and the parents patrolled them. These were in the shallow sunny waters at the edge of the lake and I waded through, so naturally the adult fish attacked me; my little legs must have been the size of oak trunks to them. They butted and pushed. I shrieked. Mother caught me up to take the full assault on her own white calves. The fish were small and helpless but they were utterly without fear, and, of course, they were under water, which made them formidable. Mother explained about the tenderness of mother-love; I continued to shriek.

We had lots of snakes, all kinds. "The grass divides as with a comb." The rattlers stayed back in the rocks and only came out in time of drought, which was rare. One day I saw a harmless garter snake chasing a frog. It was the grimmest procedure I ever watched. The frog jumped and the snake slid forward to close the gap. Twenty minutes later the frog was exhausted. The snake's head was held at the same rigid angle just inches behind. There was nowhere the frog could go, no hole, no hiding place. Water was far off. An hour later the snake lay replete, one little leg dangling from its mouth, its eyes closed in content. The frog's agony was being quieted by digestive chemistry.

One late afternoon after tennis Father called me to the court; across the entire surface raged a battle between black ants and smaller red ants. Some thousands were locked in mortal combat, couple by couple, and were dismembering each other. It was Trojan and it was perfectly silent. They died the death of heroes, without a whisper of sound, their broken bodies falling in a tiny brittle litter like steel filings. After half an hour the battle was finished, their carcasses and wire-like limbs lay still with only one or two survivors lurching in agony.

"Well," said Pop, "we must get a broom. But let's eat first."

After dinner we returned, Pop and I, and stopped, amazed. In the red dusk the court was clean. Not a leg remained. They had retrieved their dead. What had caused the heroic massacre we never knew. Whether it was jurisdictional, whether the group was a migrant invader, whether the carpenter ants were defending our house foundations for their very own destruction, whether they had deliberately chosen the tennis court as an open and decisive tournament zone we never learned. I have not seen the like since.

There existed always except in September a blur of insects, a sea of insects, coming and going, always new, humming. Life. In spring disagreeably thick, in autumn gone.

There was a procession of flowers. All summer they moved in and enchanted us and then disappeared. Before the tree leaves were out, the mountain ash bloomed smokily and in the moist black earth there were jack-in-the-pulpits, trillium, and then the various huckleberries, wild ginger, strawberries, yellow and white, the bluets and false lily-of-the-valley and, if one was lucky, the pink and astonishing moccasin flower, a real orchid, a cypripedium, blooming in quiet, decent colonies under the pines. These were wanderers. You thought you knew where they were and kept the secret so no one would pick them, and no one did pick them, but the next summer they were not there. They had just gone off and were standing privately in the brown leaves somewhere else.

And then came the violets. Oh glory! The dear things!

In May when the woods were distinct with water, from the time I was two, I used to stand rubber-booted and peer into the trees searching through green and flicker until my eyes dazzled and I could discern neither color nor distance. Then suddenly vision focused. And, behold, they were there! The violets. In the very spot they had seemed not to be, their sudden blue against the green, most strangely motionless, balanced, aerial, and stirred by water almost insensibly in their tiny island pastures, fairy-fragile beside the iris blades and succulent water plants.

There were moments when I stopped being a member of a family, my parents' child, when I stopped having identity or a calendar and became simply a part of the forest. I went back. I wondered then, as I have wondered since, how I could hold the reality of the moment, the wilderness of leaf and blossom existing beyond vision, beyond knowledge or personal experience, yet existing still, blooming and stirring.

I used to think then of good things to eat, and I longed for supper to put into my mouth and digest. And in an anguish of unexpressed energy, I pulled off the violets by their heads and carried them dying in my hot palms. The return home brought the comfort of daily certainties, like minding Mother, washing hands, and eating the crusts as well. I also found that I had a name. After such experiences I managed to overeat and, tucked away in a digestive trauma, pink fingers beneath replete cheek, pink mouth opened on even breathing, I slept hard. While behind the sealed lids the after-vision grew, a universe of soundless waters, constellations of blossom and leaf that stretched away forever and opened up the tidy comfort of nursery walls to the night.

In June there was mountain laurel and for two weeks the forest presented a sight Kew Gardens couldn't match, for in a good year and at the climax of their bloom the entire forest was taken over by pink snow. Mother used to break trees and branches of it and put them in pine crates Fred Felter constructed for her, stuffed and padded with soaking-wet newspapers, and these were shipped (Wells Fargo) to the city where her friends were entombed in stifling flats. And they arrived fresh, and that's how those dinky little railroad trains and horse-drawn delivery wagons worked.

Then came jewelweed and cardinal flowers by the ponds in the deep woods, fire lilies as red as a guardsman's tunic and, in the fire lanes, purple fireweed which only grows on charred ground; and by the roads the Canada lily with its pagoda of amber bells, and the beauty-marked tiger lily, always in open meadows, and Queen Anne's lace. It was high summer now and the fields buzzed with insects and bore their fruit and the earth rustled and teemed and suddenly all the open spaces glistened and burnished and blew with thistle silk and milkweed seeds and we were in autumn, and the yellows took over the world.

And then came the first frost and the mountain raged with color too intense to be borne. Every tree was on fire and fighting for its life, its living energy consumed in color. And in the crystalline blue air leaves drifted down, pale yellow and saffron pattering in a gentle, tireless rain, and way overhead suddenly came the honking clatter of the Canada geese, getting away, getting away, and we raised our eyes through the clear dazzle to see the tiny triangle steadily winging south. At dawn the foxes barked.

And then it was over. The forest was done. The summer had passed.

My mother, Anna Angela George, before her marriage.

My father, William Churchill de Mille, the year before his marriage.

Agnes, Mother, Margaret.

Our house, Margaret, and Agnes.

Chapter 2

◄ Merriewold lies in the southwest corner of New York State
near the Delaware River which divides New York from Pennsylvania; it is seventeen miles due north from Port Jervis, a market-
town railroad junction on the Erie line to Chicago. Earlier, Port
Jervis had been a focal point for various branches of the Erie
Canal. In this place the Delaware, although wide and swift, was
too shallow for navigation and one of the canals had been
suspended along the side of the river bluff and then miraculously
transported in wooden casing across the Delaware itself. Over in
Pennsylvania the forests had been somewhat tamed into farms
and there were several very old and charming towns. But on the
northern bank outside the skirts of the little port town, the wild
forest took over.

The hills are the Shawangunk Mountains, foothills to the
lower Catskills, Indian country, untouched and virgin. Remnants
of the tribes persisted in these parts well into the nineteenth century and roads are today marked with the blue sign signifying
raids and kidnappings. Nearby, lost in the weeds, five or six broken tombstones mark the end of the story, the family burying plot.

Cutting through the hills is the Neversink River, the trout
stream made famous by Ambrose Bierce, and its near neighbor,

the Mongaup, which displayed a drop of water two hundred feet high with beetling ledges, fern-furred between the glassy stretches above and the turmoil of water below where the water struck on rocks boiling with foam. Both rivers skirt Cuddeback-ville, a Revolutionary town of one good-sized cross road and thirty or so houses. It was here in 1906 that David Wark Griffith made his first films starring Mary Pickford, Mabel Normand, and Henry Walthall. He used the rivers on every possible location as well as the eighteenth-century house (still extant) where the company lived while shooting. North on 42 or 207 was Thompson, later changed to Monticello, a sleepy market town with pleasant houses, large gardens, assorted churches, and one business street on which operated the lawyer, the dentist, the bank, and the merchants. It was very simple. One could get through one's entire business in an hour. One had to; the way home was long, more than two hours by buggy on the back road, route 42. The main access to Merriewold was by rail and the dirt and rock road from the Ontario and Western tracks that led to Our End and ran through the woods.

The place had been discovered in 1892 by my grandfather, Henry George.

At the time of his death in 1897 Henry George was probably the best-known American, excepting Theodore Roosevelt and Mark Twain. He was certainly the best-known serious American writer. His theory was called popularly the "Single Tax," and at the turn of the century it was better known than Communism and George was more read than Marx. Henry George was one of the finest speakers of his time, a figure of international importance. He is today, according to Kenneth Galbraith, one of the two nineteenth-century writers still read; according to George Bernard Shaw, one of the three greatest American thinkers of the nineteenth century. He was a simple man. He stopped school in the seventh grade.

He had been visiting the dying wife of his editor in Liberty, New York, where the air was sought for pulmonary disorders. News had come over the Shawangunk Hills that two thousand acres of burnt tract were to be had for one thousand dollars. It was not very attractive land at that moment, looking rather like plum pudding, but the second growth had started and it would be attractive.

Henry George did not have a thousand dollars in all the world, but his friends got together and made an enclave and bought the property. There in the new woods George and his Annie lived a primitive life of idyllic working conditions and tranquillity. He was the hewer of wood and drawer of water, and she was the cook on a wood stove. His peace and his work (he was writing his magnum opus 5, the *Philosophy of Political Economy*) was interrupted by the arrival of a group of politicians, who wanted George to run for mayor of the City of New York. They had a party organized and a very respectable representation. They were fighting Tammany head on, and they wanted him to spearhead the fight. At the name of George, Tammany grew frightened enough to offer him enormous bribes to stay out of the campaign. Henry George needed money all of his life, but he didn't take bribes. "Incorruptible Henry George."

So in 1897 he ran for mayor, against the advice of his doctors, who warned that a political campaign would bring on a stroke. Nevertheless, his friends encouraged his action, saying that if he were mayor he would be able to implicate, or at least certainly advertise, his reforms. He went to his wife, Annie Corsina Fox, saying, "Annie, at the time of the Phoenix Park murders you said to me in Dublin, 'Parnell couldn't have died better than among his people and serving his cause.' Now will you allow me to risk my life for my cause?" And she replied, "if you think it right, do." And he did. And it seemed he was very likely to win.

Four nights before the election in a hotel in Union Square, Annie woke to see him standing alone in the center of the floor looking up. "Yes, yes, yes," he said, and fell unconscious. He was dead within hours.

George's funeral was, in effect, a state occasion. It was a hero's funeral, international and memorable. The catafalque was borne through the streets to torchlight and followed by a crowd of fifty thousand. It passed all the borough City Halls and, as the procession approached, the bells were set tolling. The monument on his grave was erected by public subscription at the instigation of Joseph Pulitzer: "The truth that I have tried to make clear will not find easy acceptance. If that could be, it would have been accepted long ago: if that could be, it never would have been obscured. But it will find friends, those who will toil for it, fight for it, if need be, die for it. This the power of truth."

Merriewold was sealed with blood; our little plot of wilderness had been dedicated by a great death.

George was a genius. But in his family he was a sport, and his near relatives, his siblings and cousins, although upright and staunch, were not all of them very bright. (His older sister never learned the way to the bathroom and got lost one night in the dark for two hours in her own dining room.)

It was an alert, if not brilliant family, with the one notable exception (although I suspect my grandmother of wit, I know she had wisdom). I didn't realize this until years after I was grown. But they all had very great charm which revealed itself through sheer goodness of heart. And they were upright and they were brave. The Georges were what Mother termed "blue-blooded, Philadelphia Episcopalians." My Grandmother George was a Catholic, an Australian, an exotic. She was also a remarkable waltzer, indulging in two-hour heats with the orchestra hired to play through supper, a frivolity curbed by poverty.

On my father's side, Henry de Mille, my grandfather, must have had an element of fantasy and nonconformism, for he forsook his clerical studies for the stage, believing he could influence more people with plays of moral message. These he proposed to write. But he chose David Belasco, an extraordinary craftsman, as his partner (he was Belasco's first collaborator) and Beatrice Samuel, a British elocutionist, as his wife. Both wife and collaborator were Jews and this was odd for a North Carolina high church Episcopalian. My father's Jewish strain added worldliness and zest to the almost undiluted high-mindedness of the Georges, and the alloy was welcome.

Belasco's instinct was not so much to improve as to dumfound —he was an instinctive theater man and not a reformer, and their joint efforts have not survived. In any case, they split up over Mrs. Leslie Carter, who cast a spell over "The Wizard," Belasco. She became his star, and Grandfather de Mille became a respected memory, for he died shortly thereafter—very young, thirty-six— of typhoid contracted from a bad oyster. He left two adolescent boys, a five-year-old daughter, and his widow, all poor. He also left an unblemished reputation for kindness and upright behavior. My father told of his sucking the infected matter from the throat of a child dying of diphtheria, quite the most heroic act I had ever heard of.

Father, aged fourteen, Cecil, aged twelve, and little Agnes, five, tragically orphaned, were brought up by Beatrice (Bebe) de Mille, a strong-minded woman.

Agnes, in turn, died at six of spinal meningitis and was laid out in an open coffin in the hall. Bebe took the boys down to the hall at night and forced them to look at the dead child lit by tapers. She then commanded them to kiss the little cold face in the coffin and swear that they would never ever in their lives do anything to any woman that they would not wish done to their sister. This awful scene was one they never forgot, though from time to time they lapsed in remembering the moral. But Bebe did not, and on the young men's marrying she wrote a kind of certificate for their purity to their prospective brides. She had brought them up to be pure like their father and it followed that they were pure. What is more, Cecil truly was, having his mother's implicit faith in sexual continence. Father came to have doubts, and there were some pre-nuptial confessions that shook Mother, as she had expected a virgin, just as he did. But her love was great and she forgave.

All of this was not unusual for the time. It laid edge to passion. Sex was in very truth a life and death matter. There were barrings from the home, and suicides and murders, and a fall from grace, even a hasty one, was as permanently disabling as the loss of a limb or a disfigurement today, often worse. Father's greatest hit was a play called *The Woman* (1911), in which a husband forgave his wife an indiscretion committed ten years before the marriage. It was considered a very daring play and of highly dubious influence. It sold tickets.

Earlier the family had had a taste of the tragic results of light-hearted philanderings. Bebe had run a boarding school called Pamlico, at Pompton Lakes, New Jersey, and one of the pupils was a lovely girl named Evelyn Nesbit. Her fiance shot and killed the gentleman who purported to be her guardian, when it turned out he was, in fact, nothing of the sort. The blackguard's name was Stanford White and as he was the best-known architect of his time the trial accordingly became a national sensation in which all our family figured. Evelyn's diary was read in court, describing among pertinent matters her fencing master, my brilliant young father, as "Bill de Mille, that pie-faced mut." After this sensation, Bebe's injunctions to the other students can be imagined. But Father, obviously, was not intimidated. He adored Mother, but he flirted.

The de Milles were quick, flashing, adroit, and, on a superficial level, intensely mental; they made a marvelous first impression. My father was dashing and he was agile, handsome, and lean. Mother was "completely smitten," to use her own words. He excelled in track and got medals for running, jumping, hammer-throwing, shot-putting. He fenced and boxed, but above all he played tennis, with passion and skill.

He had a long narrow face, brilliant eyes, and an aquiline nose ("the nose of a Spanish grandee," said Seymore Thomas, the portrait painter). His hands were long-fingered and strong, his torso long, his feet narrow with high insteps. He had curly brown hair but was going bald shortly after I met him, in his late twenties.

Once he elected to grow a small Imperial while in New York for conferences with David Belasco. When he returned to the woods I greeted him at the gate, "Oh Pop, you look worse than ever." I was passionately attached to him but deliciously frightened always. He laughed at me and his laugh struck terror. He laughed that night at the gate and I blushed.

He was very sexy. Sex, indeed, meant a great deal to him as I discovered long after his death when going through his papers. Mother liked Father to be admired, but she kept a pretty stiff rein on the flirting. For his part, he was constantly roused by her sprightliness and charm and she knew this. Indeed, it was the keynote of her well-being. Being a good wife was a very exercising occupation, and she was well content. But Father could not refrain from flirting with all females, and they in turn adored him and spoiled him. They thought Mother a very lucky woman.

Mother did not consider herself the lucky one. She, the beautiful baby of a world-famous man, had been raised as a little princess. She was small, five feet, wore a size one shoe (she wore exquisite shoes and displayed her foot frequently) and child's gloves; she had showers of red hair that hung to her waist.

If a woman had fine hair in Mother's day she literally gardened it. The hair of yesteryear streamed, waved, flowed. The girls lay in it, rolled in it, and, whenever they could, sat on it. Their husbands stroked it, kissed it, rumpled it, wound it around their faces and hands. I never saw Father do this, but he wrote her very specifically and intimately about her beauty and, since her hair was noteworthy, I'm sure he carried on in private after the fashion of his time. Her skin was milky, her eyes blue and of an intensity to stop speech, and when she grew angry she looked as if she had holes in her head and you could see through her to the sky beyond.

Beauty in those days did not mean as much as sensitivity or refinement, but, of course, it helped. Like the ladies of her era Mother used nothing but rice powder. Her age and her way of spending her time were exposed to the world. Her expression tended to be tense. That was because she was trying not to miss anything, to see that everyone did his or her best all the time, without respite.

Mother considered that she came of blood royal; Father felt the same about himself.

Mother thought Pop only slightly imperfect as a man, but as a playwright she believed he was all that his father had failed to be, an unquestioned genius. She claimed he had the wit of George Bernard Shaw and the tenderness of James Matthew Barrie. He had nothing of the sort. He was a journeyman craftsman who could tailor a well-made plot (usually with help) and turn out dialogue which acted very well and which was sometimes extremely funny. His work possessed, however, no real distinction or style. He knew his rules: he could hold attention, build suspense, and make a point. That's a lot, but it doesn't last. His works date, except his one-act burlesques, several of which earn royalties to this day. His vaudeville sketches (*The Man Higher Up*) were unabashed melodrama, but played in that unkind medium like a knife act.

He was sufficiently vain to bury his shortcomings under his singing, tennis-playing, and after-dinner speaking, which was brilliant. If he could not be one he acted the part of a great playwright and his minor skills made him able to bear better the fact that he wasn't a first-class writer. Because Father knew, although he never let on.

Great and successful playwrights in those days were Dumas fils, Dion Boucicault, Edmond Rostand, Henry Bernstein, Henry Arthur Jones, James Matthew Barrie, George Bernard Shaw, and our own Merriewolder, Charles Klein, who was certainly at least successful. They were very, very rich and had themselves photographed in their studies (lots of books and ormolu and knickknacks from their travels and mementos of their triumphs) and they had eight- and nine-page articles about themselves in *The Theater,* and they had an entourage and were personalities. They read their plays to assembled casts and went to rehearsals carrying canes, took long lunches and rehearsed late, until six or seven in the evening, and had four-month summer vacations when all of the theaters closed because of the heat. Father had all of these appurtenances except the ormolu and he was known and he was successful and Mother was tremendously proud of him.

The first summer residence in Merriewold had been "Crowsdale in the Pines," a gothic pleasance. Crowsdale was the editor of George's newspaper, *The Standard,* and his wife was dying of tuberculosis. But although there was small chance of the poor woman enjoying it, he built her a nineteenth-century summer villa in case she lived. It was a multiroomed, dark, mysterious stone house designed for maximum inconvenience to housekeeper and servants.

The housewarming, the last festivity in Merriewold that George attended, was noteworthy, accompanied by children waving ferns and Japanese lanterns and chanting the Single Tax battle cry to the tune of "Marching Through Georgia";

> "Sound the note of freedom, boys,
> And send it far and wide . . ."

The women's high sopranos wavered through the pines, particularly Mrs. Henry George, Jr.'s (Aunt Marie), who had an ardor unflagging and a piercing soprano reinforced by professional hope:

> "The land, the land,
> 'Twas God who gave the land
> The land, the land
> The ground on which we stand.
> Why should we be beggars
> With a ballot in our hand?
> God gave the land to the people!"

At George's death this house was acquired from the editor by Mr. Gordon. Mr. Gordon was a real Victorian gentleman, that is, very nearly intolerable, mean and totally disagreeable, and he ruled his women hard. The trouble was he attempted to rule his neighbors the same way. He suddenly laid claim to our Pine Grove. This was dedicated land, and one of the finest stands of white pine in the county. It was communally owned and not to be purchased by an individual. Not only that, Mr. Gordon laid claim to all of Merriewold not already bought up and he forbade anyone to use the station road, putting a chain across and placing a man with a shotgun on guard. Until they removed the shotgun the neighbors were forced to use the Sisters' Road over to the convent, a good seven miles out of the way.

Gordon's maneuver was strenuously resisted and finally refuted. Meanwhile, feelings ran very high and Mr. Gordon forbade his women to speak to anyone else in the park for the rest of his life. I think it's suitable that the shingles on the house, the outhouse, and the icehouse were black.

The second house at Merriewold was built five years after Henry George's death by his children. George had died at fifty-eight. His widow was fifty-six. But she seemed an old woman: the light had gone out. Nevertheless, her three children built her a house with the help of local carpenters, the family doing all the painting and scraping. Henry George's Annie moved in, but not for long; she died there. She had a doctor who had tended her hero-husband and who was in Merriewold because of his other patient, J. I. C. Clarke. I suppose there was an undertaker; the country folk had to bury their dead. But there was no Episcopal minister, so the Catholic poet, J.I.C., officiated, reading the psalms with a resounding voice and Irish lilt. Mother covered her mother with pink steepletop. "That was all the flowers there were." (So I know Grandmother died in August.)

Mother and Father had been married the year before Grandmother died, Annie giving Mother away, and the bridal pair had spent two summers in a tent behind the George house. The third summer Mother was bundled off to New York (five hours, three trains and a ferry) and in mid-September I was born on 118th

Street, delivered by a lady doctor because everyone thought it more modest.

George, Jr., Mother's brother, inherited the George house when Annie died. He was a congressman and quite exceptional. "Do you want a man in Congress," queried one election tract, "who is known to progressive statesmen of the world, Lloyd George and other liberal leaders of England, Irish members of Parliament who inherit the traditions and teachings of Michael Davitt . . . Do you want a man in Congress who, on his visit to Russia, was a guest of Leo Tolstoy's, the greatest prophet and reformer of the modern world, whose lightest word goes to the uttermost ends of the earth, freighted with greater power than the arms of the Czar's Cossacks?" This may not have been unusual electioneering for the time, but what might strike the modern voter is that on the strength of these high-minded pleas, the seventh district, from 101st Street to Spuyagnduyvil, from Park Avenue to the Hudson—in short, Harlem—returned him to Congress.

Tammany had placed young George in Washington and then, to their discomfort, found him just like his father, unwilling to take orders. But they let the situation rest. One or two honest men could not upset Tammany's grand arrangements and would serve as a kind of camouflage for their deadlier intent.

George, Jr.'s very young wife, Marie Septima Morelle Hitch of New Orleans, played the piano and liked to sing. Her touch on the piano was merciless and she missed not one of the notes. "Mother was about to go on the concert stage," writes her daughter Jane George, "when she married Papa. I have the gold medal she was awarded from the Chicago Musical Academy by Mr. F. Ziegfeld, the father of the great Flo." Before that she performed before the visiting Princess Eulalia of Spain, although her mother refused to let her conform to the monarchy by wearing the Catholic school uniform.

She practiced professionally four or five hours a day. Or rather she did until her marriage, but then she faltered, young George being jealous of her piano. He didn't mind her showing off; he minded her practicing. So she transferred her zeal and her digital dexterity to the keyboard of a typewriter and made transcripts of her husband's definitive George biography and his congressional speeches. These he didn't mind her doing daily. He had a little special shack for writing, but Aunt Marie had to keep the typewriter in the house where she could keep an eye on the children and the stews. Now and then she sneaked forty minutes at the piano and hoped Uncle Harry wouldn't hear her working. But, of course, in the woods that was impossible. He heard.

Mary Beatrice, "Bea," the eldest of their three children, was high-minded. Jane was my age and was my playmate, and my target for bullying. I bit her "until the jelly came," my small sister Margaret being not quite ready for biting. But fortunately she became so in about a year and then I could spare myself the long walk down to The Other End and the Georges' house and I could spare Jane who was getting to be big and tough and also resistant.

The son, Henry George III, wilted under his heady name and gave evidence through the years that the expectations raised by his heritage were nearly crippling. His brows were knotted from the time he was five. Mostly he lay around whimpering in a state of despondent exhaustion. In due time he called his own firstborn Henry George IV.

Opposite the George house and across the cornfield was the Pine Grove, the grove Mr. Gordon had erroneously claimed. This was a stand of white pine as fine as any in the state. And it was thick. Underneath not a sprig of green could grow and one walked on carpets of needles and through shafts and splinters of light. The only sound was the perpetual soughing in the top branches, the gurgle and chuckle of the small waterfall that poured in glistening sheets over moss-bright rocks, a noble stand of trees which had escaped the holocaust, black in summer against the surrounding forest green, green in the winter and always there sighing. It was a place for contemplation, a place for picnics, a place for secrets, a place for wandering and speculating. It was a haven for many hearts. And it was our signature.

Up the road from the Georges and over the tiny brook lived Joseph Ignatius Constantine Clarke, Irish poet, journalist, and playwright, and the one who pronounced Annie George's eulogy.

At every possible excuse he elocutioned his own poetry, with splendid nineteenth-century gestures and rolling Irish tones, booming as he stroked his yellowed mustache, his aspirants haloed with spittle. He also tried to kiss all the little girls, who fled his tobacco-stained mustached embrace, not always successfully.

But there was a lot more to him. "An Irish Patriot" said all his obituaries, which meant that he had been a Sinn Feiner and known English gaols and had, on arrival in this country, always supported the Irish Cause. He was, for a decade, the president of the American Irish Historical Society.

He was also a prominent journalist, on the staff of the New York *Herald* and managing editor of the *Morning Journal* and the *Criterion,* Sunday editor of the New York *Herald.* The New York *Sun* sent him to Japan for special reporting. He was co-founder with another Merriewolder of the Nippon Club. He was also the first man to do a public relations job for Standard Oil, preceding Ive Lee by a decade. John D. Rockefeller was considered at the turn of the century a public enemy, the prime one, but since he owned a great part of the mineral assets of the United States, he didn't care. For years he didn't care. But gradually the accumulated persistent enmity of all the editorialists began to make him uneasy. He could not understand why he was not loved. The fact that he had amassed billions while people starved in slums, second only to those in India, struck him as his own business, not theirs. He was smarter, that's all, and he was first. Be that as it may, J.I.C. got him at a vulnerable moment and said, "You've got to say something. You can't just sit silent and rake in the boodle. You've got to talk, and I'd better do the talking for you."

And Clarke was forthwith hired at a salary of twenty thousand a year (today's equivalent of about seventy). From that moment on John D. began to move slowly but steadily out of the role of predator into that of public benefactor, quite a feat of persuasion, because the rights and the basic royalties did not change hands. And from that moment financial reporting became an essential part of every big newspaper. Hitherto it had not been mentioned, like something indecent, which as a matter of fact it frequently was.

But Clarke's activities were only partially journalistic. He wrote plays, and he wrote poetry, notably a ballad on the sinking of the *Maine,* called "Kelly and Burke and Shea." This gained national approval. All the verses ended with a refrain:

> "Well, here's to the Maine and I'm
> sorry for Spain,"
> Said Kelly and Burke and Shea.
> "Well, here's thank God for the
> race and the sod,"
> Said Kelly and Burke and Shea.

That's not all there was by any means, but that's enough. He wrote even worse verse, framed excerpts of which were found later in his attic. But when he recited them with gestures, they were patriotic and riveting and, as I have indicated, liquid.

He had a special cabin at Merriewold for writing poetry, far from kitchen interference. All the men with intellects thought in separate, reserved places, guarded from family disturbance, like shrines.

He and his family lived in a little white house in the pines, with stained-glass windows, odd-shaped porches and fretwork trimmings in every room. The fireplace was a white valentine of shelves, curlicues, arabesques, parthenons, pillars, and mirrors. Between parlor and dining room there were dividing curtains of glass, bugle beads which moved with an endearing tinkle.

Auntie Clarke, his wife Mary Agnes, a well-rouged mummy, was the first lady to have a laryngeal, or whiskey, voice I had ever heard. They had two sons, Bill, my father's tennis and drinking companion, a young roustabout, and his brother, Harry, called Boompty, both brawling Irish lads of incredible sexual energy. They laughed with terrifying, provocative male laughs, but they didn't try to kiss us. They didn't dare. Father was watching. How Auntie Clarke put up with these three men I never grasped. One would have thought all the fretwork and crockery would have tumbled down at the first gust of male excitement. Auntie Clarke remained always to me a kindly, bone-collared residual, with a rasping whisper and a thick brogue. At their fiftieth wedding anniversary J.I.C. "clothed his Mary in gold." His Mary was very old and vague. I think she tippled. It was thought by some that at the anniversary celebration she was not quite conscious.

So these houses, along with several cottages by the lake, constituted what was called the Western or Other End. The lake was important because we all met there to go swimming and the Gordons had a big pavilion in which we could give picnics and such when he wasn't looking. These first houses were soon surrounded by some two dozen others either built by members of our family or by the George Disciples, which meant that they were intellectuals—writers or enlightened businessmen and scientists. Everyone knew something about the Philosophy and Faith and subscribed in varying degrees. Only gradually other elements infiltrated—people with no thought of public good—just a liking for the terrain.

After Father had become head of a family and author of two Broadway hits (*Strongheart* and *The Warrens of Virginia*) he bought (1909) a little house of his own at Our End up the road in the burnt section. Almost no one lived up there. Nevertheless, the land had increased in value just as Henry George had predicted. The price was now fifteen dollars an acre.

Our house was built by Charles Klein, the playwright, a one-time cockney tailor who had written three smash Broadway hits that made him a millionaire (no taxes then). They were *The Lion and the Mouse, Daughters of Men,* and *The Music Master,* in which David Warfield starred. (Klein's brother was Emanuel, the conductor of all the great hippodrome shows, with the diving bell and the bevies of mermaids.)

Charles Klein was considered the dean of Merriewold playwrights. He was certainly the richest. Klein had been brought to Merriewold by his collaborator, the Irish Clarke, and Klein had built himself a little peak-roofed cottage and the best tennis court in Sullivan County.

Klein's income may have been grand, but his tastes were simple and, as in the style of the time, dreadful. Mrs. Klein did burnt poker-work right up the stairs, black fleur-de-lys. The walls were paneled in three-inch strips of unknotty pine and varnished—the ceilings too. The wall pictures were tinted photographs of Venice. Curly iron lamps dangled here and there. There were pillows filled with pine needles and adorned with mottoed covers. There were dinner mats of sweet grass and birch, decorated with Indianheads, and napkin rings of white birch and quill work. Monstrous pen and ink stands abounded, and pen wipers. (I made quite a few of these myself, several spectacular ones of baby-blue flannel.)

In 1915 Charles Klein, Charles Frohman, and several distinguished colleagues went to London on theater business and sailed on a well-appointed Cunard liner. The German Embassy printed warnings to prospective customers on the front page of the New York *Times*. Klein read these carefully and, although he was an ardent Christian Scientist and denied fear, he was a cautious and realistic family man, so he took out a million-dollar life insurance policy. The family later found this helpful. The name of the boat was the *Lusitania*.

Down our road lived more cousins and near cousins, the family of Mother's other brother and the family—a large one, romantic and part Spanish—of Mother's older sister, who died tragically young.

It is not necessary to remember all the relationships. Many of the family members did not themselves, to their grief. They have been stated to show how close-knit everyone in Merriewold was, whether blood kin or not. We called all the adults Uncle and Aunt, and were in and out of their houses whenever it suited, sometimes daily.

The world of Merriewold was filled with children—clean and exuberant summer guests and permanent untouchables, silent and staring. We clean ones ignored them. The summer children played in two separate camps—"Our End" and the "Other End" —and the mile walk between was not to be attempted lightly, but only possibly for ice cream.

Ice cream always happened at parties, as did cakes and those boring games the grown-ups fancied for our delight. (If the party was given by Aunt Marie, the ice cream was invariably homemade peach.) Every birthday child had a party, and every family had at least one summer birthday. (Aunt Marie had three.) Most of these parties were held out of doors, on tables covered with crepe paper and ferns and ground pine. The little girls wore white dresses, starched (mine were hand sewn by Mother, naturally, with hours of little lace insertions and tiny tucks), and colored bows and sashes, the boys in knee breeches and stiff collars. The Birthday Child, if a girl, wore a wreath of flowers or ferns. We played games, pin the tails on donkeys, spin the plates, and walked home at sundown, cross and colicky. We had walked down the road to the festivities in careful expectation, starched and ready, the birthday gift wrapped in paper obtained by a four-hour jaunt to Monticello.

Will Moore, the superintendent's son, always brought me a cake his mother had baked and iced for the festivities. His black stockings were powdered with dust, his high laced boots scuffed, but his shirt was freshly starched as he painstakingly and proudly carried the fragile burden up the mile-long trip. The Moores were very poor but he always brought a cake.

My birthday was in September and the day began by my sitting in Mother's chair, garlanded with golden rod and all the family presents heaped onto my breakfast plate. It proceeded through morning excitements to the Party, then exhaustion and bed with the realization that there was nothing to look forward to for another year.

In between birthdays there were plays written especially by Pop, and pageants, always one big one on a Single Tax theme, with the landowner grabbing all the pine cones and everyone else (without pine cones) in rags wailing. Eventually Louise Pitman, in cheese cloth and blindfolded as Justice, was led on, and unblindfolded; she then ordered the dividing up of the pine cones amid rejoicing and pre-adolescent piping of the land song:

> "The land, the land
> 'Twas God who gave the land . . ."

Instant ice cream and a merciful change of sound effects! Interestingly enough, I don't believe a single child, with the exception of Bee George, ever retained an understanding or interest in the Single Tax, although their concern with pine cones remained lively.

Between parties and plays there were picnics in Gordon's Pavilion or at marvelous Mongaup Falls or in our own black, mysterious, secret, whispering pine grove, moonlight hayrides, and wizards' covens, when we made brews of puffballs for undesirable neighbors, including Earl Hance, whom we kids considered our very own Peeping Tom. (It was on my lawn because I had the most puffballs; certainly there was no other reason for tolerating me.) The brew looked vile enough to teach anyone a lesson, but I believe the boys lost their nerve and chucked it away in the ferns. It would not have mattered. Puffballs are perfectly benign, although black and appropriately rotten; they are, in fact, favored by some as a delicacy. The beautiful, pure white amanitas, on the other hand, of alabaster stalk and parasol, as unsullied as any of our poetry-reading ladies, was the one to beware of, deadly and with no known antidote. There was a false amanitas, very similar and perfectly harmless. You learned the difference after you'd swallowed. Also, there was some folklore about a spoon turning black and disintegrating. I'm sorry Earl Hance was not put to the test. Puffballs remain, as far as Merriewold is concerned, what the herbalists call "unproven."

Between parties and pageants there were tennis tournaments. Unlike most country clubs we did not import sportsmen, having hunters on the premises among the locals, and keeping the tennis players in a kind of captivity down in our woods. They were world champions, and they were splendid and they were Father's. In those days it was forbidden for an amateur to earn money of any kind whatever at his game; tennis sponsors were permitted to give great players pocket money only. And since a really good tennis player can do nothing else, they lived on handouts, and it nearly always corrupted them. Today Fred Alexander of the Davis Cup team would be a millionaire. Then, he was an amateur, a world figure, and a pauper. And so he was very glad to live on Father's bounty. It was rather fancy for a young playwright (even a successful and known one) to keep his own private world champion, but in those days possible.

The Sullivan County tennis championships were held on our court, it being the best (and only) court in Sullivan County. Indeed, Father organized them and, as there was no tennis at all in a radius of fifty miles (not until one reached Tuxedo Park), there never was any thought of holding matches elsewhere. Father played every clear afternoon. He played with Fred Alexander, Ed Fisher, and the young Clarkes.

Fred Alexander had a wife and son, but he'd gotten tired of them, so he lived down there where I mustn't go, in a tent, summer and winter. It was called Kampski, and he hung his pots and frying pans on a tree, and he kept his butter and milk in the running brook.

Occasionally Mother took pity on him and his tinned dinners and asked him up to a proper meal with salad and dessert in our blue and white dishes. While she mixed the salad dressing with a wooden spoon from the pretty glass cruets he talked court surfaces with Pop, and strokes. Then he shot out his lower jaw ("rather like a boy barracuda," said Pop) and he grinned.

> "Oh, they're wearing them highya
> Highya, highya, highya
> In Hawaia . . ."

And he shot out his jaw again and darted his piercing eyes around. Father laughed. Mother thought it mildly amusing the first three times, after that not.

"Fred, don't you know another song?" she inquired.

"Yes, but not fit for ladies."

And he roared. Mother didn't.

When we moved later to Hollywood, damned if Fred Alexander didn't come along, still with his gorgeous forehand drive and serve, still a pauper. He pitched his tent in the orchard in back of our Hollywood Boulevard house and played tennis every day with Father. And every night (not every other night) he had dinner with us and the two men replayed verbally, as tennis players always do, every single point. How and why my mother stood it I do not know. I did, gladly, because I was in love with Father and because he and Fred were training me to be a tennis champion.

Fred had a tennis friend of his own, also a champion, Ed Fisher, a man who frequently shared Fred's tent at Merriewold, a man of terrible strength and pretty sound style. He lived in Kampski too from time to time with his dog Huckleberry. And like all tennis players he was beggar-poor. Father offered him a place to live. Fred offered him hash and coffee. The problem was to get to Merriewold, one hundred miles from New York. So he walked and wore his wardrobe, three suits, one on top of the other. His toothbrush was presumably in one of the pockets. It must have taken him four days. I don't know what he ate en route.

Unfortunately Ed Fisher had a cyclical mental illness which manifested itself in religious mania. The strength which was so stunning on the tennis court proved nearly fatal to his friends.

"Christ is coming," he said one spring, and decorated a chair with new leaves and spring flowers. He then went to a birch sapling and twisted two young branches off. "Christ is coming soon," he said to Fred one morning at dawn, "but He wants you dead first."

Fred pulled out the pistol he had put under his pillow for just such an occasion and leveled it at Ed's head. "Take one step nearer," he warned, "and I shoot to kill."

Ed said, "Oh, all right," and he went off singing, but he pulled up a young pine tree as he wandered into the woods.

He fetched up at the superintendent's house, then occupied by the McCormacks.

"Where's Tom?" he asked Mrs. McCormack.

"Out," she said.

"Well, tell him to come see me," said Ed good-naturedly. "I've got to kill him."

"All right," she said, "I'll tell him." Then she went to the phone and called an ambulance from the Middletown State Hospital. (This was after we got a party line, one at the superintendent's, one at the Inn.) Four men arrived with strait jackets. Even so they had trouble. Fred had to help with his gun. It was very unpleasant because Fred was really fond of Ed. And Ed could play a splendid game of tennis. He was out of Middletown State for the next tournament; he was always out by tournament time.

After tennis the men went down to the pool and dashed buckets of chilled rock water over each other and roared. We could hear them shouting and yelling down in the woods. I was forbidden to go there because I was told they were naked. I listened to them, and thrilled with excitement.

One very hot afternoon I had my bath and Mother rubbed me down with olive oil (some doctor had told her this was good for baby skin—there was no baby oil on the market then). Mother said, "Go show Aunt Bettie," and rushed back to her tennis guests. I padded out to the porch naked and glistening and smelling like a salad, and Aunt Bettie said, "Oh my beauty!" and kissed me on the back of the neck and patted my behind, and then I said, "Now I'll show Father," and Aunt Bettie said, "Oh, I wouldn't do that." But I disagreed, and marched resolutely toward our tennis courts.

All Merriewold was present. Bernardo (El Señor) Braga, the sugar magnate, sat amply in a front wicker chair, beside him his lovely Maude, in pale blue and a fine panama. Their spindly legged sons moved about. Their nephews, Rionadas, flashed brilliantly as ball boys, or lounged, gallantly dressed as Mexican or Cuban hidalgos, their horses tethered at the gate. In another front seat sat J. I. C. Clarke, the poet, behind his stomach. He stretched his feet and blew out aureoles of cigar smoke. He was gallant to the ladies, who were on high-backed benches behind him. And well behind was Auntie Clarke, silent in her rouge and her boned collar. Aunt Nan Moody was there with her enormous bosom and thick ankles and three musicians. She was being feminine and adorable no matter what the score, but no one paid any attention to her coos except the musicians. All the others were there, the Shrivers, the Collinses, the Blacks, the Hendrickses.

Behind the rows was a lemonade table set out by Mother, and she herself had hurriedly reseated herself on a flat rock with the young Cuban, José Capablanca, the boy international chess master and guest of the Bragas, the game laid out between them. Mother was lost in study. He was lost in the tennis and he did not glance around except to remark, "Don't do that. I'll check in eight moves." There was not a sound except the ball and the umpire, Fred Alexander, mounted on a flat wooden table calling out the score, and the slight rustle as all the embroidered parasols and straw hats turned from one side to another.

Into this magic cocoon I entered, glistening, slippery, smelly, and stark. Father stopped in mid-serve. All heads turned. I held absolute attention. I continued my shining, silent advance. "Go back, Agnes, you'll catch cold," said Father in the quiet.

I surveyed him squarely and left, unhurried. There was laughter. It didn't matter. Bill Clarke had seen. He had laughed and he too missed the next stroke.

That was my only lifelong exhibitionism. It was, however, I believe, splendid; in public, in the star position, uncurtailed, at the peak of the afternoon, and under all those embroidered parasols.

Mother had something to say later. I hated to be crossed. But, so did Mother, and Mother, for the moment, seemed to have the upper hand.

The tennis games were the men's games. The women's were equally intense, but having to do with reality, like food, which was their province, and money. They had no money of their own, or very little, for indeed, none of them had ever earned a penny. They batted the subject between them as an exotic, daring, carefree sport. They would have denied aggressively any suggestion of dissension and indeed I think they knew none beyond what all sisters and cousins share. "The Hen Coop," Father called them when they were all on the front porch chattering and sewing and indulging themselves in speculation that little ears should not hear. Every meal was a tournament of unyielding generosity—away from the men, that is.

"Marie, let me help set the table."

"Certainly not. You've been working."

"Marie, I insist."

"I won't have it. Put that dish down, Alice, this minute."

"You've been on your feet for two hours, and Ruth is dead—cooking in this heat."

"Alice, don't!"

They struggled.

"Drop that dish!"

Alice did. Peals of laughter.

The scene in ice cream parlors was straight opéra bouffe.

"Give me the check."

"No, it's mine. I asked you."

"But we said Dutch."

"We said nothing of the kind."

"Take your hands off that."

"Waiter, bring me another check."

He had to. The bill was in shreds.

You'd think they were protesting largesse. The sums involved were never more than $3.50.

The children had been known to run out in embarrassed exasperation and wait out the wrangling. This was a kind of love-play, but it became very high-voiced. At times they had been known to throw water and the children always got drenched.

Once Jane in exasperation got a jug of water in rebuttal. "Game's over," sang out my mother firmly and quite unfairly.

For the rest of the family every company meal was a gymnasium of competitive altruism.

"Don't give me such a big piece. The small piece."

"No, that's for me."

At home the children were served last, naturally. But because of the strife they always got the bigger and choicer allotments of everything. Then often Alice and Mother, whose dinner hours were different, arrived to consider the scene.

"Marie, why are you giving the best of everything to Henry? You are spoiling him."

What Henry was at the moment was bewildered.

"Henry, give your plate to Auntie Elmoore, that's a dear boy. Jane, your mother should have that. You don't want to eat the heart of everything and let her have remnants, do you?"

Jane went sullen red to the roots of her red hair.

Alice added, "Now Little Bea wouldn't have done that."

I looked up triumphantly. Jane shot me a mortal look. Aunt Marie said timidly, "Alice, it's my fault."

"Yes, it is," said Alice.

They didn't talk this way when the men were around. The men got the first and the best of everything as a matter of course, and meals were more or less decorous and attentive to Papa. I'm sure the children were gratified. After all, authority is restful.

We had houseguests. There were, of course, Father's collaborators, all kinds and sexes. There were relatives. The distinguished Jewish relatives from England, quite superior, with marvelous, refined accents; the American relatives; many people who were goodhearted and charming and exasperatingly dull; and Father's brother, Cecil, who was a young and brilliant and adorable man, with a very handsome wife and a small, uncontrollable daughter who, among other things, ate poison mushrooms on the front lawn and provided an extremely lively evening for the family. That is, we thought she ate them, because they disappeared after she'd been around for a few minutes. And the adult members of the family spent the next two hours in an agony in the bathroom; results colorful but inconclusive. Apparently she hadn't really eaten them because she's still here and very healthy.

Uncle Cecil came several times and was very helpful in that he had an open touring car. He drove us down from Merriewold one October, the first time I had made the trip by car. It took very nearly six hours. Cecil was interesting because he was full of ideas, such as the hunting trips he was always taking in Canada and Lower California and places like that and the new ventures for the theater, and finally new ventures for that peculiar thing, moving pictures, which he was extremely full of and in which he became anxious to enlist Father's attention. He presently went off West to his tatterdemalion schemes and was lost to the legitimate theater and its honorable pursuits as an active member, and to us, his family, as a little brother. It didn't matter to him. He did very nicely on his own, and he didn't like Merriewold much; he had never liked tennis.

John Erskine, Pop's classmate and best friend, came and I remember him well because he would not go driving in a buggy on Sunday (against his religious beliefs) and because he taught me my alphabet, letting me say "lmnop" as one letter. He later became the Dean of the English Department of Columbia, the author of bestselling risqué novels, and the first head of the Juilliard School.

We had lots of musicians. We lived on music. It was part of the Merriewold environment. We had music all the time. Mother sang with a high, sweet coloratura and a natural easy trill. She sang Mozart clearly and prettily. But she was nervous when Father sang with her. She grew more and more nervous until she stopped singing altogether. Pop sang in a true baritone and he never grew nervous, no matter who was present, Reinhold Warrenwrath, Edward Johnson, Jeanne Gerville-Réache. With a cigar in one hand and a drink in the other he sang, and, it seemed to me, he sang well. In any case, he sang with ebullience.

"When are you going to be able to accompany me?" he asked me periodically.

"Next year," I answered matter-of-factly. I was six at the time and Father sang Schumann, Wagner, and Debussy. I gave myself six months to catch up.

Every house had a piano. Father's very young Aunt Bettie de Mille Pitman played the piano beautifully, fine music as well as popular. She gave piano lessons and she played at all the Inn dances to help out the family's budget. She was the official Inn hostess and got, in exchange, free summer board and room for her whole family. Her teacher was an ancient Austrian, Professor Edward Meyerhofer. He had composed and played her wedding march and presented it to her in white satin covers with a dedication in his beautiful German script. He became my piano teacher.

At five I had hurled myself at our upright piano and spent long and excruciating half hours improvising with the palms of my hands. "Mozart," said Mother, "a young female Mozart." It was obvious.

And while Mother believed that natural talent should not be subdued by instruction, it was quite apparent that my enormous musical gifts needed some curbing, at least acoustically.

Professor Meyerhofer had arrived at six o'clock one night and was ushered by Mamie into the living room on 118th Street where I was pounding and smashing. He was very old, grayhaired and bearded (actually about sixty-odd). He sat for some minutes patiently and then as I paused for breath (my exercises required a good deal of arm action and running) inquired in a heavy Austrian accent "if I liked to play."

"Yes," I said, barely looking around, "and I'm very good."

He was mercifully summoned to my father's study to discuss terms, probably two dollars an hour or some such.

The next afternoon he came for the first lesson. The running stopped. We got down to basic German five-finger exercises, and he had no regard for my youth or my enormous personality. He was interested in fingers, and the position of the wrist and other galling inconsequentials.

He had been Theodor Leschetizky's first pupil. He told me this as I sat glowering between bouts. Leschetizky was very young, about sixteen, young Edward Meyerhofer about eight, and he had felt about finger studies as I obviously did, and he balked as I was balking. Leschetizky had thrown a dictionary at his head and his aim had been good. Young Edward had gone back crying to his father and begged to be set digging potatoes instead of continuing at the keyboard. Professor Meyerhofer laughed softly as he told me. I was swinging around on the piano stool banging my feet against the carved round supports. I was bored by all this, but somehow the names stuck. His father, who had known Franz Schubert (there are lyrics, I later discovered, by Meyerhofer to the Schubert songs), was adamant about the musical instruction and had sent him back. The pupil could not have been too happy or too successful because at sixteen he had run away to Mexico with Maximilian (who was Maximilian? who was Mexico?) and had served in the army there as a foot soldier. And when the débâcle came (who was the débâcle?) he had been captured and kept in an adobe hut by Juárez's Mexican soldiers and was slated to be shot in the morning. But somehow he and the other captives got hold of a bottle of tequila and got the jailors drunk and there was no shooting and a French company arrived and saved them.

I was six years old and not able yet to read. (Mother's home-made do-it-yourself system! I read music before words.) I did not know a thing about history. My piano teacher had known Maximilian and had served under him and had spoken to him, possibly also had seen Carlota. I had not the maturity or sense to ask the proper questions. His father had known Schubert. Oh God—the chances gone by!

(I am reminded of Carlyle's writing about Marat in his *French Revolution,* 1837. "Good God, there is an aunt of his living today in Paris.")

"Well," said Professor Meyerhofer, "that's enough talking. You're rested now. Back to work."

And we started over. The damnable Czerny, all the keys depressed and one finger at a time, striking like a hammer, and the wrist not jerking, and the feet not moving, and tongue inside the mouth, and the back straight. Oh help! Oh God save me! Oh let the phone ring! Oh Mother! Now, the same exercise with the hand opening to full stretch between each sounded note. And was that all necessary? Yes, it was. And Do It.

And besides that, my dear, there was to be a twenty-minute practice every day that he did not come, not longer because my brain would not stand it. There was nothing wrong with my brain. It was because I was bright that I could not endure the monotony of these organized digital fidgets. I hid behind the bookcase, under sofas. Mother dragged me out by the ankle and sat, poor thing, like a prison matron while I Did It.

"Now," said Professor Meyerhofer one day twenty or so years later, "you will have a whole piece to play as a reward. It is sixteen bars long. You know what a bar is? Good! You count 4/4 to the bar. It is called 'Brownies in the Rain' and it is on repeated notes. But you use different fingers for the repetitions. It gives a fresher sound. Pretty, no?"

No.

But I had fallen in love with him. So Mother invited him to Merriewold for three weeks that summer. He arrived one night at about six. I heard the wagon wheels at the bend of the road and rushed to stand on the low stone wall, and when the wagon creaked into sight I was in a good position to throw myself on his bosom, which I did with a force to take the breath from his poor old chest. I remained clinging tentacle fashion until he reached the one-room cabin Mother had fixed for him below. It was a roofed box containing a pallet bed, an oil lamp, three pegs for his clothes, a chair, and, of course, an upright piano. She had placed bowls of ferns around and on the piano a jar of pink blooming laurel. This was a nice thought, but redundant; outside the window were square miles of blooming laurel.

At nine o'clock the next morning Mr. Meyerhofer was in his bower and I was beside him, sitting up straight on my stool, my wrists in proper position. We shattered Paradise.

"Can't I have a real piece?" I wheedled.

"Let us hear 'Brownies in the Rain' with nice finger action—third, second, one."

Somewhere along about here my passion for my master just faintly filmed over.

In the afternoon he came up to our upright and played Chopin. I took my shoes off and went out on the grass and pranced about. "Look at the child," everyone said. "What beautiful hair in the sunlight!" I smirked. But Mother, who had better hair, was not impressed. Never mind the golden locks. There was something bewitched in the prancing.

Professor Meyerhofer's piano sounded through the woods, his meticulous nineteenth-century playing of Liszt; and farther up the road Aunt Nan Moody and her son, Ernest, playing Brahms on their Steinway grand (Aunt Nan had pretensions as a pianist and besides there were all her musicians); and on our well-tuned upright Aunt Bettie Pitman, Mr. Meyerhofer's favorite pupil, playing Gluck and Debussy and, of course, Brahms and Schumann. (There was a piano tuner because these amateur musicians liked an instrument in reasonably good shape. He had to walk three miles from the station which he did most unwillingly and with great trepidation, fearful of the many bears "with beady eyes." But of course there was his fee, five dollars an instrument, and there weren't as many bears as all that. He exaggerated.) The pianos sounded for half a mile, since the other sounds were intermittent, and unrhythmic and different in nature. We always knew who was playing and what. We would stop and listen in love and pleasure, down by the lake, way off in the forest. There were no other sounds, just a wagon wheel or the sudden rushing of an animal. The tennis cries could be heard too far away, even outside the confines of the park, and they were loud. And then would come the lovely salutation of melody. For us personally. Schumann speaking to us. But underneath always we heard the web of life, the matrix sound, the stillness.

There were the Volpés. Arnold Volpé was a Russian Jewish émigré of considerable musical ability. He formed the first outdoor orchestral concerts in America in Central Park. These were supported by private gifts and it was the first occasion most people had of hearing contemporary Russian music: Glazunov, Glière, Rachmaninoff. It was he who gave Mother the matinee tickets to Adeline Genée, an outing which quite literally changed my life.

He had an active and vociferous and present family, a large vocal wife and two large, clamorous children, nice enough girls, I suppose, but definitely in my way. His wife, Marie Volpé, was a formidable, handsome, black-haired creature who dragooned her two daughters into eating oatmeal by saying, "Mother will love you if you do, and Mother will love you even more if you eat it without sugar and cream." That struck me as a non sequitur, also a harsh and unusual treatment. I was never obliged to face up to oatmeal. I thought the lot of the Volpé girls hard. But then I never liked them much. They were poky city creatures, they trembled at thunderstorms and shrieked at lizards down the neck.

"Please don't put lizards down them," said Madame Volpé.

"They're harmless. They're not like snakes or spiders. There are some harmless snakes too."

"Please don't put anything down them. They're city children and they don't understand."

I scowled in scorn.

"You're not to do it again, Agnes, do you hear?" said Mother sharply. Another curtailment.

"This morning," said Mrs. Volpé, "there was an old stick standing out in the water, just where the girls were swimming. I put my hand out to lean on it and do you know," her eyes grew round "as I put my hand out, it sank down!"

"Probably a snapping turtle," I said brightly.

"Oh God! Right where my girls were swimming!"

"Yes," I added thoughtfully, "that's surely what it was. They can bite through broomsticks."

"Oh God!"

But what could I do with the girls? They were so namby-pamby and so lumpish. I sought my own cronies. I took to running away and hiding. Mrs. Volpé spoke again. "I hear Agnes has said she doesn't want to play with them because they're Jews."

"It can't be true!" Mother turned to me in real shock. Indeed, I had said just that. I'd learned it from the kids at the Inn. Racism was starting up in our Promised Land and particularly with the young. I am sure I blamed the others. Mother was as emphatic about this as anything I ever recall. She may even have spanked me. This was not naughty, this was treacherous and vicious "and your father is half a Jew, and you are a quarter." That still didn't make me like the Volpé girls. The visit terminated with parental protestation of absolute delight. The three girls stared sullenly at one another. We have never met since.

So in our haven the little boys and girls learned to despise their lifetime playmates. (We despised the Catholics too, of course.) We had in our group from the beginning notable Jews, Yancey Cohen, for instance, the writer and economist; the Hendrickses, and that is an estimable name, witty and charming, in the largest house on the premises—the largest, of course, but the great one.

Margaret Sanville, a Jewish girl at the Club, wanted to join our games. Margaret Sanville was all right for some things, but we didn't want her for our secret games. We took to running away and hiding in the ferns. My little sister also tried to join and was rebuffed. She was a Jew also, but that was not the reason. She was too little and got in the way. And she kept asking questions which it was beneath us to answer and which, because she was smart, it was impossible to answer. We went on secretly talking against the Jews. It was easier.

Even in our own family there was anti-Semitism (although unvoiced) and this was curious, when one thinks about it. Cecil de Mille always spoke of "my English mother who is an Episcopalian." The head of the family, my grandfather Henry de Mille, was studying for Episcopal orders, but he had married a Jew, an elocutionist and a near-actress. Henry de Mille died young and his ashes were kept in his mother's bedroom. She kept several boxes of human relics, quite a collection of them—Henry's and his daughter's, little Agnes, who died of spinal meningitis. And then there was, strangely enough, the Jewish wife's younger brother, the charming Mark, an Englishman. They had all been very fond of him so they kept him. When Madame de Mille herself finally died, she and her rich accumulation were laid to rest and everybody's name was put on the tombstone with all the dates recorded—everybody except Mark, whose name was not mentioned. No reason was given but, after all, it was a Protestant burying ground and they saw no reason to be flamboyant about Jewish names. Nor even truthful. There is no record whatever of his grave.

I was very lonely, I think. The girl visitors at the Inn were transient and tentative. The George girl cousins were a mile away. Like many young females I was extremely aggressive toward boys. The trouble is there weren't any, or few and not ready to hand. The boys nearby were big and rough and impatient. John Pitman, my father's young cousin with whom I was in love, scorned me. The others found me both inadequate and inquisitive.

So I made some up, and in this imaginary world I was very popular. Dickie had a large rock of his own. Gockle lived in the sunflower bed. Mother was halted by piercing screams in midsquat several times: "Gockle already has that chair!"

The real-life boys were for the most part older, and they did not play with girls—not even Ernest Moody who was more or less my friend.

Ernest played with me only at the very end of the summer when everyone suitable, that is, male, had gone back to school. Therefore I valued intensely whatever time I had with him. One afternoon when he had reluctantly agreed to a play session, I marched up to the Moodys' new house, The Ledge, which Mr. Moody was building himself almost singlehanded. The house was inhabited but unfinished. I looked forward to a really delicious dalliance with Ernie, in the open underporch which provided a kind of cave. The porch itself was littered with crates which we had been told we could have as soon as they were emptied. They were half-emptied already, with excelsior and glass littering the floor. I seized a couple of loose shingles and went into my lair beneath, emerging every fifteen minutes to bawl up to Ernest, who hollered back that his mother was detaining him with household chores and to shut up and wait. My patience was short in those days. I went yet again to shriek, "How long do you think ten minutes is anyway?" And behold, this time something interesting was happening; a fire was creeping from the straw to the wall. Well, I wasn't going to tell them about that; that would only bring on more postponements.

The next time I ascended the fire was getting along nicely. It had taken over one wall and was testing a window. It didn't make much noise. It just burned. "Oh, do come down. I'm getting tired," I yelled. (They couldn't say I hadn't called out.)

"Coming!"

I escaped below.

Ernie's shriek on arrival got me out from under, and I had the entertaining spectacle of Uncle John Moody running around, hollering like mad, and all the family emptying basins, pitchers, and bowls. I'd never seen them hurry so. Pudgy Uncle John, the Dean of Wall Street, ran like a stallion.

"Well, I'm going," I said to nobody interested.

"Agnes," said Aunt Nan, stopping for one breathless moment, "did you know this was happening?" Naturally I didn't bother to answer.

Later that night my mother cornered me. "Aunt Nan says you

must have known the house was on fire for about twenty minutes before Ernest discovered it. Why didn't you tell them?"

I dropped my eyes and whispered, "I didn't like to bother anyone."

Then Mother spoke a verity: quietly and forever. "When someone's house is on fire he would like to be told. You can count on that."

We never seemed to get older. The days were so long, the afternoons so long, unless Mother made picnics or dress-ups.

Sometimes a kid had a dirty idea, and we found privacy to experiment. But our mothers were pure and they loved us. We stopped.

I was still lonely. Margaret was not enough.

Then began my adoration of Elizabeth Pitman. The Pitmans were de Milles and Father's near relatives, and they were the most vital and glamorous of all.

The Pitmans stayed every summer at the Inn for two months. There were three children all older than I, two girls and a boy, and they became pivotal members of my life. Louise, the elder sister, wasn't a sport like Elizabeth and John, but she was a pillar of society. She helped her mother with the daily chamber pots and the slops quite cheerfully.

With John, the middle one, I fell in love. John was big-boned, sterling, and uncouth. He did not do well in school and was two years behind his proper grade. But his truthfulness was unquestioned and he was an Eagle Scout and planted trees whenever doubts assailed him. He was also an accredited lifesaver and could go on much too long hikes without complaining. I thought him the model of all male beauty. It was really his teeth which were magnificent and his throaty chuckle. Also he was blond and deeply tanned. And I was fascinated by the bones of his ankles and wrists like the strong bones of a deer's leg and so much better than any girl's bones. I proposed marriage. "Not on your life," he said, snapping his gum and flexing his strong toes inside his high laced sneakers. "We're cousins. It's unhealthy. Cousins can't marry." He went out laughing and my heart withered.

John wanted to be a general—like his Grandfather Pitman. Grandpa, a Yankee, had been a drummer boy at the Battle of Bull Run, where he had climbed into a tree to see the action, and when he climbed down he discovered that, all his superiors having been killed, he consequently was now an officer himself. He was always very patriotic and John was patriotic too. John's North Carolinian grandmother (my great-grandmother), Madame de Mille, lived in the next bedroom in Orange. Her daughter, Aunt Bettie, whose house it was, forbade them to discuss the War Between the States. So when Grandma sang "The Bonnie Blue Flag" all by herself with the door closed, the General retorted with "The Battle Hymn of the Republic." Aunt Bettie played Brahms, which was neutral. He was being groomed in tennis by Fred Alexander, and was going to be taken on in the next tournament as Fred's partner.

John was our leader and a sport, no question about that. Elizabeth, his younger sister, was a sport also. The boys said so. "She's the only girl fit to play with," said Ernie Moody, looking at me contemptuously. "But she's not a girl, she's a boy really."

It was to Elizabeth, then, that I attached myself. Her rock sturdiness drew me. She was three years older than I, and therefore stronger and smarter and bigger. She was better in every way. She could cook eggs in three ways, make Boy Scout shelters (John had taught her), beds of pine needles in the forest, help old ladies cross the street, bind up bee stings or broken wrists, and she could do long division. She was greatly gifted. And she never forgot one single time to put her doll to bed. She said grace at table when her mother had headaches, pitched a ball like a boy and was invited—invited, mind you—to play with them. She could swim with five different strokes and without water wings. And she could play the piano—not, of course, like her mother, but better than I. Well, at least longer, and she didn't squirm and she didn't whine. It stood to reason that Professor Meyerhofer loved her more.

Elizabeth was not pretty or even feminine, although naturally I didn't think in those terms. She was strong-boned and forthright, a homely young Spartan with slightly buck teeth and something approaching an Adam's apple, but strong and supple and honest and slender and swift. Her keynote was common sense and practicality, exotic qualities for me. I danced around her, my opposite, I, with my aureole of golden curls and tiny fairy feet, my vulnerability, my essential idiot femininity. She was the matrix. I adored her. And she had a plain laugh, and she only laughed at what was plainly there to laugh at, essential. Out of the vague haze which was my childhood there focused one recognition, one personality, Elizabeth. Oh beautiful name! Oh brown and beautiful girl, lean and strong! Diana.

I did whatever she wanted, anything, any time. I invented ghosts. Heavens, I knew them. I'd seen them. But she explained about the fairies, so much more orthodox and acceptable. So I gave up the ghosts. She explained where the fairies were. She discovered for me where they, or at least a good covey of them, lived: in a dazzle of motes and shafted light between the birches near the garbage dumps.

But how to see them?

"By doing good," said Elizabeth promptly. Since she was a Girl Guide and came of a high church Episcopal family, she was not to be questioned.

"Look!" she said suddenly, pointing to nothing.

"What?" I whispered, instantly checking all living processes.

"A fairy!" breathed my cousin.

"What does it look like?" I asked.

"It's hard to say," she replied with great truth. "Wait quietly."

I waited, squatting until the blood left my hams and toetips, but saw nothing. It was then that she explained that one could see the fairies only if one deserved to. This, of course, put a new and unfamiliar premium on imagination. Out of pure love I curbed my instincts and attended. We took to sitting motionless for hours, crouched in the bracken, our unblinking eyes fixed on a dead branch, and stared and stared until all the woods suddenly changed.

"I see it," said my cousin.

"I can't see it," I was forced to admit. "It's nothing but twigs still. I'm not good enough."

Elizabeth suggested we could become fairies ourselves, which seemed doubtful what with having to eat cereal every morning and wear rubbers; but if we couldn't, then at least perhaps we could acquire a relationship about which the grown-ups need have no knowledge. The means she laid down for attainment were edifying: we must do three kindnesses on three consecutive days.

"I don't know anybody to be kind to," I said.

"You'll find kind things to do little by little," Elizabeth continued, a little smugly. "Mother says being kind is an art too. (There was an innuendo there.) But you did miss Tuesday and you'll have to start all over again."

Peanut butter, fudge, mud, rubber boots, wet moss, salamanders, bitter daddy-longlegs smell, skinned knees, iodine (Aunt

Bettie Pitman was brutal about this), gum boils, insect bites, itchings, wintergreens, huckleberries, ennui.

The days seemed so long, the afternoons so very long, and the forest endured them and moved like water through the long, golden hours and waited for the big change.

And all summer long, as there were seasonal flowers and berries, there were grown-up flirtations—those that resulted in engagements and those that did not. And there was very light butterfly dalliance among the young marrieds. And Pop was wicked about this and teased Mother and the other ladies dreadfully. But there were other, more annoying, more persistent troubles. Our dream-like summers were marred in a trivial, daily way, like a hangnail, a flaw. There was the tediousness of Mother's unvarying mode of expression, and although she commanded a sprightly and darling humor, altogether refreshing, concerning things directly observed, on the Verities she mouthed the banal. In Mother's vocabulary Scintillating Wit was Pop. It was always Pop; the Philosophy, that would be Henry George's work; Blue-blooded Episcopalians and/or BB Philadelphians, the Henry George family; Ardent Disciples, Henry George's followers; Deadly Bores—none of the above. (Fat Aunt Alice irreverently called the Georgists "Woolies.") But to Mother, people were either Ardent Disciples or Tammany Rascals and/or Vested Interests. Nobody just read *Progress and Poverty* and thought the scheme would be a good idea or conversely didn't think it would be a good idea. In Mother's opinion the latter had no merit of any kind whatsoever, and since they were benighted she accordingly chose not to consider them. Indeed and truly she was a bigoted and rigid liberal. I think Scintillating Wit sometimes got very tired of all this; there were expressions on his face and there were vocal exchanges.

And then there was the matter of their two temperaments, although they adored one another. Pop was a selfish man, debonair and willful, who equated manhood with unalloyed, self-centered ego. We didn't mind. We'd never known anything else. ("Anne, come blow your child's nose.") It made him all the more wonderful. But Mother, for all her fettlesomeness, her redheaded vivacity, had bad doubts about herself. This made her pathetically watchful. This caused her hurt all the time.

I said one afternoon to her, "Mother, I'm going to have a real tennis lesson from Father—at three o'clock. He says I may skip my nap."

Mother was dismayed. "He's going to coach you?"

I nodded proudly.

"I was coaching you," she said.

Then to my embarrassment, to my horror, Mother burst into tears. She continued, "He plays tennis with you. He coaches you. He makes dates with you. You can hardly hold the racket, and the patience he has with you!"

I remembered one day when he was playing with Mother. She rushed to make an overhead smash, or, in her case, pat, and she slipped and sat down hard, racket lost, her nose through the net. I yelled with mirth. Mother started to giggle. Mig screamed. Father cut all that short. He was stony. "This is not tennis." And he walked off the court. I was frightened. Mother looked like a rebuked child and her eyes filled. I put a hand out. "Oh, leave me alone. Go to Mamie—she'll let you lick the chocolate pot."

And again:

Pop said to Mother, "Annie, won't you please not sew for a moment? Try for five minutes. Just for novelty's sake."

"I'll try. I really will. Oh my goodness! Fred is planting the ferns in the wrong place. Free-e-e-d!"

And after the matter of the ferns had been settled, the needle continued—tiny, tiny secure stitches.

Another time, Mother expostulated to me with barely controlled hysteria, "I played your Father's accompaniments, but not well—not as well as Aunt Bettie, but certainly better than you." (Give me time, Mother.)

The next day Aunt Bettie said over their sewing, "Anne, Anne, you can't be all things to your man. You're his wife and he adores you and you're the mother of his two children. That's enough."

"But I'm his pal," said Mother in a quivery voice. "I should be the first to share . . . his delights, his ideas, his work. I'm his mate (she used this word). He let John Erskine see the first act before I did."

"But John's a professional playwright!"

"But I'm his—his—" she broke down. "I love him so . . . I'd let him see anything of mine. Nobody else would matter."

Aunt Bettie's arms were around her. "He loves you, darling, absolutely, but men are different."

And he did. I know this. But something was wrong. I crept away into the bushes and put my head against a rock.

It is in these silly and fragile signs that there glints the sure clues to the destruction of lives.

Chapter 3

❧ At the Other End was the Palace, Sho-Foo-Den, and this was the sign that Merriewold mattered and that we mattered, because this Japanese house lay quite outside our homely amusements. It had international importance, and it had beauty. This was no Sullivan County cottage. And in this house occurred the tragedy, and so we never forgot anything about it, not anything at all.

Outside the gates with the classic seals was a buttercup field and my Grandmother George's gabled and shingled house in which Uncle Harry and Aunt Marie George now lived. We were all neighbors together, the rich and splendid Japanese people in that place and the tobacco-spitting Yankee farmers and us, the summer residents. The local farm children coming back from milking or huckleberrying, or we summer folks walking sedately by our mothers' sides, stopped at those gates to wonder, and lowered our voices as we passed. We often sat in the grass making daisy chains or hats of upside-down bracken, when darkly at our backs sounded the throbbing of struck bronze and a bird-like voice speaking in an ancient watery incomprehensible tongue. And we fell silent and lifted our heads and shivered.

That house had world renown and when the master was present, our flag flew and we held our heads higher. Way down in the forest, way back in the huckleberry swamps, at nursery suppers, at tennis teas and birthday picnics, we knew that we had a royal family, a Presence, and that our woods were not only lovely, but important.

The ordinary Americans lived in a world of everyday needs and comfortable coping, in which there were sometimes accidents and even misconduct. In our world Mother was the Absolute, the Norm, the Focal Measure. The way she did things was The Way, the way Mother put up her hair, the way she dressed, the way she presided at table. She had royal prerogative and set royal example, and nobody, not even Mrs. Astor, whom we were never privileged to meet, knew better—except the lady at the Great House, Aunt Takamine. She was royaler. She was better. There was an aura sanctioned and blessed about her that no one ever questioned. She had the kind of presence that made everyone rise, men of course, but women too, and without knowing who she was, not only in Japan but everywhere she went. Her tact, her courtesy, became legendary. A welcome from Takamine-san, no matter what your age, was like a diplomatic recognition. She was the supreme example, the Queen.

Mother readily conceded this. The concept was used, as for instance, when I was five and had to have my tonsils removed by surgery on my father's desk. It was important to keep me from eating breakfast, something no ordinary persuasion could accomplish. "Don't you think it would be great fun to go without breakfast and call on Aunt Takamine?" chirped Mother. Great fun, and Aunt Takamine rose to the occasion and rewarded me with one of her gorgeous smiles and gave me a peony. I returned home radiant to face chloroform from the doctor with whom up to that moment I had been in love.

And on my sixth birthday Mother said, "Today you will have lunch with Aunt Takamine in the big dining room." I was especially dressed for the occasion in my best Liberty smock and I was allowed to eat in the great dining room at the gold table under the chandelier of a hundred golden chains. I stared up while chewing at a ceiling of painted medallions depicting all the vegetables, fish, and flesh of Japan. I had been told Aunt Takamine's husband ate on the floor and I looked for crumbs or bits of rice or even a spot on the matting. But there was no sign of floor untidiness and he was not present to demonstrate. The only sound beside Aunt Takamine's musical statements and our unnaturally refined agreements was the trickle of water threading down the flat, upturned stone beside the waiting moss-covered Buddha, the tiny gurgle and swish of the streamlet splashing on pebbles toward the silent ooze of the little lake, and the soughing and rubbing of pine branches. The homemade birthday party that followed was as nothing.

About Dr. Takamine there was only awe.

In the city and for business Uncle Jokichi wore Western clothes and in these he would arrive on the Ontario & Western train at the St. Joseph station—in a flawlessly cut gray tweed suit and soft fedora. But forty minutes later, washed and refreshed in tabi and geta, perfumed (*L'Heure Bleu*), he would stroll about having a replenishing talk with Inamoto, the head gardener, concerning the planting of a lily. Since this flower was to be the one note of color in the twenty-five acres of green, they sometimes deliberated for days. We watched him as he stood in his garden all in white with his scarlet crest of eight arrowheads embroidered on his sleeve, his fresh pink and white skin gleaming beneath his white hair, flicking a scarlet fan, and we thought him the most stylish figure any of us had ever seen.

He was not aloof, he was just different, and superb. He played poker, for instance, with Pop, Manuel Rionda, and Bernardo Braga. It was a very friendly, jolly, all-night game. Will Clarke,

Father's tennis chum, burst in completely potted and accused the Doctor of having cards up his sleeve, which considering that it was a kimono sleeve was an ample and serious accusation.

Uncle Jokichi used to do all sorts of everyday things, like fishing, and not for goldfish either, but for bass and sunfish. And once he took his position by old Mrs. Shriver, who was deaf as a post, and wore a kind of clock on her bosom so that she could hear. But she never could hear very much. He fell out of the boat and set up a tremendous thrashing and flailing. "Tasukete, Tasukete!" he shouted. She didn't hear, but she did notice the disturbance of ripples. Without turning her head, and indeed she looked like an Easter Island figure with a pole, she snapped in her flat, deaf voice, "Walk." So he did. He was, it turned out, in two feet of water. And when he got to shore he turned, with the skirts of his kimono dripping in his hands, and giggled. Easter Island giggled back. The pole waggled. He must have told on himself because conversation with Mrs. Shriver was impossible. No one ever listened to her high monotone. It was very endearing of him to tell of doing anything so plebeian as drowning in two feet of water.

Another time I remember a sort of cabaret given at the Inn to raise money for new tennis nets, and Laura Graves danced a ragtime dance and sang a song then current:

> Peaches are ripe in the summer time
> And that's the time they'll fall;
> Go get your girl in the summer time
> Or you'll never get your girl at all!

She wandered around the dining room floor singing and posturing until she came to the Takamine table. She didn't look at young Jo, the older Takamine son, at all. She went up to Doctor Takamine and whispered, "Go get them! Go get them!" And she

Drama: *Dreams,* a play with a labor message by William de Mille—Agnes, Elizabeth, Margaret Sanville (losing character fast), Louise Pitman.

Fred Alexander, Bill Clarke, and Pop off for three days of fishing on the Neversink. So accoutered, they walked the six miles to the location and back

In Morningside Park with Great-grandmother Samuel. All our outfits were designed and executed by Mother. My costume here was bottle-green with pleated silk on the hat and moss roses. Margaret, my sister —as suitable to one of her years (three)—was in virgin white.

The same, two years before. Other coutures.

Owie, Pop, and Maggie Ming.

Elizabeth de Mille Pitman and her mother, "Aunt Bettie."

Aunt Bettie in her wedding dress.

Ruth, our cook.

Mamie Harlow, our nurse.

had the nerve to chuck him under the chin—the Doctor! The Samurai!

All the rest of us gasped. We expected him to disappear in a cloud of incense. His handsome son, Jo, put his hand over his mouth and began to shake with laughter. The Doctor smiled, rose, and bowed and turned to his diplomatic guest and talked in Japanese. Both older men laughed a good deal. This was a side of the distinguished man we certainly had not guessed. For a moment he was a whole lot less august and paternal. Then Laura came over to my father and did the same (Laura, who was shortly to be burned out, dared to do this). Mother went scarlet, while Father, I regret to say, looked delighted. But Auntie Takamine didn't turn a hair. On such occasions she chose not to notice. But she did say as she passed my mother, "Vulgar little thing, isn't she?"

From the Inn's gossipy informants we learned that any situation dealing with proper Japanese protocol was of course totally different, the time the Imperial Noh dancers came to Merriewold, for instance. Father and J. I. C. Clarke were asked because they were theater men. Besides, J.I.C. had been to Japan and presumably knew what he was looking at. Father didn't, his experience being limited strictly to the West. And so he disgraced the family and his profession and had to be led outside by Mother and quieted down. He not only was bored, he was outraged, and, as always, vocal. A difference in culture seemed to him no excuse. They were charlatans obviously or, at best, deprived people, not having been exposed to Aristotle or Shakespeare. Or even David Belasco. The host, Dr. Takamine, was graciously tolerant, for he had long grown immune to Western ignorance. His wife less so; she had expected more from a ranking playwright. Father's tennis cronies, the Clarke sons, Bill and Boompty, abetted him, alas.

The other guests were just numbed. As I recall, none of them were asked back to the Great House that year.

But we were neighbors and we were asked back eventually—I mean the grown-ups were; I was too little. There were masquerades in honor of the Takamine boys' birthdays, three days apart. (There were lots of masquerades then. Every house had a trunk of dress-ups and every opportunity was taken for bare arms or legs—as in Brünnhilde or Cave-dweller.) All the stone lanterns in the garden winked with candles, and each guest carried a paper globe on a stick and the line flickered and bobbed around the little lake and up the terraced stairs to the great golden rooms. The birthdays were in August and the grounds were twinkling with fireflies.

Bee George was old enough to be invited but we young ones weren't. So we slept on the George porch and listened to the festivities across the trees. And the sound of music was framed and sonorous as it always is when heard through trees and slightly distorted in pitch as though removed in time and, although heard on the instant, already legendary. We lay still, in a sense of awful prescience, for the place put a spell on everyone.

No one could tell where forest ended and garden began, so subtle was the marrying of the two; because except for rhododendron hedges there were no walls or barriers of any kind. The gates to the Great House were never closed, being symbols only. One stepped from ordered planning to wilderness and the unbroken woods, or one stole back, drawn inevitably. In four strides the happenstance of the wild, wild woods became, without fence or marker, the mysterious living work of art that is a garden. The garden was our promise of magic and chivalry, our own gorgeous anachronism.

Naturally we trespassed whenever we could. The owner and

his gardeners always wore native dress, that is, not native to Sullivan County. We spied on the family as we crawled on our bellies beneath moss-paved footways and under arched lacquer bridges, as we played forbidden games, "rode horseback" on the five-hundred-year-old stone lions, one curly haired, one straight, as we climbed over gods, and sat impiously on the flat hat of Emma-hoo, God of Hell; we spied on them, venturing our heads and shoulders inside the stone lanterns (what would have happened had a child got stuck in a granite lantern weighing two tons?—iron mallets? dynamite?). We always stopped as we played and watched them from afar, but we never, if possible, directly crossed the threshold. They knew we were there. We were aware that they were standing still in the footpaths or behind the hedges watching us. But they only nodded and smiled with their crooked teeth and went about their business. Their voices were quiet and musical, but we had no way of knowing what they were talking about, and there were terrible swords hanging on the inside that could slice a newspaper to fringe; we'd seen the butler demonstrate.

One time some of us did get inside the house. It had been a clear day, and then suddenly there was a hurry of leaves, the sky crumpled with thunder and the rain was on us. The underporch proving too close to the copper gutters, we took refuge above, on the porch where only three of us had ever been before. We waited in shaking excitement, flattening our wet noses against the screen door put up in deference to Sullivan County's mosquitoes. Inside—ah, inside looked like pure grandeur. We could dimly see that it was all gold leaf with frescoes of great pine trees and scarlet Japanese maples—an enormous Chinese lantern, pendant with fine golden chains, a lamp fit for the palace of heaven. The piano—there was a Steinway—was ebony, with iris worked tastefully on the legs in the best Parisian art noveau style. And a table with fish. We could make out mysterious persons inside the house who moved about on silent feet.

As we watched from the porch, the rain stung off the curving tin-tiled roofs and bounced in a haze from the red lacquered porch that gleamed in the reflected light of water. The tall, black, naked pine trunks glistened. On the bright moss, pink salamanders tried the soft wetness with their dainty cold toes. The great wooden gong, shaped like a fish, creaked overhead. The bronze porch lanterns sounded, knocking dully as though with muffled clappers. The smell of laurel, rhododendron, and pine came to us in great whiffs. The ground opened before us and breathed suddenly. The green of moss and grass was more brilliant. Leaves were glossy as metal. A mist of water-like perfume rose and hung over the uneven garden steps. And then on the instant, way below by the lake among the blue iris, a wild doe arched on stiffened forelegs, broke cover and bounded off through the bracken to the shelter of the deeper woods.

We waited in a tent of water, expecting at any moment the fire of hell to rip and run the length of the copper ridges and outline the house with green horror. Trees had been struck in the garden and the tearing of wood had merged with the wicked crackling and spitting of the electric spark. But now, though the great branches flung about with a terrible swishing and the ground worked at their feet, the trees held fast. Nothing struck, nothing ripped. The house continued.

We went crazy. We called out imbecilities over the drumming on the roof and the racing sluiceways. We shouted and stamped and ran.

Suddenly Aunt Takamine appeared behind us. "Children, don't make such a racket! Why, you're soaking wet. Come in! Take off your shoes and come in." So we entered the gold hall— we actually entered—and barefoot and wet we tried to sit politely without touching the brocaded chairs. The house smelled of pine and sandalwood and another perfume I have never smelled since.

And then, unfortunately, Minnie Dickens appeared, gaunt and censorious, self-appointed keeper and companion of Aunt Takamine, who never let anything go on that she did not attempt to supervise—except, of course, what the doctor and his sons did. "How can you let those children track wet over your beautiful carpets?" she admonished. "Send them to the kitchen. Let them wait out there until their mothers fetch them."

"Don't be silly, Minnie," said Takamine-san. "Their mothers probably have no idea where they are. They've got to get home as fast as possible and put on dry clothes."

"You're not all that wet," said Minnie, narrowing her black eyes at us. When she did this, she almost looked Japanese herself. She took great pride, she often said so, in the fact that sometimes people mistook her for the wife of the doctor. "Where have you been?"

"Under the porch," we replied primly.

"Doing what?" said Minnie, much too sharply.

"Getting out of the rain."

"Hmm," said Minnie, and added quite vulgarly—she sometimes slipped—"I'll bet!"

"Oh, Minnie, let them alone. We'll have tea, dear, in my room. Come away," and Aunt Takamine put a soothing arm across the gaunt shoulders. Then she turned to us. "Here's Jo. Jo will see you home."

Jo? The Prince? The heir apparent?

Aunt Takamine gave us a large oiled paper umbrella to make our way back under, and Inamoto, the gardener, in a rain cape and hat of straw like those around chianti bottles, brought us another.

"Mother, they're not infants. They're young ladies."

We died. Jo smiled at us under his black waxed mustache and his teeth gleamed, his skin was amber and clean and smooth. He had a chuckle that was pure wickedness, male and light.

"I'll see Little Bea home. She's liable to colds." He tilted her chin up with his finger. She went rosy to her hair. "As for the rest of you scamps . . ."

"Tell your mothers to give you hot baths and put you to bed," called the hostess in her lovely voice. "You may have caught your deaths."

Not us. Once beyond her supervision, we bolted for the woods again. We looked back to see Jo and Little Bea under the large brown and black umbrella, walking along the path. He had his arm around her shoulder. We all blushed. We were all in love with Jo. Big and little, then and for a long time after—the beautiful, the gifted, the tragic Jo. Well, never mind, we'd been inside!

The Great House was used by the Japanese Embassy as its summer residence and it welcomed guests of world-wide distinction. Uncle Jokichi was the best-known, including the Ambassador, and the richest Japanese in America. Years later my cousin, Jane George, traveling through Japan with a group of students, became separated from her companions and lost in a Kyoto department store. She understood not a word of the language, so she said the only two Japanese names she knew—Jokichi Takamine. The manager of the store was instantly summoned and Jane was sent home in a taxi with a box of chocolates and the manager and his colleagues bowing her off on the sidewalk. This was nine years after Takamine's death.

We were so proud to have any part of this nobility! Mother always took our guests to visit and Aunt Takamine was gracious about this and we boasted. I should think so. Down a dirt road and right there, between lunch and swimming, was the most beautiful Oriental garden on the continent, and ours—sort of. We had a presence, if not a neighbor. (One did not rush to Sho-Foo-Den to borrow a pound of butter.)

And we were proud of "our" family, the great world-famous doctor and his beautiful lady. We were proud, and we all partook. They were beyond frailty or imperfection whereas we at the Other End, we Americans, were untidy with quarrels and misunderstandings and although special, of course, and certainly exciting were nevertheless messy and could be expected to prove, all too frequently, quite ordinarily human.

But the Takamines and even the high-minded Georges, who acquired superiority through propinquity, were flawless, of unblemished excellence, with no signs of trouble.

Chapter 4

❧ While the Takamines with their Great House were something like having a branch of the royal family in residence at Merriewold, it was only something like. There was always curiosity, but there was not always respect; that is, behind the family's back. I can't imagine anyone being disrespectful to Dr. Takamine in his presence, or to Aunt Takamine either. But the Inn porch bore witness to the danger of the Yellow Peril, as to that of the Jewish invasion.

I heard the gossips quite often, but Aunt Takamine heard them only once, or once that I knew about. She had walked up to the Inn to use the telephone—I believe she was phoning the Japanese Embassy in Washington. She was accompanied, as always, by Minnie Dickens, and by her Japanese butler.

Marian, the guest of the precocious and stuck-up Laura Graves, tilted back in her wicker chair and said quite loud with a high carrying laugh, "Japs or Chinks, or whatever you like, they're not like us. They don't mix. They'll be letting in niggers next. I don't know any other resort would let in people like that."

Aunt Takamine had a lovely voice and she never raised it. She stopped a minute, set her lips, and then stepped back on the porch. Her heeled, high-laced white shoes clicked on the wood.

She walked up to Marian, who sat staring at her. The girl had the grace to turn first white, then strawberry color. "Young woman," said Auntie Takamine, "obviously you come from some place that does not teach history. The Japanese achieved one of the great civilizations when your ancestors were living in wattle huts and dressing in wolfskins. They also, then and now, set great store by manners. For instance, a Japanese girl would rise when an older woman addressed her. Also, I believe she would not have presumed to make unkind remarks based on ignorance." With that she unfurled her pongee silk parasol and glided away, followed several paces behind by the butler and his basket and by Minnie Dickens looking sanctimonious. Their skirts swished and scattered the pebbles.

"Well, excuse me for living!" said Marian, but none of the ladies knew what to say, and after a bit Marian went indoors alone.

In spite of the Yellow Peril, Sho-Foo-Den was worth any danger, especially when the sons were there. When the boys were at Merriewold the whole atmosphere of the park changed markedly.

Jo would arrive in a white Stutz Bearcat, with which he terrified the neighborhood, an astonishingly professional racing car. Little Bea and Jane were waiting for him with sponges and bath towels and buckets of soapy water, and for a promised five-pound box of chocolates they cleaned his car of every bit of the trip (one hundred miles of dirt roads). They worked very hard. Indeed, they nearly removed the finish. But Jo always paid up promptly and he smiled at them and pinched their cheeks. Jo was dazzling, his glossy mustache, his black glossy hair, the flawless amber skin, the teeth and the wicked eyes. Jo's eyes, slanted, mysterious, made their hearts stop. And besides, he was theirs, and he always gave them chocolates. And then he went off on nocturnal trips and his brother Eben went with him.

Before the days of the Stutz both boys used to ride on motorcycles through the muddy ruts of the country road six miles to the local hot-spot, Monticello, their only light a Japanese lantern on a stick held in the left hand or in their teeth. They roared bawdy Japanese songs as they went, by way of warning. On their return they boasted of the number of "chickens they had killed," and they were not referring to barnyard fowl. They even brought some of the "chickens" home to see the palace in which they lived. There was one young lady who had limited allure. "What does he see in her?" asked their mother. "She has scalloped teeth."

Never mind the teeth. She was there and she was available to him. Their mother was troubled. The Doctor remained, publicly at least, silent, using his money and his gigantic prestige to extricate his sons from their more spectacular predicaments; and they were always forgiven. One smile from either and arms opened.

"Eben was sweet and warm; Jo a little terrifying, with the possibility of being untrustworthy," said the three Beatrices, daughters of Aunt Marie, Beth, and their little sister, Elmoore. Jo was tender and elusive, small and sophisticated, the one the women feared. Eben was taller, bland in a kind of boyish way. None of the older girls were allowed to go out with Jo or Eben, even though they were so rich, even though they were all dying to, none except Laura Graves, Laura, only fourteen, who was going to be burnt out in two years. Laura went out with Jo all the time, and it was a fast thing to do because Jo, although the heir to great things, was Japanese and out of bounds.

Jo knew the score, but Jo took her out. He was probably lonely. Jo, in some sort of love cruelty, took Little Bea, Jane

George's cousin and his, along as chaperone. It came near to breaking her heart, but it also gave her the chance to be with him. She went out riding in the back of his Stutz Bearcat and was given a quarter not to tattle on them, and she'd canoe them over to the other side of the lake to Camp Columbia and somehow Jo made her feel it was an act of love and devotion not to look closely as she paddled in the back waters and Laura Graves and he lay whispering on the cushions. Rather than disobey Jo, Bea did it all summer and never told.

When Jo went down to the city on his father's business, Laura begged to have Bea's great Teddy Bear because it reminded her of the outings, and she held it in her arms all night, weeping. The Teddy Bear was four feet high. It used to lie in the canoe with them—"an added chaperone." Laura clung to it because it had shared their spooning. Bea let her have it temporarily because she knew she'd outlast Laura and any of the other summer flirtations. Bea was established in the heart of the situation. She was blood-keen, and she loved Jo forever, and although he used her in these strange torturing ways he must have loved her also. But it was mean of him.

Jo was a brilliant scholar, a really first-class mind, but due to his escapades, he didn't always achieve what he intended. So it was good news when he heard that he had been accepted at the Kaiser Wilhelm Institute in Berlin. Good news to his father and mother, at any rate—not to Little Bea.

And not to Laura Graves. When she learned, which was soon, her little heart broke. She urged Jo to elope with her, but that much of a fool he was not.

He wanted to go to Berlin to study and to the Institut Pasteur in Paris, which he later did, but his being sent off just then, and in that abrupt way, was very likely a family maneuver to get him out of trouble with the summer girls. He recognized this, but if he resented it he said nothing. The butler and his mother packed his trunks.

I suppose in a way he was sorry to go. He walked the woods several days holding Bea's hand, and he kicked at stones, and sometimes he sighed. He sat for a long time on a log and smoked. He didn't look at Bea, and Bea thought she'd better steal away and leave him alone, but he reached out and pulled her back and sat slapping her little hand on his knee. He did it so long her hand was quite swollen when they went home. Then he kissed her on the eyes and sealed the grief in.

Jo was getting very used to having his love affairs pulled awry. Older, more mature, more suitable girls he was simply not permitted to meet or get to know—the sisters of his Yale classmates, for instance. For a lark it was amusing to meet an Oriental in their brothers' rooms, the son of a scientist of international fame, but something quite else again to go to visit a Jap in his home, no matter how opulent. Parents absolutely forbade it. So Jo brought not so nice girls to his mother's home, actresses and such, with very white faces and very red lips.

Aunt Takamine sighed. Mothers in Japan were treated with respect, and normally she would have been, but Caroline Takamine was a white woman, a Caucasian. Although she was Auntie Marie's sister and, like her, a New Orleans Creole, and although she had been raised in the South to expect quite other treatment, she found herself helpless: not all of her money, her international affiliations, not her intelligence, nor her Southern charm could procure her boys a decent, dignified life. The boys were Japanese and they could never be anything else in this country except by act of Congress. They were Japs. Japs were yellow—and there was the Yellow Peril, as Mr. Hearst kept drumming into us, and there was the Oriental Exclusion Act.

But if Caroline grieved, and she must have, she never let on.

She was proud almost to the point of arrogance. She kept her mouth shut. In her way she was as formidable as the Doctor. "She never talked. She never complained," said Minnie Dickens. Above all, she was loyal. She was loyal because it was her nature to be, because her rearing had reinforced this virtue and because she was Japanese. She was, legally; with marriage she had forfeited her United States citizenship.

Although there are not reliable records, Caroline Hitch Takamine was probably the first American and the third Caucasian to marry a Japanese, the first to bear legitimate half-caste American-Japanese children. She went to Japan before Lafcadio Hearn and Pierre Loti. She went when it was an absolutely unknown world, and she cut off all her ties, national and familial, to do this.

She was the first great lady most of us at Merriewold had ever known. When we children first knew her, Caroline Takamine was in her early forties. She was tall and not slender, but none of our mothers were. They ate what they liked and they corseted. Her back was always as straight as a major-general's and her walk a royal progress. She wore white a great deal and round jade earrings of considerable value. She had been a beauty when young. She now was queenly with a fresh energy, a delicacy of manner that set her apart even among Edwardian ladies who made a cult of personal style. These were the days before makeup. She needed none. Her velvet cheek still had a bloom over it, very like the soft fuzz of a peach. Her brows were heavy and shaded large gray eyes, her abundant brown hair was worn in a braided crown on her head. Her mouth was delicate-lipped, pale pink, and often partially open over a dazzling smile. It was then considered hopeful and winning to keep one's mouth partially open. Caroline did whenever possible, and she could to advantage because she had pearly teeth. Her smile did not flash; it twinkled. She had the kind of grace Ellen Terry is supposed to have had. All her efforts were glancing, deft, and evanescent. Nothing was ever bold or frontal. She was in essence quiet, but at the same time, always without exception, imperial.

She never raised her voice; she never had to. Once was quite enough, no matter how softly. Part of the effect she achieved was by her absolute assurance, and part was the voice itself, for her speaking tones were pure enchantment, cadenced and girlish. She had the most beautiful voice I have ever heard except that of Jane Cowl or Eleanora Duse, but Caroline's voice was fresher and seemed always young. She took singing lessons to enhance it. Her clothes were marvelous—evening dresses from Paris, full-length furs, velvet hats with cascades of ostrich plumes, egrets, paradise. Her jewels? George Frederick Kunz, the master gemologist of Tiffany's, designed for her a superb set of tiara, earrings, and stomacher in the stone named after himself, the Kunzite, and set it in just plain diamonds of no particular name but considerable carat value. Once at a dinner party at our New York flat I saw Aunt Takamine standing in front of Mother's bedroom cheval glass. She was in orchid pink chiffon with ropes of paste, liquid and dripping, and spangles. "It's too shiny. It's vulgar," she said. "I'm going to have all this removed." She ran her hands through the brilliants. I was on the floor clutching the brass bed rail. I could not restrain myself. "Oh, don't," I implored. "Please don't!" Aunt Takamine favored me with her ravishing smile. "You like them? I'll think twice about it then."

She was always turned out impeccably, even if entertaining children. Once in the winter she dressed with awesome splendor (black spangled net with long sleeves and a high collar, black os- trich plumed hat, chains of diamonds) to take her niece and nephew, Little Bea and her brother, to the Hippodrome. The kids never got over it. There were no grown-ups present. She did it just for them.

One childhood friend, a Japanese, remembers the great painted rooms and the elegant atmosphere of the Riverside Drive mansion. "The first and only time I ever visited Mrs. Takamine was on a sleety New Year's Day when my father took my brother and me on a formal call at her Riverside Drive mansion where there was an elevator that took us up to her drawing room. I was overwhelmed by the opulence, the thick carpets, the uniformed maid, the large bouquet of fragrant violets on a small table, the shaded lights, the French bonbons—among them pale lavender lozenges tasting of violets. That was fifty years ago—I must have been about six years old. We came home in a musty hansom cab with the snow swirling past the small windows on either side. Queer odors—wet leather, dust, sweating horse, huge coachman, the cracking whip . . . What odd memories on this thrilling spring morning in 1964," she wrote me from Tokyo. "And the mist of cherry blossoms, the red camellias and the white . . ."

To us who had never heard of tact, Caroline Takamine's manners were a lesson and a precept. For instance, she was herself not a smoker and she frowned on the custom when practiced by nieces, but she invariably took a cigarette after dinner, and smoked two or three puffs, so that her female guests should not be embarrassed to ask permission.

But she was on the other hand very strict about being considerate, to one's hostess, of course, but also to the servants—never under any circumstances democratic to one's servants. Beth, her sister, was always offering to share chocolates with Auntie's chauffeur, LaRue Kinney, which distressed the mistress. "Don't do that," Caroline would remonstrate. "You mustn't be familiar with the chauffeur."

"Caroline Takamine," said Beth, "you'll not tell me what to do. I'm just as fine a lady as you are. Have another, LaRue."

"Caroline is getting beyond herself," added Beth. "She really is. Servants exist for us, not the other way round. And if we want to be friendly, that's our right. And it's not as though she were pals with them. Believe me, she is not."

If Aunt Takamine seemed unapproachable, as all perfect beings are, the Doctor moved quite apart in an aura of mysticism.

Uncle Jokichi was white-haired when I knew him, short, round-faced, and with a pointed waxed mustache in the Prussian style. His voice was husky, growing harsher under excitement. His accent was somewhat Dutch; his Japanese accent being noticeable only under stress. Occasionally he would beckon to one of us, chuckling, and from a sandalwood closet select a toy of excruciating difficulty which baffled even our parents. He had the traditional Japanese kindness and sweetness to all children. He was especially kind to Bee George. Aunt Takamine loved her as the daughter she herself never had; she called her "my white-headed boy," and asked her to go places more than any of the others, and gave her a sapphire when she turned eighteen.

Aunt Caroline's four sisters, the Hitch girls, were not in any way grand, just nice American ladies with noticeable faults and untidy hair. There was a fierce and clannish sense of family responsibility among them and there was a transient population of visiting nieces and nephews either at Aunt Marie's or at Aunt Takamine's. I was not related to Aunt Takamine, but by marriage to her younger sister, Marie, and it must be understood that only blood cousins had the courtesy of Sho-Foo-Den, not the kin by marriage.

Little Bea was Caroline's niece and of the Blood, and she was asked to stay for weeks at the Palace. We inquired what it was like. She said it was scrumptious and sometimes, she said, it was frightening.

One night on returning in the dark from a bathroom, she had

crashed into a suit of armor, bringing it down to the floor in a tremendous clatter. It not only came to pieces, it moved, great terrifying mask, horned helmet, breastplate, shoes. First she thought all the pieces were alive because they kept moving on the matting and then she thought she'd broken a treasure. She shrieked. Young Jo appeared in his kimono holding a candle and knelt beside her smothering her cry with a strong, fine-smelling hand. He held her in his arms until she was quiet. Then they sat together for a long time rocking with giggles.

He put his head close to hers suddenly and quietly kissed her throat. She *thinks* he did. She can't quite remember. She was surprisingly aware of the roughness of his finely shaven chin, and the clean musky odor of his glossy hair. He led her back to her room and blew her a kiss as he shut the shoji.

She lay trembling for an hour. When she woke in the dawn she found that she had wet her bed. She was nine years old and had not done a thing like that for five years. She tried to wash the sheet with the water in her pitcher but only made a worse mess, so she bundled the sheet up and hid it in the bottom of the tansu, then made her bed perfectly and stole through the dawn woods to Aunt Marie's house. Jane George heard her. Little Bea said she was going to sleep on the sofa, but Jane made her come into her own bed and she finally drifted off, jerking and muttering in her sleep. She was scared, as they all were, of Aunt Takamine.

"Little girls are little princesses," said Aunt Takamine, "and they don't do gross things like wetting beds, not after they're six years old. Little boys are different. They're more like—well, animals."

"Why are they?" Jane George asked boldly.

Aunt Takamine didn't like Jane very much. "That is one of the things you will learn when it is the proper time."

"When will that be . . ." Jane began.

But Little Bea pinched her. She did not want trouble with Auntie. She wanted access to the house. This night her shame was agonizing lest Jo learn, because she knew he did not think of her as a child although she was one, and this was her great joy. This, it turned out, was close to the heart of her life. But he was already a man, thirteen years older, and they were first cousins. The family kept reminding him of this, and reminding her when she was old enough to grasp their meaning: cousins didn't marry.

She told her mother Beth about the bed-wetting. Beth, the family beauty, gathered Bea to her pleated and flounced bosom and said, "Of course you did. Perfectly natural. I daresay we all would have."

"Except Aunt Caroline."

"Except your Auntie Caroline."

"Did she never do anything weak or foolish?" begged Little Bea, her face comfortably nestling in ribbons and lace.

"Never," said Beth. "That's why she's practically unbearable at times. But don't ever, ever repeat that. This will be our secret. That we know we're human and forgive ourselves. She can't, poor thing; never could," and Beth laughed with the Hitch laugh which was like shallow water on rocks, and rose to admire her loveliness in the looking glass. Bea was always dazzled by her mother. "Do you like the blue at my throat? It's good for my eyes, I think."

And Little Bea smiled with that radiance misted over with shyness and hope that made her smile irresistible to all, and unforgettable, and that always caught at Jo's throat so sharply it was like a physical blow.

Little Bea was our darling and she came of curious heritage, although by no means as strange as her cousin, Jo Takamine. Hers,

one could say, was raffish rather than alien. Her mother was one
of the five Hitch sisters, younger than Caroline, older than Marie,
more beautiful than either although not so distinguished-looking.
Bea's father was the widower of my mother's sister, Jennie
George. He was also, unfortunately, the manager of our Inn and
as chief real estate manipulator for Merriewold he entangled the
Club's dealings so that to this day clear title cannot be proved on
several properties. Straightforward he was never, although lastingly influential. Mother believed he was crooked and that it was
a good thing her sister, Jenny, had died before she became aware
of his chicanery. His family, which was powerful in Merriewold,
took an alternate view. Will was "idealistic and a very easy
mark," said the Atkinsons. "Of questionable business ethics," said
Mother, distraught as she was that her beautiful, beloved sister
had died so young, at twenty-eight, of a heart attack. Obviously it
was Will's fault. The struggle for the guardianship of their surviving infant son endured without quarter for decades.

Bea's mother, Beth, Marie's beautiful, sexy sister, after an early,
inconsequential divorce had found herself temporarily out of a
spouse and temporarily an actress. Due to her good looks and
lovely contralto she had been taken on as Maurice Barrymore's
leading lady. But, like so many of her time, she became abruptly
stranded in the Midwest and on the way back home sitting up in
the coach she met, by chance, Will Atkinson, who paid her way
and, being a gentleman, offered to marry her. He brought her
back to Merriewold, where she was already quite well known.

By marrying back into the family Will established a series of
kinships that bordered on incest, for there were shortly a plethora
of half brothers and first cousins who found each other mutually
to be of deadly and enduring fascination.

Of course, Mother had treated Beth coolly. She was her sister's replacement. Father thought her amusing, an irresponsible and incorrigible flirt.

Beth grew tired of the marriage to Will, but married or separated, she considered herself irresistible to all men, was tirelessly devious about obtaining favors and imperious about commanding service, a Creole from New Orleans, a fatal dazzler.

Our Little Bea might prove to be, in her turn, very lovely, a princess, but her mother, Beth, was certainly the reigning queen. There was not a man in the Park who was not aware of her dusky, exquisite, floating voice, her velvet cheek, her soft mouth, her pansy eyes, and her multiple wardrobe, so ruffled and so varied and all starched and pressed out each week by Mrs. Seoles and Beth's younger sister, the Honorable Mrs. Henry George, Jr. Beth was a Southern Belle.

Bea divided her vacations between Aunt Marie Hitch George down at the Other End and Aunt Maud Atkinson Braga at Our End. Aunt Maud's husband, Bernardo Braga y Rionda, was very romantic, in fact rather exciting, because between rests at Merriewold he was industriously, with his uncle, Manuel Rionda, gaining control of approximately one tenth of the Cuban sugar. There were also for Bea happy interludes at Sho-Foo-Den.

She was first cousin to all of them and lived in close relations for stretches of time during the course of which imperceptibly her cousin George Braga fell deeply and lastingly in love with her, while her cousin Jokichi Takamine came to realize that his feelings were far from those of an older, amiable relative. And although she was too young to fall in love in any adult sense, yet she began to know that Jo was rooted into the heart of her life. It was forever for both of them, and it was forbidden.

The Takamines didn't build Sho-Foo-Den. As always, the Doctor used ingenuity and he could seize opportunity because he had money. His desires were special and precise; he wanted a home like no other on the North American continent, and he got it.

In 1904–6, with the Russo-Japanese war raging, Japan was aware of needing friends. So for the Japanese exhibit at the 1904 St. Louis International Exhibition the Imperial Government sent a complete garden, ornamented with stone figures and lanterns and great native trees. The buildings were two large houses similar to a type of Shinto temple found near Kyoto. The exhibit attracted interest as perhaps the first authentic example of Japanese architecture in the West and went a long way toward counteracting the popular Halloween misconceptions promoted by *The Mikado*.

At the conclusion of the Fair the buildings and covered porchways, mitered and joisted together like jewel boxes, the garden, trees and stone decorations which otherwise like all fair exhibitions might have been lost were given by the Japanese Government in answer to a request of Takamine, who sent a group of upstate New York carpenters to St. Louis, to be instructed by the Japanese artisans in taking the buildings apart, the pieces of which were labeled and numbered and brought to St. Joseph's in freight cars. The crates arrived in the snow. Thirty-five sleigh loads were drawn through the winter forest. With the first thaw the boxes were prized open and the astonished locals saw that every piece matched the plan in Will Moore's hand.

The gardeners took seventeen years. Jokichi had bought a fine, large piece of property in Merriewold next to Caroline's sister's (Aunt Marie's) place. A rise of ground on the property was chosen as house site, but Inamoto, master gardener, wanted a larger hill. So they made one and the hole from which they took the rocks and earth became a lake. Fifty cartloads of rhododendrons were dug up in the swamps of Old Sixteen on the road to St.

Joseph Station (Mother showed me the places) and dragged down to the gardens. Thirty cartloads died; twenty were coaxed to live. The living twenty lined the driveway which led up to the house in an enclosed way. The pines at the Other End had withstood one holocaust and these were trees in the classic Japanese style with lower limbs trimmed off for a height of fifty to one hundred feet. There is no similar grove on this side of the Pacific.

These buildings, two large houses and a carriage entrance all connected by open porches or breezeways, were of unequal height and the roofs undulated and topped one another in rhythms of red, the red tiles being by design the only color in all the place. The important guests entered by the carriage entrance and the important guests left poems to the hosts on the walls; that is, all did who could handle with any elegance a two-foot camel's hair brush and the classic ideographs. The great front steps of red lacquer led into a broad descending flight of rough rock and flower-embossed moss. The flight was not straight but curved in a meandering ellipse so that the eye was blocked and teased and led on, and one escaped visually over hedge after hedge until one found there below, among the tall pine trunks, the lake, marshy with iris. Trained and warped pine branches bent over the water, a mirror surface glistering with dragonflies. The fountains splashed all day. Under lily pads a whole civilization of frogs fretted the stillness and overhead, way up high, the tops of the pines were never still.

The gardeners came from Japan, sent by Takamine's family and friends. They worked every summer day, sun-up to black. They worked as only the Japanese can, unceasingly and with passion. Stone lanterns, stone figures, some six and seven hundred years old, were brought across the Pacific as ballast in ships, and took months in passage. A pair filled an entire boxcar in the transcontinental trip from Seattle to Port Jervis. Wood carvings arrived wound in cloth and packed in straw—panels five hundred years old, the wood golden brown and soft with age, the color rubbed away except for faint dusty indications, the aroma of color, one might say, gold dust flaking in the crevices.

As long as the doctor lived he worked on the building of those terraced gardens, adding farm sheds and kitchen patches and rustic devices as the grounds opened toward the highway, until finally there was a country bridge and a water mill and a thatched fence as a definition of property and in the thinning woods pump houses, all with charming red roofs. And the gas house, or tragic omen. That was there, too.

The muralists came, in particular Shugoro Sawabe of Kyoto, with their saucers of paint and their long, long brushes and their white mats for sitting on and their gold leaf and they painted the golden walls with branches of pine and scarlet maple interlocked. Mother said she remembered the white mats they put on the floor, flicking strokes on a wall two yards away with the modulation of wrist as subtle as a brain surgeon's. Over the front door was the owner's name in gold leaf. On every gable glowed a rosette of eight medieval feathered arrows, the ancient crest of the house of Takamine.

The house was lit by carbide gas. Everyone else relied on oil lamps and candles. But the Takamines had fashionable carbide. The gas was stored in a little low Japanese shelter, decorative but extremely dangerous. (And in one instance fatal as they were long later to find out, for the house blew up one day, blinding Charlie Dill and tearing to pieces LaRue Kinney, their beloved chauffeur. A special train was dispatched to St. Joseph's but not in time, for he died on the way to Port Jervis.)

The house, of course, attracted sight-seers, many unbidden. Aunt Takamine woke up from a nap one day to see four strangers staring at her. They'd climbed up the wisteria vine of her bedroom.

Just down the main road was the farm, Japanese style, with barns of unpainted wood satined by weather, and behind it stretched wild, rocky hillsides which the Merriewolders called "the golf course" and on which foolhardy folk actually attempted to play, teeing off from the shelf of granite at the top.

There on the very top, commanding a view of two counties, Dr. Takamine had put a teahouse as a courtesy to his neighbors. It was a perfect and unmodified example of Japanese architecture except for glass screens protecting the shoji. We could keep clubs and balls there prior to losing them in the wilderness below (we children were no good as caddies) or make tea (for it had a complete Japanese kitchen), or we could just sit and look. To the right the Convent of St. Joseph clanged its bells. Aunt Takamine was always spellbound by this. And one could see the dormitories, like dollhouses, scattered about with the black and white figures of the Dominican nuns scurrying toward salvation.

We seldom saw Dr. Takamine on our porches, but the grownups talked about every noteworthy thing he did. There were his cherry trees, for instance. He thought it would be nice if the United States capital, Washington, D.C., had a really fine display of cherry trees. So he persuaded Yukio Ozaki, the Mayor of Tokyo, to send as the gift of that city two thousand young plants. They were found on arrival to be infested and had to be burned, but he cabled the very next day for more. How the porches buzzed about that! And in the following March, with all the Washington Georges present and also the First Lady, Mrs. William Howard Taft, the project was formally inaugurated. The trees didn't look like much, Jane said, just naked, spindly sprouts. But Uncle Jo said we should have patience, that they'd be lovely later. And they were, too. The Washington cherry trees were very lovely. I remember Bee George's face when she described the first blooming. (She later became a landscape architect, so she knew all about such things. She used to study Sho-Foo-Den like a textbook.) Bee tried to teach us about the cherry blossoms. We weren't interested; she told us anyway. She named the order of flowers: first, Yoshino, clear pink and feathery fresh; then Shirayuke (snow white); Ariake, single white or faintly pink; and then in a great burst all the pinks and roses, Mikuruma-Gaeshi (returning court carriage); and last the Imperial Cherry or Gyoiko, greenish yellow flowers which turn to clear pink just before dropping, all chosen to prolong the period of blooming as long as possible, five weeks.

And then there were the scholarships Uncle Jokichi founded, both here and in Japan. Aunt Marie talked a lot about them, and the Rikagaku Kenkiojo in Tokyo patterned after the Kaiser Wilhelm Institute in Berlin, the Japanese Association in New York, a development of the Japanese American mutual aid society he had previously helped organize to combat the anti-Japanese agitation on the West Coast. It was the NAACP (Japanese-style) of its day and it proved extremely valuable to us in World War I, although not, of course, in World War II. He was a man bursting with useful and stimulating ideas. He founded with J. I. C. Clarke the Nippon Club at 161 West Ninety-third Street in New York.* (Mother always said to me as we passed, "This is the club Uncle Jo founded.") It was established to make it possible for young Japanese to meet with Americans because there was absolutely no other place for them to do this, socially and pleasantly. And there were many, many students he brought to his laboratories and paid to work here.

* And now housed in a large building on Fifty-seventh Street between Sixth and Seventh avenues.

"He is giving his life to helping young scientists," said Bee George. "He is a very great humanitarian."

"And," added Aunt Marie, "he has given an incomparable gift to humanity. It is the dream of his life to promote better understanding between our two countries. He is helping all the young Japanese."

As soon as the great house was up, the family moved in with a double staff of Japanese and American servants. For big parties, caterers and musicians came up from New York.

Then began the glory. The Prince and Princess Kuni visited. This had been the culmination of the Takamines' social life, and was never surpassed. This time the entertaining was awful. The neighbor children were told absolutely to stay out of the grounds, and chains were put across the forest paths. All the local farmers and handymen were sworn in as deputy sheriffs and posted on the roads with makeshift badges and guns to watch for interlopers or spies, and there they sat day-long, spitting tobacco juice and shooting chipmunks for want of other targets.

The Imperial guests came with complete entourage on the five-hour trip from New York City and were met by LaRue Kinney and the car and five horse-drawn station wagons.

The little girls, the Cohens and the Georges, were pressed into service and starched almost to immobility, their hair in glossy braids or symmetrical curls topped by new crisp butterfly bows, they bore bunches of garden flowers to present to their Imperial Highnesses. The lucky chosen ones were stationed behind the rhododendron hedges by the private lake.

The royal party got off at the carriage entrance where the sons of the house waited (on good behavior for once). Bee George held the bouquet of honor. She heard the soft Japanese laughter behind the hedges and then more Japanese and then there they were, the whole party. The children, having been reared on Andersen and Grimm, naturally expected proper princesses. So they stood openmouthed and unmoving, certain some dreadful mistake had been made. The royalty were in Western clothes. The Prince and Princess were short and squat, the Princess's rotundity emphasized by pregnancy. (She was about to give birth to Nagako, who later married Hirohito to become the present Empress of Japan.) The young mother wore a large hat with osprey—she looked like a mushroom, while he was myopic and wore extremely thick glasses. Bee gasped, loathe to give up the bouquet. Her Imperial Highness, with determined graciousness, took it firmly and smiled with bunched teeth. Evelyn Cohen snickered. Caroline went white. She called on her sister, Marie, and Mrs. Cohen later and told them what she thought. She said she couldn't believe her senses. Surely their daughters were more grown-up and understanding than that. In truth she was in a very awkward position. A Japanese child would have permitted herself to be disemboweled for the privilege of handing a bouquet to royalty. The Takamines were profoundly humiliated. This visit was to have put the family on the map.

The Japanese Imperial line (Aunt Caroline emphasized this) extends unbroken for seventeen hundred years, a family well established when Charlemagne assumed power. One would have to turn to Egypt or Persia for comparable dynastic duration. It is the oldest royal house existing. Besides this lineage the Germans on the British throne seem like parvenus, and Edward and Alexandra visiting our forests could not have caused a greater stir among their expatriated subjects than did this royal couple.

Auntie Takamine had always claimed that she did not like to entertain—that she endured it for the sake of the doctor. This time it was excruciating.

Nothing in the house that had ever been used before could be used now; new floor matting, new linen, new blankets, new dishes, new glass, new silver—all new. "It was a strain," said Caroline. "I don't know what I would have done without Yamanakas. They were sweet enough to lend me dozens of little jade bowls and lacquer. I could never leave the Princess's presence (she and her ladies spoke only Japanese) and I was adept only in kitchen phrases and, of course, one addresses royalty in special forms. And there was the household and the meals to see to—we had extra cooks, naturally—and the whole protocol of royal procedure. The Princess was not very well, not at her best or at ease. We sat creaking on the porch swings trying to make conversation until I could manage somehow to get away. As I say, it was a strain."

One evening while listening to the conversation (in court-style Japanese, using the proper verb forms for royalty) Marie grew restive and, thinking to demonstrate her independence as an American, as the wife of a United States Congressman and as the mother of three, and with her relentless and innocent lack of tact, she placed her arm casually on the back of the Princess's chair and leaned forward in affable attention. (These chairs had been made in Japan of enameled teakwood, crested and embossed with gold and cushioned in brocade, the male throne somewhat larger and considerably more beautiful—no one else has sat in them since.) Caroline rose, crossed the room, removed the impertinent hand, and returned quietly to her seat without speaking. Marie understood. She might stand on her rights in the House of Representatives but there was no escaping the fact that in this home democracy did not flourish. This home was not part of the United States.

Aunt Caroline's little sister, Elmoore, had been introduced to Japanese protocol somewhat earlier. When she was visiting Caroline a couple of years before in Tokyo she had been asked by the

American Ambassador to accompany him and his wife to a party at the Imperial Palace; there she had been introduced personally to the Emperor. But the older sister, Caroline, could not go because she was Japanese and because she was not of sufficiently high rank to warrant the honor.

The royal guests took the Merriewold visit in good part, even American democracy, even perhaps the lapses in decorum. In the photographs they look very jolly in sneakers and canvas tennis hats, smiling toothsomely as they display their quite small trout. Even the Princess is smiling gallantly and a shapeless sweater covers her celestially auspicious condition.

Both Exalteds left their poems on the walls of the carriage house, painted freehand.

It was a great house and a great family. There was wealth here and graciousness and international fame and achievements that benefited mankind. The House of Takamine should have stood for generations.

But the people who moved through those golden halls were doomed; the seeds of destruction were in their pattern. The Takamine-Hitches walked straight into the blaze of the new century, the concept of the single world. It was their flesh that soldered the ties.

This was a family around which legends gathered. There is, of course, a family-approved biography by K. K. Kawakami, a Japanese journalist who wrote in English, an unusual achievement for the time. It was written under the supervision and at the request of Caroline and it reads like a public relations tract.* But every member of the tribe has a different version of the story. Mary

* Published in 1928 by William Edwin Rudge of New York with a foreword by John Finley, President of the College of the City of New York.

Beatrice, Elmoore's daughter, thought Caroline was a woman of unblemished grandeur of spirit; Jane George thought her haughty and selfish; Little Bea adored her and was perhaps the most temperate of the lot and the most observant; the daughter of the Japanese scientists had little but contempt; Mary Beatrice (Bee) George had nothing but praise; and Minnie Dickens, Aunt Caroline's lifelong friend who was there from the beginning— mean and jealous, perhaps, as the cousins say, but also keen and knowledgeable—saw it happen.

Chapter 5

❧ Everyone agrees on the beginning. It has become the cornerstone of all the family legends. How many of the Merriewolders knew any of this story, I don't know. But I am curious by nature, and much later I asked questions. Some wouldn't talk; but some did.

During the Civil War, when everything was lost to Louisianians except what they could hold on to with bare fists, a Yankee captain leading a small contingent of men on a foraging expedition for General Benjamin F. Butler's troops fetched up before the Field house in the Bayou Teche outside of New Orleans. The master was ailing and bedridden; the stepmother was a New Englander and her feelings were, on this occasion, understandably mixed; in any case she remained indoors. It was therefore the youngest daughter of the house, Caroline's mother, Mary Beatrice Field, a fifteen-year-old girl, who faced the soldiers at the top of the steps. She faced them alone. Her slaves stood abashed below.

Captain Ebenezer Hitch made his position clear. "We need fodder for the horses and food for our company—pigs, eggs, butter, milk, yams, green vegetables if you have them . . ."

"Don't move," said the girl to the slaves. "Don't one of you stir."

"Miss Field," said the Captain, "I must have these things. I've come for them."

"If one of you lifts a hand," said the girl to the slaves, "I'll have you flogged."

"Miss," said the Captain, "this is war. I have orders to shoot if I must."

She did not reply. She was half French, and she tilted her little black head scornfully, her black eyes snapped. The frightened, ragged negroes, the soldiers, the woman and the officer stood silent in the thickening dusk. The slave women attempted to still the children's whimpering in their skirts. They swayed but did not stir apart. Mary Beatrice Field looked unmoving at the Captain.

"Take that man on the left," said Captain Hitch. The wretch fell to his knees. "Detail . . . Ready . . . Aim . . ."

The girl set her lips. The guns were raised. The Captain lifted his hand.

"All right," said the girl. "All right. Get them what they want."

She turned around and walked in the front door, slamming it behind her.

"Miss Field," shouted Captain Hitch to the closed door, "when this war is over, I shall return and marry you."

And so he did.

Oddly enough they never got on, although they had thirteen children. For when Captain Eben Hitch had put down his sword and sent his soldiers away, he found himself quite unable to cope with much, particularly with Madame. In authority he was no match whatever for the bright-eyed, white-capped creature who stood head for head with him. She gave the orders. She made the plans. Indeed, she was the man, except in maternal functions, which, as I have remarked, were ample. For although the Captain may have found himself harassed, frustrated, and exasperated by his black-browed wife, he could not resist her. Indeed, no man could. Papa's chief gifts were not as administrator but as raconteur, and he was a dazzling one, and as amateur musician. He took a job as controller of the port which, mercifully, kept him away from home a lot. He did come back, however, several times a year and that was his undoing.

But there were, of course, diseases. The New Orleans annual epidemics and plagues brought ghastly mortality, and even with a Hitch baby every year, there were also tragically many deaths, six to be precise. Three daughters went in one year with yellow fever. There were several stillbirths. The only boy, Freddy, the hope of the house, the heir who had mercifully withstood the scourges, accompanied his mother one day to the druggist and took a sip from a cup standing openly nearby, a cup containing, as was not infrequent on the public counter, prussic acid. He fell dead at her feet.

So that left five sisters, who all came to Merriewold—as Marie's or Caroline's guests. Caroline, the gentle and responsible; Kate, the reliable; Beth, the wild beauty, who was to become the mother of Little Bea; Marie, with a sense of merciless altruism and a stubborn selflessness that never yielded to anyone's inclination, with iron ideas about singing, castor oil, vegetables, loving kindness, and God; and lastly, the curiously named, Elmoore, the baby, spoiled and darling, who wanted everything Caroline and Beth had, and who attempted to get it by conduct not permitted to any of the others. They were all beauties (or nearly) and they all had exquisite manners and real charm. They raised hell in their different ways all their long lives, but they had charm.

Caroline's early photographs show a loveliness that would

have been classic except for an overhardness of the chin, a characteristic of all the Hitch sisters. Her walk was a legend even in her
teens, and she always wore high boots to keep her ankles slim.
Except for the click of her heels, her footfall was soundless. She
glided.

Caroline did a good deal of the housework as Mama's eldest
helper, dressing and undressing the little girls and each day tying their ribbons before she took time to dress herself. Right then
she formed the habit of looking after their manners. Because fed
or unfed, smart or shabby, those girls were reared as ladies—no
chewing gum, for instance—and "thank you" and "please" and
curtsies with "how-d'you-do" and for all occasions clean fingernails and combed and curled hair, and dainty dresses with plenty
of material left by the dressmaker to accommodate growing
bosoms, but never cut low, Mama holding the notion that lady-
like modesty was sexually attractive. One time Mama, an acknowledged beauty, took exception to the unusually low décolletage of a pretty visitor, considering the exposure an illegitimate
ruse. She rose from her chair, snatched the roses from a near table
and pinned them (ladies then always had pins handy) firmly
across the offending bosom. "I've always wanted to give you
flowers," she said to her astonished guest.

They learned deportment, loyalty, and pride. The domestic
arts, on the other hand, were rather neglected, although they always made their own beds. Since Mama couldn't cook or sew,
none of the daughters learned. Mama wouldn't and didn't, the
girls couldn't. Mama figured that if they were ladies with grace
and taste, they would marry well and have servants. They needn't
learn.

She bargained for lessons in the graces. She wished them to
learn French from the Academy next door and took the three little girls, exquisitely dressed, with her to see Madame Vitrelle.

Mama could be enchantingly persuasive and adorably charming when she wished to be. And "the Three Rosebuds" sat with their feet straight out in front of them and their bonnets on straight and their eyes round. Unfortunately, three days before, Beth had thrown the good lady's cat into the cistern and then urged her young stooges, Marie and Elmoore, to practice long-distance spitting with the poor cadaver as the target. Mama beamed. Madame Vitrelle snapped, "Madame Eetch, take your children. I would not have these three devils in my school for all the tea in Japan!" Oh, prophetic words!

But above everything else, Mama valued education. All the girls learned languages, history, and philosophy—Ingersoll and Felix Adler, for instance. Mama heard about the interesting theories of Henry George, political economist, and read *Progress and Poverty,* five hundred and sixty-three pages of closely reasoned economics and philosophy, aloud to her daughters, aged seventeen to four. They were bored to tears and vowed never to have any more of that!

Papa's job may have kept him away—good! But it also brought in very little money—not enough to support Mama's fancy taste. So she went to work herself, but in a genteel way. She had a seat on the Stock Exchange and went regularly every day to manage her affairs, using Papa's savings as capital. These savings she lost. She later persuaded a boarder, Edward L. Moore, to let her invest his savings, and these she also lost. Mr. Moore was not bound like Papa to stay, but he nevertheless did, and he forebore to withdraw his trust and his friendship, which is remarkable. The youngest daughter, you may have noted, was named Ellen Moore, shortly condensed to Elmoore, and this curious nickname she retained all her life. Beth, who could be spiteful and who resented the attention paid to the pretty baby, always explained, "Elmoore was named for Mr. Moore. Mama made up the name herself as being appropriate."

But the rest of the family believed that Mama, although totally innocent (Caroline said Mr. Moore did not take up lodgings with them until Elmoore was five. Elmoore had been baptized Ellen Bader Hitch), wished to discipline Papa and therefore used the nickname. Mama was a great tease.

Mama's relations with Mr. Moore, like her relations with Papa, had their ups and downs. Marie once caught her standing on a chair outside the favored boarder's door, dropping bits of flaming paper through the transom, but whether it was a sign of displeasure or a symbol of passion, Marie could not be sure. Mama could be, as Marie said, "very difficult."

One day she hid in a closet until the little girls were distraught with anxiety. (This was much later in Chicago when they were living in a tall building with dangerous windows and Mama was, as they all knew, unreliable about heights.) They wept; they called; they raced from room to room, fearing that she had thrown herself out to the pavement. When they were on the point of summoning official help, Mama emerged and complacently discovered herself. It had been, she amiably explained, a test to see how much they really loved her.

Mama saw to it that Caroline had the best music instruction. But even her fantastic flair for bargaining failed to obtain the services of the finest French and German music masters, so she determined on Federal endowment. This was three quarters of a century before the term had been coined. She went to Washington by coach to persuade President Grant to give Captain Hitch a military pension. Leaving Caroline to keep the home, she took along on this junket her three "Little Rosebuds" as persuaders and she obtained a pension for life, a nice day's work for a Southern aristocrat who had been robbed at the point of a Yankee gun.

Minnie Dickens, whose family estate was next door to Mama's and who was Caroline's girlhood companion and confidant, never understood Mary Beatrice, nor did Minnie's stepfather and mother. She was domineering, Minnie said, and selfish and always arbitrary, often cruel to Caroline. Minnie's mother said she admired and felt sorry for her, but her father couldn't abide her. He was the one man Mama failed to enthrall. "Too bossy." Minnie never forgave her for what she did to Caroline or to the Captain either.

But, of course, Mama was in some ways very endearing. When Mama had any money at all, she took the girls to various spas and resorts—all of them and Nana, the nurse, but not Papa. Holidays never included Papa. She always wanted to go to Europe but she waited the whole of her life until she could take all of the children at once. She would not take just one or two, or go alone. Poor lady, she waited too long. She never went.

But there were local trips, although not always peaceful. At a mountain resort the innkeeper's wife suddenly appeared, babe in arms, and implored, "Madame Hitch, please go. Take your children and go. My husband admires you so, when I see how he looks at you it curdles my milk."

Even local trips suggest a certain amount of affluence. There was none, or only very little, and at intermittent times. Mary Beatrice was hard put to it to cope—the children kept coming year after year. God knows, there were doctor's bills, and Papa's salary was broken and inadequate. But the stock market would suddenly reverse and Mama then bought the best of everything, the finest wool, the finest linen and hand-embroidery. She herself always wore French silk and hand lace and her bonnets were from Paris. Clothes were new or worn as fortunes changed; they were never shoddy. Mama refused to sleep on anything but pure linen and she had fresh sheets on all the beds every day. This was the prerogative of a lady, and being a lady was the Hitch métier.

She decided to move where she could take in more boarders. They had been living in the American quarter of New Orleans, which was the stylish part of town. They moved to the older, unfashionable French quarter, the *quartier,* where she purchased an enormous house. The money required for this transaction was borrowed at the bank, using what as security she never told. What's more, she fitted the house top to bottom with new furniture and did over every room. Her family remonstrated with her on the expense. "But it's such good security," she countered.

The house was dilapidated and had no running water or plumbing, but it was for these reasons cheaper than the one they'd had, and it was roomy, with spacious high-ceilinged rooms and great gilt mirrors. The front gate opened straight from the street into the courtyard, on one side of which were the old slave quarters and on the other a mansion of three stories with iron-trellised balconies over which the girls used to hang to watch the household work below, the great tubs of water boiling for laundry—all the water needed in the house was collected in great open tubs—the coming and going of supplies, charcoal, wood, and the weekly hoses for cleaning the privies.

Beth (an extremely beautiful child of precocious sexual attraction and daring invention) once bribed her baby sisters, Marie and Elmoore, to ride up and down the three stories in the chained buckets that serviced these privies. They became disenchanted with the trip en route and their screams brought Mama and Nana and the entire household staff. By the grace of God, Papa was away on a trip or possibly Beth, who was fifteen, would have been in no shape for the elopement she shortly undertook. Papa was heavy-handed with the switch. This was all part of the household fun.

The mansion was elegant and they loved it. Mama decided to take in boarders, but only special ones.

Mama had the house repainted and cleaned, took off her cap, put on her bonnet (she had a row of false curls sewn inside her caps and bonnets so she wouldn't have to waste her time arranging her hair), and went down to the Chamber of Commerce to make known her plan, which was nothing less than to invite the Japanese officials, then visiting New Orleans for the Cotton Centennial celebration, to board in her mansion. Two young Japanese gentlemen, Takamine and Watanabe, were representatives of their country and they also proved to be exotic exhibits.

Hardly anyone had ever seen a Japanese—Chinese yes, but not Japanese. Mary Beatrice decided to kidnap them. She had no particular claims to them, but she looked very smart in her French hat and real lace and curls, and she spoke with authority. The Chamber of Commerce bowed; the Japanese gentlemen were notified. Mary Beatrice suggested dinner and wrote a formal invitation.

Caroline was aghast. "You're going to have them at table? You're asking me to eat with a Jap?"

Caroline was a docile girl and did whatever she was asked. As the oldest, she had taken the full brunt of her mother's and father's early adjustments. She was battle-weary by the time she was five, and she had discovered that if she remained aloof, cool and passive, she could step in and get what she wanted while the others were still grappling. She seldom committed herself. She found it effective not to notice—what she did not like she did not choose to see. She shut her lovely long gray eyes, and her gentle mouth, the flush waxed and waned on her downy cheek and she said absolutely nothing. But Japanese dinner guests were too much and she had not yet learned the absolute control she later mastered. She would not, she declared, eat at the same table, and her eyes snapped with something akin to her mother's fire. Caroline stood at bay alone; Papa was away from home.

Mama said nothing further; Mama had never been crossed successfully in her life. She went into the kitchen and gave orders. She went into the dining room and laid the best table her fine linen and silver permitted. She tidied up the begonias and gloxenias on their rosewood pedestals. She polished the arrangements of wax flowers under glass bells which were her only domestic devising and her especial pride. She put on her watered silk and her garnets and a newly starched pristine cap. The door pull clanged.

Caroline was in the parlor, practicing the piano in a torn cotton housedress, her soft brown hair hanging in braids. (Her braids were as thick as an arm.) She looked untidy but, even so, quite lovely. She let out a girlish squeal as though she hadn't expected callers—the minx—and lit up the three flights of stairs to her room.

Two very small Orientals stood bowing on the doormat. Takamine had a waxed pointed mustache in the Prussian manner. They wore flawless occidental clothes. Otherwise they looked just Japanese, which was extraordinary enough. Mama welcomed them, French style, colonial style, exquisitely, and bade them to be seated.

The little girls were beady-eyed at the door cracks, but the first daughter of the house was upstairs, shivering with excitement at her first unwonted show of revolt (her last) and with trepidation at the certainty of immediate discipline.

Beth beckoned Mama with a smudgy finger. "Caroline's upstairs and says she won't come down."

"Beth, it's not your business," was Mama's reply to this treachery, but her eyes snapped.

Mama no sooner got the young men comfortable than she

marched up all the flights, forced Caroline to unbolt the door, and, taking her literally by the ear and elbow, pulled her, strong and unwilling as she was, downstairs. She dragged on past the bedroom doors where the little sisters held their breaths in sheer awe, past Nana, whose "Please, Madame, not in her dressing gown!" went unheeded, past the goggle-eyed negro maids, past even the cook, who had heard the hubbub and came to the pantry door. They arrived in the drawing room, Caroline whispering and protesting the whole way. "No, Mama, no, please no! Papa wouldn't like this." Mama's hold hardened. They arrived, Mama hardly flushed, Caroline a wreck, wrapper awry, hair in wisps, cheeks scarlet, eyes welling, mouth shaking. An unwashed hand clutched the housedress together across her maidenly bosom. Mama presented her with a gentle flourish.

The oriental visitors rose and bowed again from the waist.

Caroline wept without check through dinner, the tears flooding her soft eyes and threading her cheeks. She sniffed into the enormous hand-hemmed table napkin. Her appetite was poor.

Caroline later told about that dinner, and so did Beth, who was perfectly furious that she was not old enough to sit with them. Tattletaling with Beth somehow became Act III of any Sardou drama.

Caroline barely touched her fork or spoon. Not so the guests. They ate with relish a really superb French cuisine. Mama had outdone herself and the cooks cooked for dear life, knowing what was at stake: next year's wages, to be precise. The gentlemen took no notice of the weeping member of the group as Mama sought to bring out the facts of her visitors' lives.

They were students of chemistry, she learned. "How interesting," said Mama. "Caroline, pass Mr. Takamine the preserved kumquats. Your wrapper is slipping." Takamine explained that he was the son of doctors, a profession esteemed throughout Japan for more than a thousand years.

Young Takamine had been sent as the representative of several business firms to the Exposition. He had high, but unspecified diplomatic connections and a certain amount of wealth. This also was left imprecise.

Throughout dinner Takamine deferred to Caroline, taking no notice of her discomfort. Both men, in fact, behaved as though entertaining in a dressing gown with one's hair on end and weeping eyes was a feature of American table manners. It occurred to Caroline slowly, but irresistibly, during the course of the meal that she was sitting beside the most courteous and considerate gentleman she had ever met in her life.

Young Takamine's voice was very soft. He spoke good English with hardly a trace of accent, perhaps a slight Dutch slurring. Occasionally he rolled his "r's" Scotch style.

Madame Hitch was enchanted. The Japanese had brought small gifts, but she was neither foolish nor gullible. She was intrigued by the quality of mind, the curiosity, strength, feeling, and grace of her new friends. She hoped they would make her home their lodgings for the coming year. As a matter of course, she asked for a letter of reference. Mr. Takamine proffered one (translated) which Mary Beatrice found acceptable. (The original was, of course, in ideographs.) It was, she gathered, from someone distinctly superior.

They moved in.

At this time little was known about Japan. There were in 1882 few tourists to Japan, few travelers' reports, newspaper items, or foreign friends. Diplomatic relations had been established (a consul but no ambassador), traders, missionaries, and foreign advisors were being welcomed but the general public had little information and the same was true reciprocally of Japan. Gilbert and Sullivan's *The Mikado,* misleading as it was, had yet to be written. Lafcadio Hearn and Pierre Loti were still to visit the Imperial islands. Ignorance about Japan was almost total and the curiosity about the islands off the China coast was almost as great as the curiosity lately entertained about the Iron Curtain countries.

On the other hand, the first few visitors from Japan were equally astonished and curious. They intended, however, to find out all they could as quickly as possible.

All popular Japan intended to find out everything quickly. For if the world knew little of the Empire, they were in considerable ignorance of all that had happened outside the boundaries of their own country during the past two hundred years. Only the elite, the rulers were conversant with the discoveries and inventions of the West. When the ordinary Japanese people had last heard a bit of foreign news, Charles I sat on the throne of England.

The surprise came in 1853 when Commodore Matthew Perry, carrying a message from President Millard Fillmore, sailed his fleet (and, as President Fillmore expressly pointed out, it was a "powerful squadron") into Edo Bay and landed at Uraga. The presidential message to the Mikado was a pretty compromise between silken devoirs and Yankee bullying and the flagship that brought the message of friendship and reassurance had its cannons at the ready. The Japanese had perfected many skills, but their armaments were not their strongest. Since they were a closed country they had no need. Their weapons were still those of the early nineteenth century and no match for the invaders.

But President Fillmore had offered bribes with his threats!

"Our great state of California produces about sixty millions of dollars in gold every year, besides silver, quick silver, precious stones and many other valuable articles. Your Imperial Majesty's subjects are skilled in many of these arts . . ." There it was, the direct invitation.

Out of Pandora's box came his last temptation: "We beg your Imperial Majesty's acceptance of a few presents. They are of no great value in themselves, but some of them may serve as specimens of the articles manufactured in the United States . . ."

Caroline often said, oh so often, and with sadness, "We invited them. We brought everything on ourselves deliberately."

For the West the way was open for painted lanterns and paper fans and pretty silks. For Japan it was something more and the two young men who moved into the Hitches' second floor and gave such enchanting suppers were among the vanguard of a great and incalculable historic movement. With unmatched energy and a remarkable sense of reality, the farsighted Japanese recognized that the West might have its drawbacks, but the West had moved way past feudalism, wallowing ahead for three hundred years in experiments with war, religion, revolution, travel, invention, and intellectual exchange. An Imperial rescript enjoined every Japanese to dedicate his life, energy, and brains to lifting his country within a generation to scientific and technological equality with the West. It was to be a Homeric effort.

Takamine's vision matched in many respects the Western vision of world adventure: the real estate seizures of contemporary Americans, the expanding and octopus-like building of railroads, the monopolizing of mining, wheat and cattle, the shipbuilding, diamond mining, and colonizing of the English. He, too, wished to join what James Truslow Adams calls "the period of the dinosaurs."

Of course, no one in New Orleans at that time took the young visitors seriously. They were just Japanese. They did not seem to expect to be taken seriously. It is true they were well-acquainted with caste and had practiced rights and privileges that even an ante-bellum plantation owner might envy, but they expected, wherever they went, ignorance and condescension, which they were prepared not to resent. Japan was well aware that it would have to endure the slights of the West if it was going to match the achievements of the West. The plan was to go out and learn, and never mind the snubs. Later would be something else.

The visitors had been reared in a tradition of courtesy—what am I saying?—of princely generosity. There were small amusing gifts for casual hostesses and children and there were costly, if odd, gifts for Caroline and Mama. Packages of rare and quite bitter tea began to arrive wrapped up in fine handmade paper and colored prints. These were quaint and some were even pretty in an odd oriental way, but the household threw them out along with the other wrappings because Mama liked the rooms neat. The donor remarked that next time it might be nice to keep some since people were beginning to collect them in Boston and London and other places, and the artists ("They were really artists?" said the little girls. "The prints were not just prints?") were becoming known—Hiroshige, Hokusai, Harunobu. (Oh, said the little girls, they could never remember *those* names!) The Fogg Museum in Boston was making a real fuss about tea wrappings. The prints, however, were gone in the trash bin.

So the boarder unwrapped some dolls made like warriors and princesses—"No, court ladies," said Takamine—the ladies wore long red silk trousers, padded, and straight black hair to the floor, and they carried lutes, and other lesser dolls, the ballad singers, had lutes, too—"No," said their soft-voiced friend, "samisen." Oh, said the little girls, they'd never remember *that*.

Caroline began to remember all the words and all the names and the next time some tea came, she took the prints from around the japanned tea chest and carried them to her room and studied them—and they were beautiful and worth keeping.

Caroline once asked Takamine and his friend, Watanabe, to lend costumes for a masquerade ball and they enthusiastically supplied two complete ladies' outfits—under linen as well as over kimono and the accouterments, obi, tabi, geta, and all. The donors were somewhat taken aback to see that twelve girls had outfitted themselves and were waltzing and polkaing about in the most intimate pieces of Japanese ladies' wardrobes. They made no comment at the time, congratulating all on how enchanting they looked. The young gentlemen became very, very popular. No one took them seriously, of course. They were Japanese.

Takamine talked to Caroline about tea-making and she tried to understand, but the tea was bitter! She took the cup in her hand, though, and turned it twice, and bowed to him, and drank just the proper amount. So did Mama. Mama, however, refused to sit on the floor where Jokichi and Caroline were gravely nodding at one another. She sat on an Empire chair and a silk cushion. Her manners were no less respectful for that. Beth wished to join in, of course, but was forbidden to. Papa wandered past the doorway at one of these sessions, raised his eyes to heaven, and left silently. Papa was on terms of formal politeness with Jokichi —but that was all.

Mary Beatrice had borne thirteen children and considered herself middle-aged. She was at this time (according to Caroline but not according to the census) thirty-two years old, four years older than Takamine. Whatever her true age, she was at the height of her physical beauty. Papa was away from home these days for longer and longer stretches of time, and while there has never been a hint of anything but the most honorable and gracious friendship between them, in view of what followed it is safe to infer that on all levels of sensibility she was taken with the young

My sixth birthday party with bows and wreaths.

Maggie Ming in dress-up as bride.

Mother, Grandmother (Bibi) de Mille's English sister, J. I. C. Clarke, Aunt Bettie, Auntie Clarke, listening to J.I.C.'s poetry.

Sho-Foo-Den.

Caroline.

man. She was a woman of intense feeling; the situation was intriguing and mysterious.

During the year Mama and Jokichi had ample opportunity to get acquainted, and so did Caroline. She used to practice the piano in the early morning in the parlor without heat. Jokichi felt sorry for her and said so. She began to trust and confide in him. He confided in Mama. He taught his anthem to Caroline. Her voice was light and quavery but true, her time sense accurate. She sang the ancient Japanese with a soft New Orleans accent.

But she didn't speak much when Mama was around. Mama spoke. Mama was drawing the doctor out.

He had been born, she learned, in the castle city of Kanazawa on November 3, 1854, the year after Commodore Perry had sailed into Edo Bay and unlocked Japan for general Western intercourse. Jokichi's father was a retainer to the Maeda family, the then Lord of Kaga, a peer of the realm. Jokichi's father was a doctor and he could speak Dutch. "In the Japan of feudalism and chivalry," writes Kawakami, Takamine's biographer, "the physician was perhaps the most respected of the civilians. At once a philanthropist, a scholar, a littérateur, he was a man of culture and refinement versed not only in the science and practice of medicine, but also in poetry, in fine arts, in the classics of both Japan and China, in the tea ceremony, in flower arrangement. A sworded samurai with the usual prerogatives and accomplishments of the warrior class, the physician was not a fighter but a man of peace and humanity whose mission was to heal and cure with little thought of remuneration."

Lord Maeda had had the prescience to send young, hopeful men to study Western ways and a Western tongue at Nagasaki, where Dutch traders and a few Portuguese, the only remaining Europeans, had been permitted to hold out during the long years of seclusion. When Jokichi was a young, hopeful man of twelve, he had been dispatched alone to Nagasaki six hundred miles away from home by horseback, boat, and cart, there being no railways yet, and lodged with the Portuguese consul, but on learning that the consul could speak Japanese, his lordly patron removed him to a completely Western household, this time Dutch, where to his chagrin he was forced to work as a houseboy. The humiliation, however, was only temporary. He was transferred at eighteen to a medical school at Osaka, where he discovered that he had a flair for chemistry. That year, 1872, four years after the Shogunate had been abolished by official statute, he continued on to Edo, the brand-new capital of Japan, where he stayed six years at the brand-new center for the study of science and engineering. He was one of twenty-three students selected and supported by the government for training, and on graduation he was sent, still at government expense, to England and Glasgow. There he lived with a family named Brown on the fourth floor of a stone house and was forced to attend family prayers in half-hour sessions morning and evening, which bored him wonderfully; he was a Buddhist. He was also forbidden to drink any alcohol at any time. He was very annoyed at this. He wrote all the strange events to his mother. He wrote her regularly. Mary Beatrice nodded with approval.

Takamine said then, as he said throughout his life, that medicine would prove to be the great civilizing influence of Asia, the great cohesive force among the nations of the world. Mama nodded again.

Young Takamine was particularly taken by the display of South Carolina phosphates and minerals at the Cotton Exposition. His interest was sufficiently keen to warrant a trip to Charleston, South Carolina, where he visited factories and learned how the rock was transformed into fertilizer. Mama showed a most unexpected interest in these unsocial commodities, and what is more, she seemed to grasp what he was talking about. Caroline remained attentive but only partially understanding.

He had theories about ferments and yeasts. He wished to tap Japan's chemical and soil resources, which he believed (wrongly as it turned out) were enormous. He wished to harness its water power. He wished to bring his country into a closer industrial and scientific community with the Western World. He wished to introduce patent law into Japan and was studying assiduously the United States' patent laws. He wished—he wished to marry Caroline.

Mama thought this a good idea. Mama had determined to annex the chemist with the dynamic ideas and the unusual character.

The match would be without precedent of any kind. A few Japanese diplomats of the many sent to study in Europe had married highborn German ladies, and there had been any number of illegitimate and unrecorded unions between occidental men and Japanese women, but this was to be the first case on record of an American-born lady marrying a Japanese. Yet Mama urged marriage.

I think Mama did not grasp the situation properly. She, who was so impressed by the advanced ideas of Robert Ingersoll and Henry George and the tantalizing theories of this young chemist, was in reality contracting with a gentleman of feudal Japan. Very possibly Jokichi had persuaded himself that he had accepted the 1868 Restoration psychologically. But he was still far from the American way of thinking.

Mary Beatrice had met the one man she could not dominate, the strongest man she had ever encountered, even possibly including President Grant. His strength was undoubtedly his root attraction for her. Mary Beatrice was as ambitious as Jokichi and as unscrupulous, with this added element, which even she as a devoted Southerner could not gauge: that what he did was not only for himself and his family but also for his fatherland. How deeply the paternalistic culture had shaped the young scientist no one who had not grown up under the same influence could guess. Because of his enormous charm and consideration she did not realize all this, but she came to know it later, bitterly.

The same drive that put the younger sons of Europe's feudal lords on the high seas and got them entire countries of their own beckoned young Takamine to Europe and America and to Western scientific learning. There, small in body, alien and alone, he would be at every disadvantage. Nevertheless, the possibilities for advancement were not defined beforehand. And he had the wit and the curiosity and the energy of his century and the patience and discipline of his heritage.

At that time in Japan a Caucasian wife was not only a rarity, but a mark of social status because everyone knew it cost money to maintain a Western wife. Caroline would be a symbol of distinction, and Mary Beatrice would be a strong claim on the Western world. Was it really Mama he wished as his Western root?

Caroline surveyed her life. Helping with housework, helping with little obstreperous sisters, helping—never, never speaking her own mind, never, in fact, knowing her own mind. More of the same seemed unattractive. At sixteen Caroline was still a sort of *Backfisch*. She had not yet even attained her full growth and at the moment was exactly as tall as her suitor. If this marriage seemed risky, it was also adventuresome and it would make her special, and she would go far, far away. And so, she said, she "accepted her fate." Caroline was a great believer in fate, which is another word for exhaustion.

All their friends and neighbors were aghast. This was a

misalliance for proper, not like marrying a negro (which was illegal), but it certainly was not like marrying a white man either. There was general outcry and remonstrance. Aunt Emma van Pelt wrote an outraged letter from Paris, Aunt Lizzie Head from Germantown, Pennsylvania. Captain Hitch was hard put to endure the clamor; Madame Hitch did not even turn her capped head to listen. Minnie's stepfather said flatly, "If she's just marrying to get away from her mother, bring her home to us. She can have a place to live in my house as long as I live. But I'll not condone that wedding. I'll be out of town."

Captain Hitch took his daughter aside and faced her quietly. "Caroline," he said, sitting her down and looking at her squarely, "do you want this of your own will? Do you know what you're getting into?"

"I think so," she replied gravely. "I think I do."

"If you want it, I shan't interefere," said the Captain.

"All right, Papa, don't," she replied.

"That's it then," said the Captain and went back to sea.

But it was not to be just yet. Mama had encouraged the engagement and looked upon the marriage as a good job behind her. She believed in early marriages, the earlier the better, and lots and lots of children. She believed in these things forcefully, notwithstanding a perfect disregard for connubiality or community of interests in her own life. Caroline was of a marriageable age and had to be settled. She settled her.

But before taking the final step, Jokichi asked Caroline to wait while he departed for Japan and broke the news to his own folks.

His family was appalled. He, the son of a doctor, marrying a poor Creole of mixed French, English, and American heritage! They took it very hard.

He had troubles on all sides. On returning to Tokyo he had been offered an appointment in the Division of Chemistry in the

Department of Agriculture and Commerce, and an assistantship in the Bureau of Industries, but the latter post carried neither remuneration nor power, and the former very little. However, he had brought back with him small quantities of the South Carolina phosphates, "the first artificial fertilizer ever introduced to Japan," says Kawakami. The value of the phosphate was not appreciated at first; but after a time Takamine's enthusiasm and persistence was such that the Department of Agriculture was persuaded to distribute the fertilizer among the farmers in small quantities with the order that the results be reported.

I do not know how these tests were actually conducted. Japanese farmers were certainly not ignorant. Literacy was widespread and farming techniques intensively developed. Natural fertilizers, animal droppings, night soil, and vegetable matter had long been used. But chemical fertilizer was indeed a novelty. It seems likely that Takamine put the phosphate in the hands of village elders to try out in selected plots.

On the other hand, the family with its scanty and imperfect knowledge of Japan imagined their hero, the young brilliant innovator, standing in the fields explaining, standing before the farmers, poor medieval creatures, bow-legged, bent-backed, explaining as they turned their listening faces under their straw hats, squinting with eyes that had never known glasses, gaping with teeth that had never known dentistry, trying to understand science; why the earth was not sufficiently enriched by their own droppings, what chemicals meant, what the earth which crumbled in their hands consisted of. Takamine, exhorting and explaining, firing them, overwhelming them at the risk of direct starvation. Highly romantic and highly dramatic and not true! But the end result was good. For in the event, "the reports submitted," Kawakami states, "were enthusiastic about the 'miracles.'"

There was as yet no international wireless telegraphy. The Pacific Ocean was three weeks wide and there was another three weeks, the continent, to cross. They broke out a bottle of champagne in New Orleans when the letter recounting the success finally arrived, and Caroline slept with the paper under her cheek.

Vice-Minister Yoshida urged the government to establish a fertilizer factory under Takamine's direction. The government declined. Takamine and four friends, Shibusawa, Masuda, Okura, and Asano, leaders in Japan's industrial world, thereupon built one of their own and named it "The Tokyo Artificial Fertilizer Company." Takamine ate his heart out for his faraway love and wrote letters constantly that always took months to reach her.

In spite of bureaucracy's indifference, Takamine shortly introduced Western products into Japan—Bakelite, caustic soda, aluminum (he helped form and owned the Asia Aluminum Company), asbestos (which had been known in the eighteenth century as stone-cotton but was not readily available in our commercial form—what a boon to the country of wood and paper houses!), acetate of lime, bromides—all this, claims his biographer, without thought of personal remuneration, entirely *pro bono publico*. Yet it must be noted that the interests he retained in the Asia Aluminum Company and the Sankyo Pharmaceutical Company were to furnish the bulk of his wealth, and for decades his wealth remained considerable. But that was later. Jokichi had practical forethought—"vision" they called it.

After two long years his enterprising young friends offered to send him west once more on a trip to gather further information through Europe and North America. When he finally worked his way back to New Orleans, he seemingly had a substantial job and his mother's blessing on the marriage.

Caroline, during these lonely years had, like any well-brought-up engaged girl, been occupying her time in doing nothing. She could not accept invitations or go to dances. She sat at home while her younger sisters, carefree and unbespoke, disported themselves. While Beth, for instance, ran off in an attempted elopement that was only forestalled at the station by Papa, Caroline hemmed linens and sewed lace on the edges of underwear. The weeks passed very slowly and the word from Tokyo was not explicit. The weeks passed and passed, and so did her first youth—her time for parties, and Mardi Gras, and picnics, and rides with young men, and church socials, and innocent, idiotic, girlish pranks. She was an engaged young woman. She held herself in suspension and two whole years went by.

When Jokichi returned, Caroline was two inches taller than he. She subsequently grew another inch.

Madame Hitch set the day of the wedding in June. Several close friends, including Minnie's stepfather, left town precipitously. With unblemished aplomb, Mama readied the house for the nuptials. Smilax was looped all over the doors and balconies, and Japanese paper lanterns, an intriguing innovation at that time, were hung in the grills. Superb gifts arrived from Japan, including tea from someone highly placed—the family was vague —that *no one* could stand. Caroline wore a dress of white embroidered crepe and Brussels lace. The wedding breakfast was held on the iron-laced balconies and in rooms thrown open to the night, and the meal included avocado pear salad, unknown up to that point in New Orleans.

With the marriage, Caroline lost her United States citizenship by the then international law and became a subject of the Emperor. Her legal and social status was that of any other Japanese wife—low and legally quite unprotected. Her social status was odd, not altogether accepted by the Japanese, but recognized as an exotic and valuable acquisition. With the marriage the bridegroom estranged himself from his clan, not legally but emotionally, crucially damaging his social and business contacts. The feudal class distinctions had been formally abolished with the 1868 Restoration but prejudice remained. He had not explained this to Madame Hitch. Perhaps he had thought it would not be so and it was such an ignominious and insulting thing to admit. But it was so.

The bridal couple departed the day after the wedding for Washington, D.C., where it was uncomfortably warm, but where the doctor had pressing business with the copyright and patent office. He studied the international laws as thoroughly as any lawyer. He presented his wife to the Japanese Embassy and the people there met with grave courtesy the tall young woman who was now their new care and entirely within their jurisdiction. The legations of both countries looked on the match with astonishment. No one expected the union to last.

The bride and groom continued the odd honeymoon with a trip through South Carolina to consider and collect the local phosphates, to buy machinery for the manufacture of chemical fertilizer, and finished up with a swing through New England. They were just conventional enough to add a quick weekend at Niagara Falls—plenty of water power there, always a subject of interest to the groom.

Jokichi then took his bride across the Pacific. The trip was made on a Japanese steamer and took three weeks. Everyone was enchantingly courteous to her. The people seemed to be like flowers, bending and nodding. If she put out a hand, they yielded and swayed to her touch. They were as solicitous as good fairies about a new princess. Of course she could not speak to them and so could never get a direct answer. And the Pacific seemed never to end. She walked the decks under the great skies and wondered. She was only twenty, but marriage was forever, and each hour she was putting the world between herself and what she knew.

Jokichi was adoring, a perfect and loving bridegroom. He explained everything. He tried to instruct her in all, he tried to share. His patience and kindness were inexhaustible. But the moment he spoke to a steward, or an officer, or a passenger, she was an alien and had to stand aside and wait for translations. The most Caroline ever said about any sort of situation was that it was "something of a strain." It must have been.

There were besides some curious lessons she had to learn. It was understood between them that she would live as an American wife and not be restricted to the decorums and limitations of a Japanese. This had been readily agreed to. "For, of course," said Jokichi, and kissed her eyes, "if I'd wanted a Japanese wife, I'd have chosen one." He could not protect her from everything, however. She was in a Japanese world.

On unpacking his suitcases, she had found several cards for Japanese brothels. He did not explain. He smiled and turned away. No doubt he was astonished at her surprise. (I have never understood this story, since Caroline could not read Japanese, but it was told me by Aunt Marie. Perhaps there were pictures. Perhaps Caroline was unduly suspicious. Perhaps the cards were merely geisha cards.)

On arrival in Tokyo no delegation came to greet her. There was certainly no imperial welcome of any sort, indeed no special attention. Several of Jokichi's business friends, in careful Western dress, were waiting on the dock. They spoke a few words of English and they brought her flowers.

The wife of the American Consul called and they were invited for tea at the Consulate and Caroline enchanted the entire legation. "We'd better watch that situation very carefully," they said. But, of course, she was no longer a legal responsibility.

She was taken to be presented to Jokichi's family. If she could get through this, she felt nothing else would ever daunt her. She was very nervous and had a sick headache for three days before. But she didn't complain. "She never once in her whole life complained." She wore her going-away dress, pale dust blue, with a jabot of real lace, a folded blue silk belt on her waist and inserts of pleated lace over mousseline in the skirt. (Mama had had it made by French seamstresses in New Orleans.) She had to bring low slippers so that she could remove them easily—the high button boots she usually wore would prove awkward. Her hair was high under a little bonnet with French roses and soft feathers. Jokichi had given her one good pearl and she wore that on a chain at her throat. She was very white, so white her lips were bloodless, which was unusual. Jokichi noticed and was kind. He kept squeezing her hand. She shook a good deal and on the long train ride to Kanazawa she was quite sick and had to resort frequently to the smelling salts in her handkerchief. Jokichi had her put her head down to her knees, which was difficult because she wore corsets. They were in second-class and there was a little Japanese lady in the compartment with them who was very kind, got cold water for Caroline's head and ministered in every way to the first Caucasian she had ever seen—this extremely tall, beautiful, low-voiced, very sick girl. The husband had murmured explanations. "Hai," said the little lady. "Hai, hai," bowing to Jokichi and patting Caroline's flaccid hand with a touch like petals.

Then the train drew up. Caroline adjusted her hat, pushed her hair in place, took a final sniff of the salts, laid her gloved hand on her husband's arm, and stepped out to a new life.

The family was there, all but the mother, in dark kimonos,

bowing and murmuring softly and politely. She could hardly see. They all bowed and then the women offered their right hands in occidental formality. They'd been practicing with embarrassed laughter at home. When they extended their right hands, they pushed back the kimono sleeve with the left in a whispering flourish of the most lovely grace. Caroline took their hands in her white-gloved trembling fingers and they went into rickshas. The ride at a good running pace in that fresh-smelling town rather restored her, although there were bumps and joggles in the ruts. When they arrived she felt less dizzied. She got out and went through the garden, her heels crunching on the gravel. It was late morning and she was aware that the garden was lovely, but she couldn't seem to get air. She was breathing heavily and shallowly. She left her slippers at the doorsill and put her cotton stockinged feet on the soft responding matting and moved forward. They entered the largest room of the house.

There they were, in serried ranks at the far end, the entire family seated formally, immobile, the men in front of the women. In the center of the back row was a tiny white-haired woman in dark plum and black. Jokichi had described her, so Caroline, even in her terrible nervousness, knew who she was. Jokichi pushed her forward and put his hand under her elbow and she was down safely on her knees and bowed her forehead to the tatami twice, as he did beside her. He could not help her up. He was prone beside her. She moved forward to her mother-in-law and bowed again to the floor, hat brim to matting. She felt two delicate hands, soft as a child's, touch her hands on the matting and draw her forward, and she looked up into an old, wise face and into the black eyes, which gazed at her. They were without expression of any kind.

Then she met, as they sat in a row, even those she had originally met at the station, all the uncles, aunts, brothers, sisters, cousins, nephews, and nieces, and bowed to each, not so low to those of her own generation, which was fortunate because she simply did not have the strength in her thighs to go down and up again.

They sat Japanese style on their heels—by this time Caroline was in real pain—the men on one side of the room, the women on the other, and drank ceremonial tea and ate little cakes. She tried her few phrases of extreme politeness which she had carefully learned. Suddenly the room went dark. "Jokichi, Jokichi darling . . ." she murmured and fainted dead away.

She was lifted to an adjoining chamber and ministered to by the women which involved, to their great astonishment, loosening her stays. They'd heard about these things, but they'd never seen them. They couldn't believe women submitted to them voluntarily. Western men must be very cruel!

When she was brought around, she found Jokichi kneeling beside her holding her hand. "Forgive me, forgive me," she whispered.

"You did brilliantly. It was a strain."

She put her head on his shoulder and closed her eyes to hide tears of weakness. She fell instantly asleep. He sat for an hour supporting her without moving. After that his sister took his place, and then Jokichi returned.

Takamine-san, the old lady, sat quite alone, bolt upright, staring through the shoji at the garden leaves. She had not liked Caroline.

Caroline realized she faced disapproval and hostility, that she was not to be naturally accepted as the oldest son's wife, which was a very special position, but must win their hearts on her own lovableness.

Caroline was shy, but tried to hide her uncertainty under iron control. It produced in her a semblance of haughtiness, in reality quite false. Minnie said this may have been unattractive to her new family because while they also practiced enormous reserve, they had a system of formalities and rituals to bridge every situation, and of course she had none.

And her bridegroom? Kind, courteous, sympathetic, and remote. He listened always. He never explained or changed his opinion. She could argue and argue in her soft, lovely voice, and he would smile affectionately, the ends of his waxed mustache twitching up and his eyes crinkling with love, and then he'd do just what he'd intended to do in the first place. "When I was with them," said Minnie, "it always made me very nervous to hear Caroline trying to persuade him." Jokichi listened, emitting soft little "Ahs!" which might mean anything, but which encouraged the speaker, but he was intransigent in a velvet, silent way.

She did not look for close companionship in marriage; she had never seen any. It was enough that her husband was able and that he kept her at his side without running away constantly like Papa. In Japan he reassumed his position as head of the family and, while always courteous and gentle, he knew his rights, which were neither democratic nor American, but based on the submission of women. And in Japan they did just that without argument. This was not altogether hard for Caroline. In spite of Mama's example, she had been brought up in the Southern woman's code of deferring everything to the man. Yet this was different from anything she had experienced in New Orleans.

Nevertheless, he sought to make her understand his business and plans but since these involved a good bit of scientific knowledge, it is inevitable that many of his ideas were beyond her.

Jokichi rather showed her off. She did not walk behind him, but shoulder to shoulder, and she was taller. Occasionally on nar-

row footways, she preceded him, and at this, male passersby, even
the polite Japanese, turned and frankly stared.

She ate with him on the floor trays and she ate Japanese food—
there was no other—but soon he ate with her in Western style at
table and, although this was absolutely without precedent, she ate
with him when he had male guests. She could not join the conversation, but she was present, the officiating hostess, and his
friends had to accept her.

The mother-in-law was not pleased. All this was contrary to
custom and therefore diminished his standing. Caroline was mix-
ing into the men's world in a way that seemed unseemly and im-
proper. Peasants ate together in mixed company (the women always last, of course) but not ladies and gentlemen, and for good
reasons: the presence of a young wife would hamper and modify
the men's talk, as it did now.

So Caroline found herself in almost total isolation, ignorant of
social usages, unable to speak the language, unable to confide in
women, and not only just because of language difficulties; forbidden to speak to men except under the most formal and public circumstances. She had not even confidantes in her servants, as
Mama for all her outrageousness always had had, because Caroline had a rigid sense of hierarchy, a sense of unbreachable
decorum. She never let her hair down to anyone, not one single
time, and therefore her daily life presented daily loneliness.

Think of not being able to make a joke, or use the vernacular,
or be aware of everything taken for granted by others; think
of never being able to refer to shared experience or custom or
family crotchets, of living under the necessity of explaining every
nuance of feeling or of letting it go unremarked; of never knowing American news, of waiting months for home word; or wearing stockings and corsets, and corset covers, and camisoles, bus-
tles, and boned collars, and buttoned boots with heels in a world

where women slid by on tabied feet in soft, soundless garments; she longed, she wrote home, "for red beans, bouillabaisse, French bread, bananas, steak, pralines, and shrimp Creole. And, oh heavens, how I would love a glass of fresh milk."

Caroline had expected oriental glamor. What she found was different. What she found hardest to accept was the stench of the fertilizer, for the family lived, by Jokichi's choice, very close to the factory. Indeed, Caroline had much to contend with that even the extremely old-fashioned New Orleans home had spared her. This land of cherry blossoms and tea-making could be uncomfortable. It was bitter cold in the winters. Oh, the cold! Her feet and hands grew inflamed and rheumatic with it. One huddled about the hibachi. One sat wrapped in cotton quilted futon all day and slept between them at night. The wind sang under the raised floor of the house and shook the shoji, and Caroline's feet blistered with chilblains. Thank God for the soft wool undergarments Mama sent her. In the summer the heat was stifling and there were mosquitoes. The house had only primitive plumbing. There was little privacy.

She felt like a traveler always, forever, with no relief. And what strange, small humiliations and disagreeableness she was forced to meet daily with perfect aplomb! She never spoke of any of this. Years later her daughter-in-law, a European, on coming to Japan as the honored bride of her son, found that she could not bathe until all the men were finished and that she was given the honey bucket last. There was first Papa Jokichi, then Jo and Eben, and then the daughter. But Caroline never complained, never even remarked. "She was cool always," said Minnie. "Not passionate. Cool."

There were Mama's letters, of course. Mary Beatrice wrote every single day, but as the ships sailed from San Francisco only twice a month, the letters came in accumulated packets and there was never any sense of immediacy, although they were letters of news, of gossip, and above all of instruction and advice. Mary Beatrice was still ordering her around, she who knew nothing whatever of Japan. Caroline wished she wouldn't, although she was grateful for home news; the advice was simply inapplicable for, of course, Caroline had written not one word of her problems. Mama had brought her up not to whine, and her loyalty was now to her husband, absolutely and totally. Mama understood this intellectually, but still it did not suit Mary Beatrice to step aside for anyone, not even for Jokichi, whom she adored.

The civilization that Caroline was now entering as a member was alien to her in many fundamental ways. It was not retarded or backward as Westerners believed because, they argued, Japan had been cut off for two hundred years from free commerce and intercourse with themselves. The Japanese were worldly enough. Their cities were large and busy. Their trading and banking systems were among the oldest and most highly developed in the world. In matters of urban trade they were indeed well advanced, having, for instance, department stores two hundred years before we did. Their public education was on a par with anything in the United States, while their arts, painting, pottery, poetry, prose, and theater were among the most sophisticated the world has ever produced.

But the craze at the end of the nineteenth century was for accepting anything Western. It turned out often to be the superficial West. Baseball took over rapidly and, not so rapidly but much too soon, our hideous Western dress, and a people who could not cross two sticks or arrange three vegetables or tie a printed handkerchief without grace accepted easily pure Western ugliness. For unfortunately the Japanese idea of Western style was gleaned almost entirely from missionaries, traders, and commercial travelers, always untrustworthy advocates of esthetic subtleties.

So Caroline lived out her first year as a bride, webbed with ceremony. She stood perfectly alone at the zero point between great opposing pressures and watched the forces of civilization regroup and gather, while she bargained for vegetables and cooked them in unfamiliar pots with peculiar recipes, while she tried with love and patience to learn the rudiments of chemistry.

Caroline was pregnant, and it was a hard pregnancy. "Let it be a boy," she prayed. "Let it be a boy. This is no world for girls."

She resented the fact that it was a man's world entirely, yet she had no thought to change matters. She was against votes for women and spoke against the English and American women who began to agitate for the franchise and who wished to obtain rights over their children and their money. Equal rights would not be needed, she thought, if one had any subtlety. She believed this absolutely and she was firm in asserting that a lady should be faithful always, no matter what, under all circumstances. Infidelity or brutality on a man's part was no license for similar conduct on the woman's. "She had no respect for passion," said Minnie, "except when expressed through music."

Mama learned the news about the pregnancy in April and offered to come. Caroline said, "No," her first independent decision. She turned sick at the thought of the confrontation between the two mothers-in-law over the birth of the heir. Oddly enough, Jokichi also was relieved, although he had kept in constant correspondence with Mama. Caroline would be safe and cherished, her wrote Mary Beatrice. Many people had been born previously in Japan. He would get her the best medical attention.

From now on Mama's letters were full of detailed physiological instruction. Caroline was to continue her cold baths. (Caroline had stopped her cold baths with the independence of marriage, but she did not relay this fact.) Caroline was to sleep so many hours. Caroline was to drink milk (an impossibility in Japan), and so on. But if any harm came to Caroline she would not hear for four weeks.

Caroline put on her kimonos and kept them on, discovering the first true ease of her young life. She put her feet up on a stool and read the letters with firm lips. She did not read them to Jokichi. But Papa's letters sent love and felicitations and droll anecdotes and amusing comments about their family. Caroline read these aloud. In any case, Mama was writing directly to Jokichi, letters which concerned business and they were very shrewd indeed. Jokichi told her about his discovery of a wonderful new diastase.

Two sons were born: Jokichi, Jr., born August 28, 1888, and Ebenezer Takashi Takamine, August 3, 1889, nationals of Japan. They were descendants of *Mayflower* passengers and distantly but legitimately related to the Roosevelts through their mother's ancestry, but due to the 1875 Oriental Exclusion Act, they were barred forever from United States citizenship except by special act of Congress.

Caroline gave birth with the help of the local midwife, with whom she could barely communicate. By now, however, to a degree, she had assumed the place to which she believed she was destined. The situation of being always a curiosity, the object of unusual concern and attention twenty-four hours a day, in some sense suited her. She had been the oldest and most beautiful of five, but had been completely dominated and overshadowed by her mother, then by her mother-in-law—now, no longer. In Japan she was not only the wife of the oldest son, but the very special wife, claiming special prerogatives as an American. Lonely or not, she was noticeable. She got used to every single head turning every time she went down the street, and she got to enjoy it. She had need of what comfort she could take from this aspect of the situation, for they were living in straitened and disheartening circumstances.

The government officials were openly resistant to subsidizing private enterprise and the farmers, despite the "miracle," were still slow to adopt the chemical fertilizer. But Jokichi was working on a wonderful plan.

Before his discovery, diastase, which converts starch into dextrin and sugar, was obtained only in germinating grains and animal fluids, sprouting barley being universally used. Takamine's new technique shortened the fermenting process of grain alcohol from six months to forty-eight hours and eliminated barley. It does not take great scientific knowledge to see where this can lead. Mary Beatrice, in New Orleans, took note: what a boon to the liquor business.

It is remarkable that the position of mother-in-law, so powerful in Japan between daughter-in-law and husband's mother, should have become reversed in this quaint trans-Pacific version. This needy and harassed American gentlewoman put her life behind the young scientist. She was his business partner, his patron, his root in the New World. She gave her entire faith to him, without stint, as she had never done to the Captain. She sent him what money she could, her savings and sums raised from friends, and he accepted the loans without hesitation because he knew that he would one day repay her. She made possible his Western career.

Mary Beatrice's life had never been easy, and at this point it was dreadful. Things had gone from bad to worse in New Orleans. In 1890 the Hitches moved to Chicago, where Mary Beatrice took a house and re-established the New Orleans program of boarders and business. With them went the perennial boarder,

L. Moore, to be joined, the year of the Chicago Columbian Exposition of 1893, by Minnie Dickens and her mother, who were able to help with the rent. Mary Beatrice immediately opened a stock brokerage office and set to work in her customary bustling fashion.

In Chicago they struck cold weather, hard times, and the rough and tumble of gigantic industrial expansion. Mama did not flinch. She had lived all her life in the South, but although she was an aging woman—by that I mean she was in her forties—and in an alien climate, she softened her disciplines not a whit. She still stood up in a tub of ice-cold water every morning and poured it over her shoulders and chest, before walking briskly through the north wind to her office. The little girls were administered to in the same manner before school, whimper as they might.

Mama always had her distant son-in-law on her mind. He belonged, she felt, where there was less ceremony and more dividend. It was her idea to form a company for the manufacture of whatever Jokichi held patents for, a really daring and farsighted plan considering that he was seven thousand miles or a month and a half away from the scene of operations, had no American affiliations and no prospects of any, was unknown in this country, and was a member of a race beginning to be looked on with considerable distrust (Hearst had been very busy). In short, Mary Beatrice organized the company quite legally and soundly, selling stock to the butcher, the baker, and all trades people she knew, even using the stock (but not her shares) as barter for the necessaries of life. When driven to extremity, she sold her jewels.

One way or another Mary Beatrice formed the Takamine Ferment Company to manufacture diastase, fully protected under American patent laws. She was the president of the company and determined the business policies. Jokichi agreed to this—well, what else could he do at the time? Barely in his life in either country had he heard of a business run by a woman. Jokichi as partner was to concern himself with science, Mary Beatrice told him. Surprisingly enough, she was offered a generous sum on the New Orleans stock market for a nonexistent enterprise and she made a special trip back to investigate. But on thinking over the proposition she turned it down flat and continued to sit over the Takamine Ferment Company like a broody hen. All the little Hitch girls had their shares, and L. Moore naturally had his. The price of the shares was never high, one hundred dollars for years. The selling price at that point was zero. They were none of them —Mary Beatrice abjured them—ever to sell or give away any of the Takamine stock, no matter what the provocation. She was intransigent about this.

Astonishingly, she amassed enough to pay the Takamines' fares home; more wonderfully she had found a way of getting Jokichi a salaried position, until she could bring the projected company into something more functional than a paper organization.

And so in 1890, triumphantly and happily Mama and the Captain cabled Jokichi that the United States "whiskey trust" was interested in having the benefit of his new—and patented—technique of fermentation. How did Mary Beatrice reach the whiskey trust? What French bonnets or New Orleans dinners or display of young daughters or enthusiastic and inflaming conversations were involved? By some means she reached them. An offer was made.

Captain Eben was glad to get his daughter back from heathen shores. Mary Beatrice was glad too, but I think she chiefly wanted to resume friendship with Jokichi, and I think she believed that with the two of them in proximity, they could establish a masterful business. With him at her side, she could take on the world.

But the Takamines now faced a hard choice. After three years of struggle the great Japan Artificial Fertilizer plant (it subsequently became the greatest Japanese concern of the kind) was beginning to pay off and its ledgers finally balanced. Everywhere in Japan business and scientific projects were opening up. Jokichi knew he would be successful at home. Then came the cable. (What was the "whiskey trust"? Was it reliable? What waited in the hurly-burly of the United States for a Japanese gentleman and his half-breed children?) Caroline relates that he wished to stay in Tokyo and that she, unselfish as she always was, in spite of all the pull of home and family, did not persuade him otherwise. She urged him to do as he thought best. He put the matter before his friends and business associates, the Barons Shibusawa and Matsuda, who urged him to go to America in the interests— of all things—of patriotism, or so he said. And it is in his official biography that it was this thought that decided him, the chance to show the Western world what Japanese science could do. According to the biography there was no thought of material advantage. This unworldliness seems hardly possible.

So Jokichi and Caroline Takamine, Japanese citizens, and their children, Jokichi, two, and Ebenezer, one, Japanese citizens, left for Peoria, Illinois, to enter the not very courtly environment of the brewing business.

When Mary Beatrice saw the black-eyed boys, her first grandchildren, she cried out, "Take them away, they're not mine!" Caroline merely murmured as she shepherded them off, "What did you expect?" Minnie Dickens told me this story, but Little Bea repudiates this tale vehemently. "Outrageous and impossible! Mary Beatrice loved children and was kind. Besides, she had engineered the marriage and revered Jokichi, and she'd seen the babies' photographs. Minnie," adds Bea, "was a viperish and jealous old witch! It is unlikely that Mary Beatrice could have said this or anything of the kind, or that if she had, Jokichi and Caroline would have ever spoken to her again. No, it is unthinkable." But somebody did say it. It was the cry that greeted the boys in the New World and that followed them all the rest of their lives.

They established themselves in Peoria near the breweries.

But matters were sinister on every hand. The malt interests opened direct war. Jokichi was submitted to every kind of attack, contrived labor troubles, slander, threats, theft of ideas, arson. All this was endured while he suffered bouts of virulent hepatitis. And there was TB. Caroline's chest gave way. Too much fertilizer; too much stockyard; too many bleeding adrenals, Jokichi's current interest; too much poverty and hostility, ignorance; too much cruel effort to carry it all off with style. There was a brief visit in the mountains of Virginia, where she pulled herself together, and then she returned immediately to get on with her job.

Jokichi kept sending for young scientists from Japan, and those who came were able and experienced. Some were brilliant. They were also underpaid.

Jokichi kept saying, "Science is the great cohesive force of civilization." He also said with shrewdness, "It needs but one discovery, one great and useful idea, and we will be able to devote the rest of our lives to doing all we dream of, cultivating the arts, helping young gifted men with education and opportunity, traveling, establishing a salon that will be the forum for all intellectuals of both countries, bettering the relations between Japan and the West. Caroline, we can build gardens. One discovery and we lay the world at the feet of our sons."

He was on the brink of discovering the medical use for the diastase. He had learned how to manufacture alcohol in a fraction of the time previously required, now he worked on a process that would cure dyspepsia, the first to relieve indigestion. A young Japanese, Dr. Shinizu, continued in 1892 the experiment for him but died of tuberculosis shortly thereafter. Takamine called the product Taka-Diastase.

He had leased a house close to the abattoirs of the stockyards, which were almost unbearably malodorous (Caroline had once thought fertilizer difficult to live with!), but he insisted on staying there for reasons difficult to make clear to outsiders but which his mother-in-law never questioned, nor Caroline, since he wished it.

While the factory manufactured diastase, he conducted experiments in an old carriage house, devoting every moment he could spare from the whiskey research. He stayed there day and night, with his coat wrapped over the telephone so that he could not hear Caroline's summons to meals.

He was searching for an elusive substance, in the adrenal glands of sheep. In his Peoria carriage house in the stockyards the adrenals of sheep were daily brought him by the bloody basketful straight from the killing pens. The rooms reeked of them. The researchers' hands seemed permanently red; the stench got in their hair and clothes. But the active substance remained elusive.

Jokichi desperately needed money for the research but he could not interest any of the big drug houses. So at his wife's suggestion he invited the heads of Parke-Davis to dinner, pawning his father's watch and chain to pay for the meal. Caroline said the dinner was astonishingly good and she was at her ravishing best. He opened his heart and mind to the businessmen but received no answer of any kind, not a word then or for weeks.

As he was giving up all hope, a wire belatedly came from Parke-Davis, which promised to manufacture and market his Taka-Diastase. They would take out the patents jointly in their two names, and they wired a contract for continued research and a retainer for Jokichi in advisory capacity. The sum involved was not princely—$300 a month—but in 1897 it was worth about six times its present value, and the allotments were regular and guaranteed. Above all, the endowment was an earnest of faith. It also established a claim on anything the doctor might discover, but Takamine of course owned outright anything his young researchers might turn up.

His name was now known in the proper circles. He had made brilliant contacts in Johns Hopkins, men with new ideas were consulting with him, men with new techniques were crossing the Pacific to work in his laboratory. He felt he was about to make a break-through discovery. And he wanted to be ready for world negotiation and world traffic. It became obvious to him that he needed an expertly efficient, modern, businesslike firm, and accordingly he intended to take the control into his own hands.

Up to this moment it had been Mary Beatrice's company. She had projected it, built it, supported it. She had told America about Takamine when he was far away and himself indifferent to the opportunities here. She had fetched him back, fostered his chances, and watched the growth of his brilliant labors. This Japanese man stood in place of a weak and ineffectual husband, of a son lost by fearful accident, of a career missed by accidents of birth and sex; he stood for genius, the conquest of worlds. His achievements were in effect her lifework. Now at the moment of vindication she was about to be ordered to step aside and resume the anonymity and powerlessness of womanhood.

Caroline knew her husband was right, that his plan was the sensible and practical thing to do, but she blanched at what was ahead when Mama would be told. Jokichi assured her that Mama would be paid back, every penny, and that she would be looked after with love and cherishing all her life. Caroline just stared at him. But he continued, very stubbornly, to say that a company that was going to span Asia, Europe, and the United States could not be headed by a middle-aged woman. The president had to be a man, an able one who understood every aspect of the business, scientific and commercial. He intended to be that man. The matter was decided.

There is no record of their confrontation. The family is mum. But Jokichi told Mama that he, and not she, must assume the business reins from that time on.

Her heart broke right then. She had recurrent attacks of rage and despondency and finally, after an outburst of blazing anger, went into a coma. Marie and Elmoore and Nana were summoned from their home in the night. But she did not recognize them. She died in Caroline's home on Woodlawn Avenue in Chicago, December 12, 1897, aged forty-seven. Jokichi was at her side too, but she did not regain consciousness or speak to him. When it was over, he, being a Buddhist, went to the one temple in Chicago and spent some quiet time. He always spoke of her afterward with the most profound love and admiration.

Mama died without being able to say good-bye or tell them what she wanted. But she had left a will. All of her shares were divided between her daughters and her husband. She also stipulated that the home must be kept together with Mr. Moore, and Nana was to preside; no one was ever to sell Takamine stock; they were to live out their lives as ladies.

Papa hurried back and arranged with Nana to stay forever. L. Moore left and was not heard from again. His story closes. Caroline and Jokichi, with unparalled generosity, offered to take the two youngest sisters in, but this plan was considered inadvisable and Nana, with Papa's approval, sold up and arranged to housekeep in lodgings. Beth had embarked on a stage career.

Now freed from want and with the support of Parke-Davis' $300 monthly research fund, Jokichi was able at last to turn his attention to the big experiments, the ones that were occupying several scientists, notably J. J. Ebel at Johns Hopkins.

Later in 1897 the workshop and the family moved to New York and established themselves near Morningside Park. Little sister Elmoore had been taken into the Takamine home with their old nurse Nana. Marie was about to be married to Henry George, Jr. (Mama had arranged this). Beth had achieved her marriage to Will Atkinson.

A laboratory was established on East 103 Street and Heizo Wooyenaka, only twenty-three years of age but a trained and experienced chemist who might bring the latest new techniques, both German and Japanese, unknown yet in America, joined Takamine in New York in response to his request for a researcher.

Now at the Takamine flat and nearby laboratory on Hamilton Terrace near Central Park West once more the evil-smelling experiments with sheep and pork adrenals recommenced. "The New York laboratory was, in fact, a basement," says Wooyenaka's daughter. "It was sparsely equipped. Test tubes were few and had to be used and reused until they were reduced to stubs. The basement windows remained closed to regulate oxydization. Father worked alone, unaided and without going out, sometimes seventy-two hours at a stretch. Takamine from time to time, occasionally in silk hat on the way back from the opera, looked in to inquire about the progress of the work."

Takamine kept pressing for results. Scientists know the breathless, tightening wonder that makes possible the daylong, nightlong repeated failures, and because there were no assistants or helpers, the two men worked alone, and often in the absence of the Doctor, Wooyenaka worked night and day without sufficient rest, in the June heat, watching the dawn gild the angel on the Cathedral Church of St. John the Divine as he settled before his microscope, watching the gas street lamps flicker on the worn grass plots of the park as he trudged wearily back to his lodgings. He had more than once awakened from a dead faint on the laboratory floor as he pursued the elusive substance into tens of experiments—fifties—tens of fifties. But Takamine urged continuance without respite.

One hot midnight, June 28, 1900, Wooyenaka completed an experiment, again in failure and revealing nothing definitive. Dispirited and exhausted, he did something he had never permitted himself before: he went home without washing up the sink or the equipment, simply abandoned the mess, locked up the close and fetid room and left. The next morning, almost before daybreak, he hurried back through the gray streets in haste, ashamed, to clean and set his table in order. And greeting his reddened eyes there in the dirty debris of the unwashed tubes were the crystals so long sought—there in the filth—Adrenalin, one of the break-through discoveries of medical chemistry.

Ten days later, J. J. Ebel of Johns Hopkins University in Baltimore applied for a patent for the same formula, but Takamine had already obtained it in his own name.

Mary Beatrice was dead. She could share in nothing he had found.

Chapter 6

All this was before I was born. As a small child I was not brought into frequent contact with the family. The others, the people at the Other End, the Georges' End, didn't talk much. Being blood relatives they were quite proprietary, not to say snotty. We were all of us in awe of Aunt Takamine and excited by her beauty and importance and wealth and by the exotic doctor, of course. And the family stood as the showpiece and guarantee for our entire community. We expected it to endure forever. Well, of course, we expected everything to endure. When I became really interested I could have asked Aunt Caroline a great many things and she would have told me much, but I didn't, being concerned at the time with my own affairs.

Although hardly anyone in Merriewold understood about chemistry, they all recognized success. They soon enough heard about Adrenalin. What, then, was it?

It was the first hormone to be isolated in pure form, explains Takamine's biographer, Kawakama, "the best haemostatic agent yet created . . . non-irritating, non-poisonous, non-cumulative, without injurious properties . . . Surgery never attempted before, including eye surgery, was now possible. Heart stimulation, control of hemorrhage, heart failure from dental anesthesia, surgical

shock, drowning or electrocution, Addison's disease, asthma—
these and other scourges were for the first time brought under
control. It gave good results in morphine and opium poisoning,
collapse in anaesthesia, bleeding in surgical operations. It was
even helpful in deafness, hay fever, nasal hemorrhage and heart
disease."

By an astonishing coincidence Aunt Marie was one of the first
to be saved. Hemorrhaging in childbirth, she was on the point of
collapse and death when Caroline, standing beside her, repeated
from memory to the attendant doctor the newly discovered formula. The young father found a druggist who could fill the pre-
scription and obtained the hormones, and although the infant
died, Marie was saved.

Caroline, Minnie believed, understood little or nothing of her
husband's work, but she tried, as she considered herself his partner. Emotionally she may have been his partner, but she was certainly no chemist.

The year before the discovery, in 1899, Takamine had been
made a Doctor of Science by the University of Tokyo, but
directly after he began to acquire more honors—doctorates of
chemistry and governmental orders—but all Japanese. He was
not saluted by any American university nor did he receive the
Nobel Prize. His neighbors at Merriewold never understood this
and we were surprised and disappointed, all of us. Nevertheless,
his name became widely known and because his triumph was in
the West, he was honored as a champion of his country's prestige,
and because the copyrights, especially in Japan, were his, he grew
rich—unlike the Curies, who scorned financial consideration as
"contrary to the spirit of science," stating their credo that whatever was of benefit to mankind was to be given as a free gift to
mankind. The Curies, accordingly, remained poor, and Madame
Curie, beyond her Institute, never had anything luxurious or ex-

pensive. Furthermore, she never received a single decoration from the French Government. Takamine and his partners in Tokyo, on the contrary, became extremely rich and he was highly decorated.

In the United States he assumed a special position of tremendous affluence and influence among the Japanese, who regarded him as unofficial ambassador between the two peoples and the father and advisor of young scientists who came to him.

"These activities he entered upon with no thought of gain for himself, but actuated by high principles, the accomplishment of something of value for his country, the promotion of better relations between America and Japan," wrote the family biographer.

There were those (not family, of course) who noted that he was getting a remarkable bargain in needy talent. (Children hear things, they always do. I remember hearing in this context the phrase "indentured labor," which I did not understand, of course.) But Jo and Eben, who were taken into the Takamine laboratory as soon as they were old enough, heard much. In the laboratories there was talk of injustice, of fraudulent seizure of ideas, of exploitation and plagiarism. The public image of Takamine as the father of young Japanese researchers was one thing; the resentment and anger of the men who worked unseen and unnamed with microscopes and test tubes was something very different.

In 1901, at a medical convention at Johns Hopkins, Takamine, accompanied by Wooyenaka, announced the isolation of the active principle of the suprarenal gland, the first of all gland hormones to be isolated in pure form. After the publication of the discovery, Dr. Charles F. Chandler of Columbia University invited Takamine to his laboratory to demonstrate, but "J.T. dispatched my father instead," adds his daughter. And she implies very strongly that J.T. could not make the demonstration.

The truth is that the doctor's fortune and fame were based in part on a claim which, although quite legal and commonly practiced, was basically unethical, or so his scientists believed.

The part Wooyenaka had played in the great discovery was formally and briefly acknowledged at the time, 1900. The Takamine biographer states, "A sober and honest youth, he [Wooyenaka] seemed to have a talent for research. This man was to become the central figure in the laboratory . . ." and later concerning Takamine, "Neither von Furth nor J. J. Ebel, distinguished scientists, had succeeded in doing that which was essentially the work of one unknown young Japanese [Takamine] with inexplicable ease!" (By actual count, several hundred experiments, and not by Takamine.) "Although Dr. Takamine," says his daughter, "once acknowledged personally his indebtedness to my father,* no adequate public acknowledgment was ever made even at the time Dr. Takamine was invited by Tokyo Imperial University to come to Japan to receive a medal and a cash prize. Wooyenaka received 360 stocks at $5 apiece of the Oriental Takamine Corporation."

The question of who takes credit for a discovery where several men have worked for years under the instigation and at the cost of a director, where independent scientists in separate places have made progressive findings, is always a delicate one, involving authorship of ideas and responsibilities, inspiration, the subtle areas of collaboration and suggestion. Any accusation of plagia-

* *Journal of History of Science* (No. 79, July–September, 1966), an organ of the National Museum of Science in Tokyo, states: "Though generally accepted until now that Jokichi Takamine was the discoverer of Adrenalin, reports until now on the method and analyses that led to the discovery were incorrect. The isolating of Adrenalin was due to Jokichi Takamine's assistant Keizo Wooyenaka, whose laboratory diary establishes this fact. This was earlier pointed out by Yojiro Tsuzuki . . ."

rism must be viewed with great care. Perhaps only the men involved can ever know how much they owe to one another. Whether Wooyenaka would have made the discovery without Takamine's direction and subsidy, whether Takamine could have made the discovery without Wooyenaka's unique knowledge and skill, cannot be answered. The fact remained that Takamine became a multimillionaire and a much decorated businessman. Wooyenaka remained poor by comparison and relatively unknown.

It is important, however, to judge Takamine in the light of his times. He operated when the railroads were pre-empting whole sections of the United States, when wheat and beef markets were cornered, when natural resources of oil, iron, coal, and timber were pocketed. When frock-coated land manipulators were encouraged, as once belted barons had been, to take over. This was before labor legislation. This was before the individual was considered to have inalienable rights in his own ideas, whether the law so specified or not. Takamine, like any seventeenth-century New World adventurer, invaded and took possession by proclamation. Instead of a sword he brandished a patent law.

There is no question that the Doctor and Caroline believed he acted always with unblemished integrity. And so the legend of his genius, philanthropy, and statesmanship, encouraged by his family, grew over the years. But the hearts of his brilliant assistants smoldered with resentment. The turnover in researchers in the laboratory was constant and quick. Very few of them chose to stay. Wooyenaka was one who did.

He continued in the Takamine laboratory for sixteen years, but finally left after what he considered an arbitrary and unfair deal and returned to Japan, where he managed the diastase plant for the Sankyo Pharmaceutical Company, making improvements in the manufacture of diastase, Adrenalin, and Bakelite. Ebenezer

Takamine many, many years later brought him a heavy embossed silver tray on behalf of his father's firms. It did not seem enough, somehow.

The Doctor never considered his workers as companions or social or intellectual equals, which they most certainly were. He treated them as upper servants. This would have been in order if the researchers had been clerks or unskilled, but, although years younger, they were scientists with training, degrees, and experience equal to their boss's. Indeed, they never considered themselves employees in the usual sense, nor retainers beholden to an overlord. They considered themselves modern scientists working jointly on a parity with their director and they considered the discoveries the result of joint effort. Caroline was the boss's wife and she considered herself "better born, a Creole." But she was not better born, nor in fact nearly as well born as, for instance, one of the wives who was descended from the prestigious Heiké family, nor was she as well educated as they. The wives numbered a graduate of the first women's university in Japan. Caroline was barely educated. Yet she condescended to almost everyone, even to her own sisters, who were presumably as well born as she, certainly to all the wives of her husband's Japanese employees, and they were never asked to her house socially, although the husbands alone were from time to time pressed into service as fill-ins for dinner parties and at her Thursday at-homes. The women naturally resented this. They wouldn't have been asked in Japan, where such social customs did not exist, of course, but they certainly could expect to be asked in the United States.

I knew almost none of the facts of their lives. The legends were rife, and they were enough. The Doctor was a samurai (a baron, the Pitmans believed, who forbore to use his title out of deference to the Georges and the Hitches; this makes no sense of any kind). One out of every four visitors was noble. (Well, they had had a prince and princess, several barons and Lord High Admirals.) He was a saint; the Georges approached this view. He was good (obviously), a father to his apprentices (all the family told us this), and he was a most kind and gentle neighbor (we could see this for ourselves). Our parents, along with the rest of civilized America, knew all about the grand international progress, and we were proud.

But the boys' recklessness of behavior and their cynicism and laziness and their tendency to get violent whenever they could—these things were known also.

The Takamine boys were not the first young men to be ruined by money, too great indulgence, too careless a leaning on Papa's reputation and Papa's credentials and power. Takamine came from a land where codes of conduct were more important than life itself. Caroline descended from people who valued responsibility more highly than success or money and made out of the practice of loyalty a religion. Yet the boys did as they pleased. Of course, as I say, I knew nothing of this. But I knew they were wild and in them such behavior was tolerated, was even considered rather fun. In Earl Hance it was not.

The deal with Parke-Davis included a trip around the world for Jokichi and his whole family, including a valet and a nurse for little sister Elmoore, who since Marie's marriage to Henry George, Jr., now lived with Caroline. ("My brother-in-law took me around the world," Elmoore always said. Never "my sister took me." She was jealous of Caroline, naturally.) They made stopovers whenever the doctor wished to study. They returned after a year to glory.

Laboratories expanded. The factories multiplied. The base factory in Clifton, New Jersey, was a thriving plant sending out its products to five continents. Parke-Davis supplied Adrenalin to the entire Western World. The Sankyo Pharmaceutical Company in Tokyo, owned outright by Shiohara, who bought rights to produce Taka-Diastase with Takamine as a large shareholder, supplied the entire Eastern World. It was largely from the Takamine Japanese holdings, the Sankyo Company and the Asia Aluminum Company, that his fortune came. In three years he had amassed several millions. Takamine was now in a position to acquire business interests not related to chemistry, large shares in the Otis Elevator Company, for instance. All the larger metropolitan centers were at this point converting to elevators because elevators made skyscrapers possible.

"Carrie never knew how wealthy she was," said Minnie, "for she operated on a monthly allowance, but it is a fact, she learned later, that for many years Jokichi could write a check for over a million dollars without any modification of their way of life, and their way of life, although public-spirited, matched that of any contemporary Prince of Finance." They had two great houses, one on Riverside Drive, the other one in Merriewold. They had a car, the first many of us had ever seen, driven by a Sullivan County chauffeur, LaRue Kinney.

The New York seasons were alternated with frequent trips to Japan and Europe and Caroline once chaperoned the two daughters of the Doctor's Tokyo partner, Shiohara, right around the United States and Europe, fitted them out in Paris, got them dinner and ball partners, exposed them to museums, sports, spas, and good times generally, then dispatched them back home where they had to set about forgetting as quickly as possible most of what they had learned and settle down to the life of the average Japanese housewife. Sometimes she took friends or family. Uncle Harry George accompanied the Doctor on one trip. He brought back to his wife, Marie, pearls and a kakemono and to his sister, my mother, a dress length of fine white crepe completely covered with embroidered wisteria blooms (I was learning to cross-stitch, not very neatly, at the time and I examined the Japanese stitches with amazement). Mother wore this for her big occasions, such as Father's openings. There began to appear in our house all sorts of inexpensive ware, cotton material, rice cloth, pots, soap dishes, tea cups, cheap but charming and predating all national manufacturer's marks. (Inexpensive Japanese stores were now the rage in New York, really inexpensive; you could buy a spray of handmade [how else?] paper cherry blossoms for ten cents and little gardens of growing moss and pines with sand, bridges, and lanterns for a dollar. But I who had seen a correct garden and real blossoms was scornful and kept my week's allowance, twenty-five cents, clutched in my retentive palm.) And there were valuable gifts from the Doctor, a tansu and a samurai sword which Father hung above his desk and forbade me to touch. Fifteen years later he unwound it from its silk chords, drew it from its sheath. In all that time it had not been sharpened but the light ran down its blade like ribbon. We were pleased but not surprised, Father and I; we expected "our" sword to be of the finest steel.

They began to entertain on a government level, and while their house was not official, it was considered smart, even obligatory, from a business and social point of view, for the Japanese certainly, and for many European statesmen as well. The Japanese government officials asked to see Carrie and Jokichi before continuing on to Washington.

Aunt Marie and Uncle Harry were invited to many of the grand parties, Mother and Father to a few, but always to the theatricals (Sho-Foo-Den had the largest room in Merriewold), at which Father always presented one of his one-acters. I remember a satire on changing sex mores, *In 1999*. Mother smoked a cigarette (she nearly choked) and threw Pop on the floor. I saw it only in rehearsal, not being allowed to stay up, in truth not being invited. The audience shouted with laughter, but I was embarrassed and sad. I didn't like seeing Father thrown on the Sho-Foo-Den rug, even by Mother. I didn't like seeing him humiliated, not even in fun. He was too splendid. Aunt Caroline came as Gounod's Marguerite, Mother told me. The Doctor was too important to play-act. J. I. C. Clarke recited "The Crew of the Nancy Brigg" with gestures.

As time went on, Caroline became more and more haughty, demanding flattery, even adulation from the young, and always complete agreement from her sisters. Indeed, all the sisters were cowed by Caroline. "Lady Caroline," her coterie and certain of her nieces called her, not always with love. Those who disagreed did not get Christmas presents; this was axiomatic. Of course, after her own fashion, Caroline was generous in worldly goods, giving cast-off garments, usually fine ones, and on occasion money and jewels, as at Bee George's coming-of-age. Usually Aunt Caroline's presents were Japanese and not very costly—a source of amusement to her sisters, who were themselves open-handed, Marie to the point of immolation.

Some of Caroline's arrogance was, I believe, self-protection, for the loneliness had not ever abated and she spent a good part of her time without the company of either of her sons or the Doctor. Her sons adored her, certainly, but they had their own friends; hers bored them; and the Doctor was busy. Her sisters could not be counted on for solid advice or understanding. She had no equals—only Minnie, the dependent. The truth is that it never crossed Caroline's mind that other members of her family were on an equal footing with similar rights and expectations. She was apart, with the privileges as well as the duties of the overlord.

The Takamines began to consider themselves as royalty, certainly the boys did. Jo took what he wanted—or tried to—and it was only his mother who attempted to discipline him. His father never did, and he and Caroline had many disputes about this. He always won, although she knew she was right. And then Jo, Jr., and Eben discovered that they could go behind their mother's back. They had man-to-man talks with their father, which always resulted in their getting more money and more forgiveness. She tried desperately to curb their drinking, but the Doctor (remembering his own harsh and deprived youth, his shame as an ignominious houseboy in the Dutch household at Nagasaki, the unending work, the lack of pleasure) would have none of her fussing—and out of pity for his sons he was overly indulgent. His sons were gentlemen, he said, and had certain prerogatives, and were not to be curbed by women.

They drank, they gambled, and maybe worse. Young gentlemen had behaved so always with impunity, even with picturesqueness, said Jokichi. But America provided certain new aspects of raffishness that were more dangerous than amusing.

Then, too, the boys had begun to feel the discrimination against them even as very young children in Peoria. In school and college, it was made increasingly obvious that the sons of the distinguished Jokichi and the delicately reared Caroline were regarded as half-castes.

So they were lonely, though on the surface jolly. At first they were welcomed everywhere as the heirs of a prominent man and as quaint and charming exotics. Their parents entertained for them as only the Takamines could, but they could not join fraternities. They had porch privileges at other country clubs and were forbidden to go inside. Gradually they began to behave a little worse than other adolescents. When they went off to college, it was nip and tuck whether they'd get through. Eben never finished college. He wanted to be a doctor, but that was clearly out of the question. The boys were taken into their father's laboratory in Clifton, New Jersey, and kept there in the company of qualified and able researchers, surrounded by the most brilliant young minds possible to lure from Japan.

Jo graduated. He was bright and could get by without working. He could do anything. He was a woodsman, a carpenter, an athlete (halfback at Yale), and in spite of a certain cynical laziness a gifted scientist. All the faculty at Johns Hopkins later felt that he had a considerable talent and the promise of achievement, but that he was playing with his resources. As he grew up he developed surface manners of explicit courtliness which put off all intimacy. This offended some American men, who thought him unctuous and insincere. He was neither. Little Bea said the manner was a screen for the deepest turbulence, also a mask, like his mother's arrogance, to protect him against the slights which he had grown to expect. Life was luxurious but by no means easy.

The objections to Caroline's marrying a Japanese had at the time been based on ignorance. The general condemnation continued and was augmented by fear. Bitter and persistent anti-Japanese feeling started in California, where there had been considerable immigration, and it was, of course, at base an economic problem. Hearst fanned the hate; the Yellow Peril made good copy. Young Jo and Eben were part of the Yellow Peril.

But in her home Caroline seemed happy. No one gainsaid her there. "The Iron Maiden," her grandson was to call her. Her two establishments required real organization and tremendous discipline. There were battalions of servants to organize and hold tight with kindness—two staffs of cooks, one for the Westerners and one for the Japanese, and they had to be kept at peace. (In New York the Doctor's dinners were brought by the chauffeur, LaRue Kinney, direct and piping hot from the Nippon Club.) And the servants had to be guarded from loneliness. Meals were on time because it was "kind to them." Any interference with the servants' routine was out of the question and fooling at table was forbidden even when grown-ups were not present, because of "them." Once all of the cousins were having lunch together alone and broke up into fits of giggles because Eben came by and made some remark. They couldn't stop laughing even when the butler changed the dishes. The butler, instinctively from habit, thought they were mocking him and threatened to give notice. Aunt Takamine was furious. She not only sent the cousins straight home, but she took her parasol and went across the woods to Auntie Marie's; she told the mothers, who happened to be there on the front porch reading, what she thought. She was very precise and very cross.

"Goodness," said Auntie Marie, "just because the children laughed. What would we do if the children didn't laugh? How dreadful that would be!"

Children (house guests—not the sons certainly) ate a daylight supper, were undressed and bathed, dressed again, displayed to Auntie's other guests, complimented, undressed a second time, and bedded down without a murmur but plenty of prayers. Little girls wore high laced boots, or at least Auntie hoped they would, to keep their ankles slim, learned French, and believed in fairies. Big girls wore decent long skirts, no makeup or hair dye, believed in chastity and marital rectitude. No girls drank or smoked or had wills of their own. (No girls except her daughters-in-law— she was later to find that out.) Girls served their mothers, until death if necessary; if they did not, it meant they did not love them. Not loving a mother was very nearly inhuman. It was certainly unchristian, possibly unladylike. In any case, it was quite outside her understanding. One loved one's mother or one's aunts. Girls did. And that meant absolute obedience and prolonged propinquity.

Jane George used to get very mad. "She's a bully," she said. She loved her own mother, but she didn't like to be told to do so. "There will be no Christmas present for me this year, but I don't care. She is a bully."

On going across the rhododendrons, nieces were instructed as though they were entering court life. All of this took a lot of time and administrative attention, and it was done with firmness but great courtesy and finesse. Little Bea, who was an intimate of the house, told me stories.

"How can you have a young child [Bea] about?" asked a guest.

Auntie answered melodiously and slowly: "I considered very carefully whether I had the energy and time to look after a child before I invited Beatrice." She was the only one who called Bea "Beatrice." "I invited a little girl to stay with me, but when she arrived she was as mature and competent as any adult. She is not a responsibility, just a very considerate guest!"

After that Bea realized she'd better not have any more real fun that summer.

It was five days later that Auntie said to her, "Beatrice, I don't like you bathing in a one-piece suit. These lewd Clarke men— well, it's not that they can help being lewd. It's boys' nature and their upbringing . . ."

"But you've known them all your life. They're Auntie Clarke's sons!"

"No matter, you're not to wear a suit where your legs and . . . and so forth show. Now, darling, Auntie has an idea. Pull out that drawer and you'll find under the 'Elsa' dress a bathing suit made for Auntie in Paris. It is just the color of your eyes and I'll give it to you." (Mary Beatrice had said, "I've always wanted to give you flowers," as she took charge of a recalcitrant décolletage.)

The bathing suit was very large, very heavy, of serge, and

wired in the bosom, which for Bea was unnecessary. It pulled her into the mud and she nearly drowned, but she wore it although she swam right out of it and left it behind like a body in the lily pads. It was, indeed, however, the color of her eyes. When young Jo saw her in it he threw back his head and shouted with laughter.

"Race to the point!" he called.

She could barely do a breast stroke in all that wet serge and wire. But she had thought to wear her own singlet underneath. He pulled her out of the suit and they went to the point and back. She got tired and had to return floating on top of him, her hands on his shoulders. She could feel the great shoulder muscles working.

"There, polliwog," he said, bringing her back to the shallows. "Get into that God-awful mess. Mother really is the limit!"

"Bea drowned this afternoon," he announced at the dinner table. "She'd gone down for the third time and I saved her. Her modesty and the bathing suit are intact."

Auntie didn't hear. She had that faculty. Uncle Jo patted her hand and put some seaweed on her plate with a flick of his hashi.

Bea continued to wear the bathing suit. Auntie noticed her obedience and rewarded her—three nights later she presented Bea with Uncle Jo's Teddy bear, which the Good Fairy had left her "as a prize for being sweet and obedient."

Uncle Jo was aghast. "Not this! It's mine. I won this in a Parke-Davis foot race. I won it! I keep it!"

"The Good Fairy brought it for Bea," said Aunt Caroline with relentless sweetness.

His mother never ceased to amaze young Jo; she seemed to him equal parts Lady Murasaki and Beatrix Potter.

Later Uncle Jo put his hand on hers and said, "I'm not sure you did not run as hard as I to win this prize."

"She did," said Jo, "she did, and she will continue to."

This was the bear that chaperoned Laura Graves and Jo on their outings. This was the only time Caroline had her way against the Doctor's will—the only time, that is, anyone knew of.

Everything was planned in Sho-Foo-Den, so unlike the rest of Merriewold. I remember one summer I had a fetish about dirt.

"Get her into rompers," said my beloved Doctor Mendelsohn, "and see that she gets into the mud." No one at Sho-Foo-Den ever got into the mud. Since everything was designed, naturally the dinner seating was high protocol. But the Doctor had other ideas.

"Little Bea sits by me at table," said Uncle Jo.

"But I had planned . . ."

So soft one hardly heard it, so soft it was under speech, and with a chuckle . . . oh, that chuckle, as unanswerable as water!

"Little Bea sits by me." And Bea did, in spite of Aunt Takamine.

He spent hours with Bea painting in the garden and gave her drawing papers, colors, and charcoals like his own. Her brown toes curling inside the sandals disapproved of by Auntie, her lovely brown curls tumbling under a canvas hat, she sat beside her white-haired uncle. They spoke little as they worked and after a bit she always stopped to watch his bold, beautiful strokes. She thought he was a fool to waste his time in the laboratory. She told him so every time they painted together.

He often took Bea with him through his garden, explaining the stone figures, the badger, for instance, to whom one prayed for weather, sincerity and faith being the most important things to bear in mind, and also, of course, generosity. One placed coins in the hollows of his toes.

"If generous enough, one always got what one wanted."

"But what if I prayed for rain," she asked, "and the sun shone?"

"Then you assume it is because more people prayed harder for sun," and taking her hand he burst into the popular song, "Can't yo heah me callin', Caroline."

One evening Uncle Jo shouted on the porch from the top of the red stairs. "Come quickly! Look now by the trees!"

There was a splash of moonlight by the tree and across the gray bark. Nothing else.

"Don't you see?" he said in a voice husky with emotion and burred suddenly with thick Japanese accent. "There by the tree."

For one second, like the shadow of a memory, Bea says, she saw her. The jeweled pins in her hair glittered and quivered.

"She's beautiful! Oh, Lady!" Bea cried. Uncle Jo put out his strong hand and grabbed her to him.

"The Lady of the Pines."

"She's gone," Bea whispered.

"Don't tell them what you saw," he whispered. "You have the gift. They'll make fun of you. We saw it together."

Caroline was saying, "Jo plays such strange games with her."

"We will build a shrine to her tomorrow," said Uncle Jo.

Auntie thought it charming nonsense. Yet Auntie believed in the saints.

Days followed days, summer followed summer in the idyllic, dreamlike tranquillity, amid the fragmentary glimpses of white dresses and parasols down green and shadowed vistas, the flash of color as a kerchief showed through the hedges, the sound of the swish of twig brooms, high voices calling, the creak of the porch swing where Aunt Takamine sat in the gentle afternoons and rose to meet us if we came by calling or with a piece of news (we didn't bring flowers or gifts of jam as we would have to other houses. How do you bring presents to a palace?); the voice of Aunt Caroline's old, blind father, Captain Ebenezer Hitch, as he sat on the great swing under the fish-shaped gong and sang whaling songs or told his grandchildren his marvelous yarns about the Civil War; the resonance of the great dinner gong, and at night the music filtering in through the tree trunks, the throbbing of frogs as the sky slowly turned off and died down in the deepening west, where was Japan.

This was Sho-Foo-Den and its magic family. And Uncle Jo was there with us, honored, fêted, courted, quite feudal and protective.

All this time we were up the road at the Other End, leading our busy, entertaining American lives. Occasionally we wondered about them, but with polite discretion, and whether they wondered about us is unlikely; they were self-sufficient.

Well, there were the Pitmans. There was always Elizabeth. But it was all changing. And sometimes there were bitter scenes.

Sometimes remarks were made openly in front of us, and the violence they revealed was frightening.

"Ann," said Father one day, "have you seen my tennis charts?"

"Yes," said Mother. "I took them to show to Graham Reed—and—I meant to tell you . . ."

"You took them from off my bureau?"

"Yes, but—"

"The tournament charts?"

"He was so interested."

"Without my permission?"

"I meant to tell you and the children suddenly called and I left them, and . . ."

"And?"

"They got thrown away."

Mother giggled. And Margaret giggled with sheer nerves. There was a line of white around Father's mouth.

Captain Ebenezer Hitch and Mary Fields Hitch, at the time of their marriage.

Caroline Hitch at eighteen.

Mama in her white French house cap.

Marie Morelle Septima Hitch George, as I knew her.

Jo, Jr.; Jokichi Takamine; Eben.

Jane, Caroline, Marie, Beatrice George.

Lady Caroline with Dr. Takamine and Jo.

Lady Caroline.

"Little Bea"—Beatrice Margaret Atkinson.

Jane; Henry George III; Bee George in the garden of Sho-Foo-Den.

Little Bea at sixteen.

"William," Mother suddenly called piteously in horrified remonstrance. "William, it's only a game."

But she was talking to a retreating back. He still loved her, however, and he came back and kissed her tears away.

But why was there violence?

And then there was the time that Mother and I met up with Dr. Takamine and a dark-kimonoed Japanese lady on a backwoods road, and Mother and the Doctor chatted, but he didn't introduce us, and she obviously wasn't a guest, and Mother came away with her lips set tight. And then she began to chatter much too brightly about silly plans.

We children were not supposed to know the naughty things that happened, but of course we did. Our mothers talked privately and we listened. We sensed that there was trouble at Sho-Foo-Den, but we didn't wish to see it. None of the Georges or Bea wished to see it. We knew there was trouble in our own lives, but we didn't wish to see that either. And the grown-ups thought we noticed nothing. How blithely the grown-ups assumed whenever they dropped their voices and took on a tone of horrified wonder that we automatically stopped noticing. In other respects they were quite intelligent. They ought to have known. Any remark made in the dead of night in a silent house is important, also audible. And any remark that is cut off short is also important. We knew this. Didn't they? What we knew we told one another in places they were not likely to overhear, such as under the boathouse floor or in the tops of trees.

It wasn't going to last. Our lovely time—it wasn't going to last. Uncle Harry seemed not at all well, and Mother and Aunt Marie were worried. The whole family was worried. He was really an invalid now, frightened and desperately seeking cures. Our perfect home, and the None-Such, the Takamines' marriage weren't going to last. It seemed that if anything happened to destroy that miraculous family, all would be damaged. Somehow the marriage had to do with the goodness of all our parents and with safety.

I've often thought that just as sounds are impressed on the air and travel forever to be picked up by whatever instrument is capable of catching and repeating; and just as light can be seen centuries after it has been extinguished; so it is not inconceivable that events leave imprints on the atmosphere and will be read back when we have the proper devices. As I've stood under the pines of Sho-Foo-Den, I've wondered what beauty, what sound, what lost elegance and pride is preserved there somewhere. There must be left some hint, because it had a kind of perfection; it was so powerful and it was so brief.

And as I've stood under the oaks at Our End and looked at their dazzling heads, I thought, "How can I keep it? It cannot at all be lost, it cannot be."

Chapter 7

❧ And then suddenly it was shattered.

That summer was 1914. I remember in August sitting one day on the Cohens' porch cutting out paper dolls while the ladies embroidered.

Katherine Cohen came bouncing in, important with news. "Jo Takamine is in the hands of the Leipzig police. Mrs. Takamine is in a real flurry and the Doctor has left for Washington. My, but they've sent a lot of telegrams!"

But her mother had discovered more important news. Mrs. Cohen had opened the New York papers. "My goodness!" she said. "England declares war on Germany. My goodness!" Mrs. Cohen was round-eyed. "Think of that! Will it really happen?"

It *had* happened. The papers reached us two days late. "Harry!" breathed Mother. "And Marie and the children!" They'd been away a year in Italy and Germany because of his health. They were presently in Wiesbaden, where Uncle Harry was unsuccessfully taking the cure.

The Georges came home precipitously, with German newspapers lining their suitcases so that we might read ourselves about the British atrocities. They were absolutely and profoundly pro-

German. So were the Moodys, who were traveling for pleasure, and de luxe. "We had to come back steerage, Anne!" said Anne Moody to Mother in real astonishment and disgust. "Steerage!" Moody's Investors Service in steerage!

The Leipzig police relinquished Jo. They were very glad to, at this juncture.

There were quite a lot of other changes impending as well.

We were to go to California. We were not to live in the East any longer. And the next summer the Pitmans would have our house and the Merriewold part of my life was to be over.

It was not just that we were going away from Merriewold. Things were changing. We could all feel it.

It was going to be a big change for Pop, who hoped to better his professional fortunes, which had got into a sorry rut. No doubt he hoped also to freshen up the marriage because, although I didn't know it, that had got into a rut also. Mother's fussing and jealousy had worn down his nerves, as well as, though he depended for stability on it, her rigidity of thought. He went down to New York on business but he sent from New York for her, and years later I found his letters.

> I was very grateful for our few days alone. It was like the lovely times we used to have and the little irritations and causes of impatience and misunderstanding simply dropped away. Beside the great love and tenderness I feel for you, they are of no importance. Oh my dear little wife, my little helpmeet, how I adore you! If we could have such times in Merriewold! If it could be as it was! It will. We will both be patient. We know we love one another.

I was aware of nothing but her terrible depression. She developed an infected spot on her face, a spot on that impeccable cheek! And she told me later she was sure she had cancer of the face.

So then, we were going West. It would be hard for her, far from friends and family, far from Georgists, music, theater, but it would be a new start.

Father spoke blithely about Hollywood, but there was a look in his eyes. He was going into exile. Mother couldn't begin to think how she would keep house with strange furniture, strange cups and saucers, strange bedspreads and closets. Mamie and Ruth were to be left behind. "Who will we get?" I wailed. Father chuckled. "There are people out there who like to eat too. I think we will find some very nice young women willing to work for wages."

But somehow it seemed to me to be heralding the end of the marriage. How? I couldn't imagine. We'd all be together, and yet . . . Naturally, I never spoke of this. I just didn't want change. Everything was fine as it was. I tied spools to my heels, but that was a game. In reality I didn't want to grow older. I would be leaving Elizabeth, but not for too long, and she might visit us, but who could tell what might happen? She'd find another friend, possibly even a relative. There were all those North Carolinean cousins. I didn't want them in my bedroom. I would grow older. Elizabeth would grow older. And surely nothing would be better.

One of the Inn servant girls sang:

> Do you remember
> California in September,
> When we stood in the wood
> 'Neath the beautiful sky?
> I made you cry
> As I whispered goodbye.

"They're going there," said Mamie and took my hand. I smirked with importance, and excitement. There would be mountains. How did one keep from falling off a mountain? How did a house stand there? Mountains were pointed. I drew them to study the problem. They were pointed all right.

And the woods. I would be leaving the woods. There were few trees in Southern California (Grandma Bebe had visited Uncle Ce in Hollywood and reported) and very little rain, none at all in the summer. The hills were burned brown as a dog's back, and no brooks and no lakes, just roses and poinsettias, which belonged properly in pots and not around all the time. No rain!

Every time there was a change in weather, I used to run on the porch to watch the trees stand out electrically against the sky. And I listened as though I would never again hear the sound of drops on a tin roof. "Oh, it does not rain enough in California—I shall forget." I used to wrap my arms around the tree trunks holding my face against the bark until I was sure I could feel the sap move against my body. I stopped often in the middle of the road to gaze at the trees' mellowing heads in sheer ecstasy of love. The sudden unaccountable winds in their high branches, the steady quietude at their feet, the light and shadow down the fire lanes, the enchantment around the corners of the forest—all these I knew would be with the others when I was gone. I would think of this across the world, afternoon by afternoon, going on in the tops of the forest. "This is my country," I sang in a kind of litany, "this is my land. I shall die for love of it if I am taken away. I am the queen of the forest."

The forest and I had always been indivisible. The forest was myself. And then it was the scene of all I had been and would be. Just when the trees had stopped being magic presences, symbols of potency, beloveds, and became the background of romantic adventures, I do not know. It happened. It was happening. I was an older woman. I was dead. I was a child with all to do ahead and the day was midmorning. Here was life and here was death and here was my parents' love and the promise of mine to be, with death down in the forest! To give my bones to the rain, to lay my body on the damp beloved floor, there to disintegrate gently, to dissolve against the moss and the rotting wood, until wintergreen and Solomon's-seal grew through my hair and my flesh mildewed and my fingers turned to threads among the ferns and the sweet-smelling creeping things; to give myself forever to the floor of the trees!

I remember one night sitting on my chamber pot, alone and saying, "I shall never forget this moment." And I didn't forget: the candle in its aureole, the feel of the china against my flesh, the overwhelming night silence, the noises of small animals. There was nothing else but my clenched will to save the moment from the night, from the ten thousand nights, pristine, durable, the child watching the candle, saved from the night, from the wash of time.

I tried to memorize the graining of the wood in our nursery, the arrangement of the dishes on the shelves downstairs, the warp of the kitchen floor. Margaret and I swept the daddy longlegs out of the playhouse and called Fred Felter to board it up. The croquet set and the tennis net Pop gave to John Pitman (as a loan), who ran off impatiently, barely saying, "Thank you." The raincoats and rubber boots were put in an old trunk with the dressups. Elizabeth helped me. "You won't need these in California, I guess," said Liz. And then the deer skull. "I shall certainly throw that out," said Liz.

"Oh, please don't. It's important to me."

"I can't think why," said Liz in her most sensible Girl Guide voice.

"It just is. I want to come back and find it."

"It won't be long," said Aunt Bettie.

The autumn of 1914 was the most glorious of all. Somehow we all knew it was the last. We looked at everything to remember for always. I walked to the station with the boys. Everyone else, including my small sister, rode in the station wagon, Frank Felter driving. We were the last summer visitors to leave Merriewold. We waited at St. Joseph's station as in a vision, unmoving for all time. Mamie was weeping openly and Mother was sad and nervous, but excited too, with lots on her mind and not all of it unhappy. Mother was the captain because Father had gone ahead and left her in charge. Mother bustled. She was terribly busy. Fat Aunt Alice George kept begging her to quiet down and take things easy. Mother just set her lips. Aunt Bettie and John and Louise and the others talked practicalities, like doctors. Liz held my hand.

It was a big change all right. It was a final change. The little locomotive came hooting and chuffing from Monticello. And we were for it. ⊱

Nous n'irons plus aux bois,
Les lauriers sont coupés . . .

—OLD SONG

We'll to the woods no more,
The laurels all are cut,
The bowers are bare of bay
That once the muses wore.
The year draws in the day
And soon will evening shut,
We'll to the woods no more,
The laurels all are cut.

Oh we'll no more, no more
To the leafy woods away,
To the high wild hills of laurel
And the bowers of bay no more.

—TRANSLATED BY A. E. HOUSMAN

Chapter 8

What do very young people write to one another? News about dogs, small household accidents, how John broke his beautiful teeth against the backstop, the new car. The real news was never touched on.

Elizabeth had grown up. She didn't mention this when she wrote to me in California. Four years had gone by and she was seventeen. I pined for her and for Merriewold. California was wonderful in the winter when it rained, but the summers were desert hot, no grass, no flowers, brown earth, brown grass, bold sky. I made pools in the garden with the hose. They lasted about eleven minutes, and I found my toes not refreshed by water, but caked with hot mud. My skin, my hair, my heart thirsted for green.

What were they doing in the woods? How was my forest faring? Were there tennis and morning swimming? Were there hayrides? There in the green it stayed three o'clock for so long!

Father was a highly successful director ($4,000 a week) and very powerful in Hollywood—not as powerful or known as Cecil, who was a world figure, but famous in his field. But he seemed driven and Mother kept begging him to go back for a rest. There were no walks now, not with him along, no trips to the mountains except as picture locations, very few stays at the beach—not for fun, that is. There were outings on C.B.'s yacht; deep-sea tuna seemed to me a strange substitute for brook trout. The atmosphere was altogether different.

"Just take a few weeks and smell the moss and ferns again. Get lost in your forest—you would come back west like a giant refreshed."

"We can't inconvenience the Pitmans. They don't expect us."

"There's Marie's."

Pop just looked at her. "When I go back I want my house and my woods to myself. Besides, I can't leave my job. You go."

But Mother dared not leave him. We were living in Hollywood now and a successful director was as solicited and wooed as a head of state. Pop was ringed with female adorers.

But if they wouldn't come "could I go back alone to Merriewold for a few weeks? Could I please, *please* go back?" The parents consulted with Aunt Bettie. But the house was full of college friends, warned Aunt Bettie. They ran a kind of summer camp, the boys covered with citronella sleeping out of doors, and the girls on every level surface. No matter, I wouldn't mind. Just give me my bed in my nursery and I'd be a great help in the kitchen. I'd do anything to help.

And then I really was going back. It was all planned. A friend was to escort me as far as the Port Jervis station.

The journey enchanted me and magically was directed eastward, not westward. Pasadena first, and the fruit orchards, and everything beautiful and glowing and full under the July sun, listless in the California heat. Then came the desert lands, smoky and shimmering in the heat daze. Then came Barstow, Flagstaff, incredibly hot. Then Indian country and the really dramatic sunsets. That was two days. And then Kansas. It just lasted, it just was, it was all of that day, the middle of the week. And then came, finally, at dusk on the fourth day, Illinois, Chicago.

Chicago of course was very exciting. And I changed trains, and then was off again on the home stretch, into the green eastern summer landscape. Fireflies, deep thick leaves, heat lightning, and everywhere green, for the first time in months and years, green. My skin felt moist again, the hair stirred at my temples. I began to breathe. I didn't sleep that night. I was up at seven o'clock having one of those spanking Pullman breakfasts that were so pleasant, with a starched and friendly waiter. Everybody was complaining about the heat and what a terrible day it would be. But it would not be a terrible day, it would be the end of my trip.

I thought all the way of the games we were going to play, the games, not dolls, not dress-ups, the games which were my second life and my emotional meaning, the games played in California, but so much better and more exciting in the woods; Indians in the dappled shade where I had stood naked and beautiful, Knights, Howard Pyle's Knights by the deep pools and mossy banks (this would not be dry sagebrush, this would be oak and birch forest, the land of the troubadors). And I would be clad in shining armor, in the motes, in the shade and "burned like one burning flame together." We would be, really be, whoever we said we were—always youths unless I was dead and a martyr. I had been killed and I had lain with my lifeblood staining my dress and the dust. My eyes were open and staring. My hair lay thin in the dirt, the wreaths of dust thin and quiet beside it. But the top of the forest was flat with wind. I knew the very spot in the road. Did it happen? I remember this more poignantly than real events, and then the place where I danced my soul away. I was afraid to look at the spot. But it was there in the woods waiting for me.

This is the stuff in which all creative perception roots. It exists concurrently with stomach-ache, tempers, gum boils, sex curiosity, with salamanders, sadism, and love. It is always there, like the leaves. While we are young we latch on to it, but it is there anyway. The feeling is very sharp in childhood. It fades with hurry and practicality. It is important.

I put my face near the sizzling hot windowpane of the car and watched the landscape slide past. Farms, little towns, little stations—ding, ding, ding, ding ding—and people getting the mail out and everyone in shirt sleeves, and hot, hot and green. In the washrooms all the women complained of the heat and adjusted their dripping corsets and wondered how they'd last the day. I lasted. And then we got closer and closer and finally we rounded a bend and came alongside the Delaware River and there was Port Jervis. There was the station, and I got off. And there was Uncle Richmond Pitman to take the bags, and he left word where the trunk was to be sent and put me into the big Packard, Greyling, which was his new addition to Merriewold, and started to drive up Route 42 to home.

It was twilight by this time and still very, very hot. I looked at the landscape and realized how extremely beautiful it was and wondered why I had never looked at it before to see how like the pictures of Medieval England it was. And we went on past stone walls and farms and gardens and houses, seventeen miles. And then finally there were the stone pylons of Merriewold, and we turned in and went up the great, deeply shadowed red earth roads, the roads that led up to the heartland of Merriewold and the Takamine pines, but there was a new charming Japanese farm garden of vegetables and jolly flowers and a wattled fence of pleated straw and a mill wheel waiting to be explored. And we honked again and again, and on the Georges' porch, which was the first one we passed, stood Aunt Marie and the cousins, waving dish towels and sheets. And Uncle Rich sped on and in the deep sunset went up the road, closer and closer to home. And when we got to the top of the last little hill he gave a prolonged honk, and we were there. Before the car stopped at our path Elizabeth was on the running board, her arms clamped around my neck.

"My goodness, what a hug!" said Uncle Rich rising from behind the steering wheel, in bumbling fun. "Say, look out, there, do you want to pull the girl to pieces?" Elizabeth was dragging me bodily over the side of the automobile.

"You precious, precious lamb," said Aunt Bettie, separating us as fast as she could reach the spot. "Give me another hug. When we brought the Doody-bear out to meet you I said to Elizabeth, 'We must have the Doody-bear when our baby comes home.'" (The Doody-bear was the size of a mastiff, was mounted on four wheels and had been ridden by me all around the garden paths, my father pulling, a long, long time ago. The Doody-bear was a present from the despised Jewish Uncle Mark.) I regarded it now dubiously; the rats had got at it.

John kissed me—he had grown even more handsome. Before he kissed me, he looked as though he didn't know whether or not he ought to, but he was my cousin so it was all right. He had of course been told to do this by his mother.

There were house guests with smirks, strangers, aliens, but there, and smiling their way into our business. There was among the Pitmans at Our End, out of kinship and love, Jane George, who had left her own clan to welcome me and who was no longer a fat child, good for biting, but a slender maiden with a shower of red hair down her back, like my mother, the George hair. "Why Jane, you've grown pretty," I said, and turned my attention immediately to the others.

I stood there in the dusk, trembling, and when I spoke my voice was thick. "I'm home and I don't know whether to laugh or cry and I don't know what to do and this is the happiest moment of my life."

Then suddenly—"Look at the spruce tree! When Pop planted it, it came just to my head. Now it's taller than the house! Oh, I can hardly bear this," and dropping my purse and gloves in the grass, I threw out my arms and ran into the forest with hard uncertain steps. Elizabeth's long legs caught up with me and we disappeared in the twilight. But Elizabeth grabbed my hand with her long, brown beautiful one and we raced through the garden to the vegetable patch and sat there eating carrots. And we sat quite quietly without saying anything and watched the twilight come trembling through the leaves. And finally the whip-poor-will called and I put my head down and wept.

But presently Elizabeth said, "There now, don't be a goose. You stay here and have another carrot and I'll go up to the house and finish the dishes." I whispered, "Oh, Elizabeth—please, my first night, stay with me." But she got up just like a grown-up and smoothed out her skirts. "I have guests. Jane will stay with you." Jane was standing off in the deep twilight. "Stay with me, Jane," I said.

We went up to the house, looking at everything on the way—every petal, every rock, every stick, the new croquet set, the new hammock, everything that had been added or made (and as a matter of fact very little had, because Uncle Rich didn't do anything new to the garden or house). Now and then we looked at something or stopped to listen to the steady pulsing of the crickets. Then we came to Dickie's rock, the rock of my invisible friend.

"I remember the day I first climbed on top of it alone. I was so proud I ran over to tell Ernie Moody. He'd always had to boost me up with his knee. Now I can look over the top."

The poplars behind the rock shivered. The sky had grayed completely through. We talked in whispers.

On the side of the path, in the shadows, stood Fred Felter. He looked dreadful and he reeked of whiskey. He smiled sideways.

"Hulloa, Agnes. I'm glad you're back. It's all different now. I've missed your father."

I murmured something and rushed on toward Mamie's kitchen. Fred smiled crookedly and breathed after me. His whiskey breath penetrated the dark. "We miss you, we miss your Pa. Pitman doesn't pay me. (This was quite untrue, I found out.) It's not the way it was. (This was true.) You need a new icebox." His whine diminished into the darkness. He was drunk. He was faded, torn and dirty. "Stingy!" He didn't belong there at this hour. He'd waited there for me. "Mean." He was destroyed and he was still young and now I was able to see and understand.

I left Jane in the dark and went in the dusk to see what the others were up to. One of the boys was there with Elizabeth and they were slapping each other with a towel.

"Can I help?"

And Elizabeth said, "No, it's quite all right, we can do it alone, thank you. Why don't you see the grown-ups?"

And so I went to see the grown-ups, who were having a talk about things that didn't interest me. Finally Aunt Bettie said, "The child is beginning to look peaked from the heat and I think it's time she had some bed."

And I thought: "My room—my beautiful room with the mosquito nettings and the shining wood ceiling and the windows that open to the night."

And to my astonishment Uncle Rich said, "I'll get the car out."

"Why?" I asked.

"Well," he said, "you're staying at the Georges'."

And Aunt Bettie said, "You did realize, because I explained, that we had house guests. (They had at least fourteen guests every weekend. Aunt Bettie liked an entertaining household; it kept her brood at home.) And we don't have a single extra bed, and you are to stay down at the Georges' and live with them."

And I said, and my mouth shook, "But my house . . ."

And Bettie said, "You can come up every day."

And with that they put me in the car with Jane and Elizabeth didn't even come.

Aunt Marie was waiting up with blueberry cobbler and thick country cream, which I could not eat, and sat there urging me. I sat, staring. Aunt Marie said, "Come along Petty, it's late and you're exhausted.

I lay listening to the bats squeaking until finally I got up and pattered down the stairs to Jane on the porch.

"Jane, are you awake?" I whispered.

"Yes."

"I can't sleep."

"Neither can I."

"I guess it's the branches outside," I said. "I'm not used to them."

"Go to bed, Petty," said Aunt Marie, instantly awake.

"Ag, dear," Jane whispered, "I'm glad you're back."

And there was the wilderness train crying its mournful wail.

I was awake with the first wagon wheels. It was a glorious day, the sun glistering on the pine needles and lying in a silver haze on the grass. A bluebottle bumped noisily against the screen. The bees were beginning to bother the syringa blossoms below. I waved a comb at Jane and put my chin on the warm sill. (I was sitting on the floor and slowly, very slowly, combing my hair.) A line of ants, I said, had formed across the path. Crows could be heard cawing in the silent sunny morning. There was a faint breathing of convent bells as the trees stirred. Aunt Marie was using the pump on the back porch. I closed my eyes in ecstasy. "Jane, Jane," I sighed, "I've come home."

I hurried through breakfast and bedmaking, and before Jane was ready I said, "I must go up to the Other End."

"Oh, I wouldn't," said Aunt Marie. "I'd wait, you can see them in swimming."

"No," I said, "they said to come every day."

In two minutes I was on the road and walking. I burst into the dining room, our dining room, and Aunt Bettie and Uncle Rich were sitting in Mother's and Father's places at breakfast but there was no one else.

"Where are they?" I demanded. "Where are they? I must see them."

"Oh, they're down at Kampski."

It now was a little cabin, not just a tent.

I said, "They're using Kampski, they're daring to use Kampski?"

And she said, "Of course, it's fun for the boys and they do use it."

I said, "Let me go."

And Aunt Bettie said, "Oh, I wouldn't, I'd wait till they come and find you."

But I was in the woods walking through the undergrowth, hunting. I got to the third pool, which I knew very well, where Fred Alexander used to keep his bacon and butter. But I could find no track of the old camp. It was hidden in the trees which had grown up. I began to yell. And suddenly a door opened right behind me and there stood John, saying, "Don't make such a row, you'll let everyone know where this is; it's a secret place."

He went indoors and I followed him. He resumed his coffee with his feet up. His girlfriend, a beautiful redhead, Rusty, was watching him drink coffee. There were two boys there also, cleaning up breakfast things. Elizabeth was playing chess in the back room with somebody else. I didn't know what to do. No one spoke to me. I went up to the loft and explored, sticking my head down the stovepipe holes. No one was interested. John yelled, "That's no place for a little girl. The floor isn't boarded over. You'll fall through the ceiling."

"All right," I answered more quietly than he had expected.

I began to reach with my legs for the ladder rungs. As I descended, my dress pulled up around my arms so that my pants showed. John turned away his head in distaste. Rusty grinned. "She's only a kid, John."

"Don't I know it?" he snapped. "Look," he put down his feet and coffee cup in exasperation, "look, I'll get Elizabeth out."

"Don't," I said in a pinched tone. "She's playing chess and she said she wouldn't be finished for quite a time. She said it was a difficult game. Too hard for me. I could find cards up at the house." I picked up John's Latin book aimlessly. I was dead white, I know, and my mouth trembled.

"You're still studying Caesar, huh?" and I giggled. "Easy, don't you think?"

John glowered, "No, I do not."

"I had that year before last. I'm doing Virgil now. It's much prettier."

John was gazing at me from under his brows in pure displeasure.

"But," I continued recklessly, "the part I love goes 'Nox erat, et placidum carpebant fessa soporum corpera per terras.' You won't have that for two years. It's lovely." John quietly took the book and knocked his pipe against his shoe. Rusty was pleating the folds of her skirt.

"Look, kiddo, we all know you're bright. I'm not so bright. Even Caesar is hard for me. Now run along and let the big slow boy get on with his studying."

I had humbled him in front of his girl. He was going to destroy me. Elizabeth was standing there. I turned and left. John called after me, "I know this is your father's and Fred Alexander's camp. I haven't hurt it, not one frying pan. And tomorrow we have to let his crazy friend, Ed Fisher, take over, and so we won't be able to come back. That'll please both of you."

I stood still on the wood path staring. John's voice followed me down the hill. "Spoiled, these movie people. I don't care if he is Mother's cousin." And farther down, because sounds in the woods carried most wonderfully, Elizabeth's beloved voice: "Two months, ye Gods!"

The walk back was a very long walk. I saw the lovely waiting vernal spots, the moted shafts between the birches (they were there all right), the dapples beneath the oaks, the deep moss by the pools. No Indians, no Knights, just growing up into bodies.

Jane was waiting for me at the big house. We hung around with nothing to do. The morning finally became time for swimming; that is, three hours later. Aunt Bettie said, "I think you'd better get your suit and meet us down there." And I had to walk back to the Georges' for the suit and then over to swimming with all of them, and it was public and I had not gone home nor really seen Elizabeth. After swimming it was, of course, lunchtime, and I prepared to follow Elizabeth home but was told, quite gently by Jane, that I was expected at the George house. At the Georges' there were, besides Aunt Marie's orphaned children, Little Bea and Cousin Alice George. I did not belong there. But that's where my place would be, at the Georges' from then on. At lunch, at dinner, at breakfast; at all meals I was to be there, that was now my place, and unless I was particularly invited as a special guest up to my own house. I couldn't go to eat.

Aunt Marie had refused to take me as a paying boarder but I was there. Uncle Harry had died in the meantime while I was away. Mother had helped Aunt Marie financially as much as she could throughout the years as Aunt Marie, an honest congressman's widow, was very poor indeed now and needed the money. Obviously Mother and the two aunts had connived. Mother had betrayed me. It suited Aunt Bettie and, I guess, Mother's sense of family loyalty. Mother ordained I should take as much delight in the Georges as the Pitmans, and love Jane as much as Elizabeth. The fact is, I didn't.

After lunch I set off up the hot roads, up the hill, to the Other End and my house. And there I found that the young people had gone off somewhere on one of their own forays, and that they would return to play tennis.

"Oh," I said, "I shall play tennis."

"Well, no," said Aunt Bettie, "they have their tennis matches all fixed and made out, and you're very much younger and very much littler and they will have to have special games for you."

"But it's my court!" I said.

Aunt Bettie looked extremely shocked. She pursed her lips and wiped the sweat from under her eyes. "Don't talk that way, dearie, it's not becoming; your father has given us the house while he's away. And it's our house and the young people have their own plans and their own friends, and they are delighted to see you but they cannot break up their plans."

And I said, "When am I to play on my court with Elizabeth?"

"Oh," said Aunt Bettie, "maybe even tomorrow morning." So that night after supper I went up the hill and found they'd all gone off in the Greyling Packard to Monticello.

"You just go off to Monticello like that?" I said.

"Yes, we can in the car—it takes only twenty-five minutes."

"They won't be back for a long time," said Aunt Bettie.

So I went home and had the evening with Jane and the others. Bee George told us stories. Bee is the best storyteller I ever knew. But it wasn't Elizabeth.

We sat on the great darkening front porch. The bats swooped and the chipmunks made little scurrying noises overhead; and I listened for the car. At half past ten, when we were dropping asleep in our cots on the porch (we slept on the big front porch open to the pines and the bats and in the early morning we saw the red deer in the Moors' cornfield opposite) I heard the car come back and I jumped up and watched them as they went past; they didn't stop and didn't wave; they went past up to my house—to hot chocolate, to music, to fun, to their devices, to their life without me. And that's how it was.

Of course, we all went swimming. We tramped home from the dam not altogether refreshed, with wet hair to Aunt Marie's lunch (meat, five fresh vegetables, and a pudding or pie). We did the dishes. We played around in the afternoon. I practiced dancing (oh, how I missed my regular classes!). We wasted time. We had dinner, just as many vegetables and Aunt Marie just as relentless, and in the evening there was Bee's storytelling. But what were they doing at the other house? Occasionally their car went by.

Not that the George household wasn't interesting. It was very interesting. And although I wasn't concerned emotionally, I saw all and I remembered all.

Aunt Marie no longer played the piano so strenuously because she had taken up singing. Several years into her widowhood some greedy lady had told her that she had a voice. Mrs. Fels, the widow of the great Georgist, Joseph Fels (Fels Naptha Soap), paid for all her lessons and the misguided and overly ambitious teacher gave her a lesson every day, sometimes two, and she cracked the voice. It was pathetic and needless and saddened all of us. But Aunt Marie did not yield easily. She vocalized aciduously while the pies cooled. She always chose terrible and disaster-laden songs, like "Hagar's Lament," her heavy black brows knotted with anguish and her hands clenched over her apron but, as instructed, with her mouth in an O so that the refrain came out "Dith let me in." We all begged her in vain to open her mouth. Her children did, and Caroline did, and my mother had done so, but she would not because she had been told not to. Aunt Bettie, who really knew about these things, worked with her for hours on diction, tone production, phrasing. No use. Mother at last sent her to Graham Reed, one of her own New York teachers, and there she met disapproval and rejection, also a dismal prognosis: "Ruinous habits, too old for correction." It was like Uncle Harry dying all over again.

Aunt Marie seemed overworked and driven, which I think she was to the point where she had substituted strenuousness and intent for the charm and allure practiced by all the other Hitch sisters, who were beguiling women. Allure takes time, however, and Aunt Marie had none, for her life had proven much harder than the others'. ("I think all the aunts," writes Jane, "were more style conscious than Mother, who had spent four and a half years doing everything for Papa while he was ill, shaving him, brushing his teeth, massaging him, dressing him, and all the duties of a male nurse, and she had no energy left after that ordeal to do more than try to make ends meet, and educate the three of us. She put Bee through Ambler, a horticultural school, for two years and then four years at Cornell. She later gave me four years of college and Henry seven, and she took us all to Europe for a year, and then gave me the year with the Floating University, so after

Papa became ill, she never thought of clothes or a man or herself really. She was always interested in ideas and people but not in herself or her appearance, but before that Mother had had some beautiful clothes which she finally gave me. You wouldn't remember her then, but I have some pictures of her in a lovely hand-painted chiffon that was made for her by Mrs. Thatcher, one of the fine couturières in New York. She wore it to a White House reception.")

Aunt Marie held her courage by concentrating on her son, Henry, who was heir to the great heritage. Henry was expected to be a fine citizen, a statesman, a writer, above all A THINKER. "Incorruptible" conduct was taken for granted. However, Henry George III never got his chores done. He had stomach-aches except when it was time for swimming, with the result that his older sister, Bee, did his chores for him, or his mother. It wasn't that he avoided them for fun. He avoided them for misery, and so you couldn't get angry at him—most of us couldn't. Jane could.

"Bee, did you take those milk cans back to the McCormacks?"

"It's dark."

"All the more reason. If Henry had to go without milk he'd change. He gets away with murder."

"He tries."

"You mean *you* try. A girl lugging those heavy cans down a rough road in the black of night! My goodness!"

But it was his performance after meals—every meal—that was arresting.

After lunch or dinner Henry always had a stomach-ache. He would lie on the black leather couch under the kakemono and moan, rolling about with his knees doubled up. Aunt Marie kept a copy of *Science and Health with Key to the Scriptures* on a shelf over the wood stove, and on top of that a bottle of castor oil.

Holding one in each hand, she would stand over him and say, "Choose!" Henry would stop groaning and rolling to consider.

"I'll try the Truth," he said meekly.

So Aunt Marie would sit in the bentwood rocker and open Mrs. Eddy's book on her knee. It always took Henry some time to grasp the meaning of the text and by the time he did, the dishes were all done and put away on the shelves and the pots scrubbed by his sisters and cousins.

The young were just plain mad at both of them, the older ones appalled, particularly Caroline Takamine, who, knowing a great deal about spoiled boys, felt she had a right, nay a duty, to exhort Marie to alter her conduct. Many a sunny morning Caroline made a trip through the pines to her sister's to advise her against spoiling her brood. She used to lie on the black leather couch under the six-foot kakemono (a waterfall and cranes in mist) while Marie creaked beside her and mopped her brow. Caroline came over in white shoes, freshly pressed white hand-embroidered voile, jade earrings, flicked a delicate fan against the heat and the mosquitoes, and in a voice like a fluting bird, told Aunt Marie what was what, and by implication what Henry was, although she never expected much from males. Caroline explained how Jane and Henry were being turned into brats, and they were too, at least he was, and how now that their father was dead, they needed a firm hand.

Marie demurred in her son's behalf; Henry was trying to be pure—so hard for a boy—and Henry was an Eagle Scout and had planted three hundred and fifty baby trees, and he was a lifeguard junior grade.

"I don't think that's what we were talking about," said Caroline.

"It's hard being a boy."

"Maybe," said Caroline, fanning herself. "But I will not con-

done or pardon filial selfishness. Now Jane—" and she was off
with considerable harshness.

George Braga used to come around mooning after his love,
Little Bea, who stayed for long vacations with Aunt Marie while
her mother, Beth the Belle, was divorcing Will Atkinson. Bea
had also sought asylum in her Aunt Maud Atkinson Braga's
home and Maud, although the sister of the wronged party, had
most generously taken her in. Bea and George became very close,
but George was the one who loved. He was gentle and subtle and
wise beyond his years and doggedly faithful. There was, however,
something restrained, checked, even frightened in his manner.

His father, the Spaniard Bernardo Braga, and his uncle,
Manuel Rionda, had possession of a half million acres of Cuban
cane fields encompassing three entire villages, mills, churches, sta-
bles, shops, trainyards, warehouses, and casas, which they administered strictly. ("In the cane fields," said Bernardo Braga, "we
shoot anyone who smokes. We shoot to kill." And Uncle Manuel
Rionda said often, "Don't look at the passing cars in the streets,
don't look at anything. It's your duty to think only of the sugar
business." And another time he said to a nephew who was five
minutes late for dinner, "You can never be too late in my
house. Stay away.")

George, his brother, and a few cousins stood in line to be heirs
to an estate that was just a little smaller than Rhode Island, and
the boys were going to be masters of two miles of Hudson River
frontage (the Palisades), and five hundred acres of Alpine property and various New Jersey houses. George was a good catch,
but he was subdued in spite of his wit and good nature. His lovely
mother, Maud, was dying of cancer and his father was distraught.
Even as a young man, George's happiness, his playfulness, was
filmed over with sadness, but he was obviously in love, and Aunt

Marie, being sympathetic and unstintingly hospitable, invited him for lunch at least three times a week and sometimes for dinner. George helped with the dishes and said that the food was good and ample but that the milk was often on the point of turning. There were, of course, several reasons for this:

1. Milk couldn't turn in a Christian Science household.
2. No Georgist would drink fresh milk if there was slightly old milk to be got through.
3. It was very difficult without a man's help to handle the ice blocks in order to keep milk cold.

And then there was fat Aunt Alice. She seemed to be having sex problems. No unmarried aunts were permitted sex problems, nor widowed mothers, like Aunt Marie. It was terribly shocking to see evidence of grown-ups' grief. If one could reach the state of being a grown-up, one ought to be safe. They knew how so they did not suffer. In any case their trouble was all right as long as we never saw them cry. Of course mothers cried when their husbands died and when their brothers died, that is, Uncle Harry. Aunt Marie wept very, very quietly at night.

We first became aware of bad trouble with Allie when we woke at five-thirty one morning to hear her sobbing. She was in the kitchen with Aunt Marie and their voices were muffled, but that Allie was crying hard was certain. Every one of us woke instantly. There were five of us on the porch, alert and terrified. We lay without moving, trying not to breathe, so that we could hear better.

Allie was Mother's cousin and we thought of her as middle-aged—I dare say she was at the time thirty-seven or -eight—but she seemed older, perhaps because she was so fat. She seemed always happy and funny. Allie was always funny, one of the funniest people we had ever known, and loving and full of curiosity and zest. If agony could lodge in all that mountainous con-tented flesh, where was there hope for any of us?

"Have some coffee, Petty," said Aunt Marie's voice, "and keep your voice down. The children will wake."

"Oh, God," said Allie, "why must it always be I who has to pretend to have no feelings? You can weep in public."

"Sh, darling, sh," said Aunt Marie.

"I asked him outright last night. I put it to him straight. 'When,' I said. And he replied—he replied—"

"Sh," said Aunt Marie. "There, now."

"—that he was not the marrying kind, and didn't I know that? Hadn't he made it quite clear?"

"That's strange, very strange. Here, hold your cup," said Aunt Marie. "He's been seeing you every day for months."

"Twice a day," said Allie emphatically. "And special deliveries on Sunday when he couldn't leave his mother, and flowers on all occasions, and birthdays, and the notes were love notes. How he needed me, how he relied on me—relied, mind you. This time I believed it would happen. This time I trusted."

"I don't understand," said Aunt Marie. "What happened? Is there another woman?"

"Nothing happened. Nothing ever happened. He said he was not the marrying kind. He said he would like things to go on and never change—to go on—as things—as we—as we—" she sobbed. "The same. He wanted it the same. He won't declare himself."

"That you can't permit," said Aunt Marie.

"No," said Allie.

"Do you hear?" breathed Jane, without stirring in bed.

"Sh!" said Little Bea.

We did not discuss one word of what we had heard, but for

once assembled at the breakfast table clean and neat and on time. Allie was not there. She had a headache, Aunt Marie said.

Allie came down to lunch, white and drawn. But she joked as always and teased Henry about his table manners.

"Today you are going to eat facing the table? We have much to be grateful for." We did not speak much lest we miss something. Allie hardly ate anything, but she kept joking. She talked a lot, jokes of course. Aunt Marie kept talking about more helpings and keeping our elbows out of our plates and things like that. Once when she came back from carrying a heavy platter, she patted Allie on the shoulder, without looking at her. That was unusual.

Henry began his regular post-lunch performance. This time Allie said she'd deal with him. She'd like to.

"Now, Henry," she said as she sat down quietly and opened *Science and Health,* "stop that groaning."

He didn't.

"Stop that this minute. Pay attention. I've been reading this all morning and I think I know what it means. You try now. Hard."

Henry regarded her amazed. "You're crying," he said.

"I am not," said Allie. "There are no such things as tears in God's world. Don't you know that?"

"Yes," said Henry doubtfully.

For the first time Henry Saw the Light in time to help us put the big plates on the high shelves.

After dishes and waiting until it was safe to swim, and after the swim, we decided to watch the tennis tournament. Allie was there with Donald, and Donald was beside her, her la-dee-dah beau.

"Is that wise?" said Aunt Marie as Allie was getting out her hat. "I don't think you should do that, Petty. Don't see him today."

"Nothing more can happen to me," said Allie. "I don't want talk. People will think it queer if we're not together. I couldn't bear them to know."

"It's inhuman," said Aunt Marie. "Stay home and rest. I'll read to you."

"I can bear it," said Allie. So there they were, side by side, and no one knew except all of us. We watched very carefully for a quiver or a break. She turned her lovely gray eyes on him under the white gold lashes and smiled gently. She joked as always, but not loudly, and she only once playfully poked Donald, who was not laughing at all. He looked very uncomfortable and waiting and hot. He was overdressed as always in his stiff collar and laced boots. We thought him terribly sissy, but he had always laughed so heartily at her jokes and kept his arm around her and stroked her fine soft white gold hair. "Lovely hair," he'd say.

"You shouldn't let him take these liberties," said Aunt Marie.

"Oh, pshaw," said Allie. "He doesn't take my hair down—if that's what you're talking about. You have an evil mind."

"You shouldn't," said Aunt Marie. "It's not wise."

This time Allie didn't snuggle against him or pop gumdrops in his mouth or hold his hand or stroke his fingers. She just poked him once as they sat watching Throckmorton twist in midair like a cat. She made a joke but she didn't look at him. He said he needed a glass of water and went away for a good while.

At the end of the week he left the Inn and went back to the city. We never saw him again.

Every so often in sheer bravado one of us would ask Allie, "How's Donald?"

"Oh, he's fine," she'd say. But I don't think she ever knew, because I don't think she ever heard.

I came upon Aunt Alice once on the walk between the Pitmans and Georges, sitting by the roadside apparently doing nothing, and there were tear marks on her face. The first time she just waved, but the second time she lumbered to her feet and walked beside me, making forced remarks that interested neither of us. Suddenly she said, "I miss your mother. And your father. Harry was no use. He was too ill. There seem to be no men anymore." We walked.

"It's not the way it was," I murmured and my eyes filled.

Her voice cut through the softness. "Agnes, have they let you play on your court, I mean, with them?"

I shook my head.

"Preposterous! Never mind. You have better courts in California." She went back to her brooding. I resumed mine.

Gradually, but not soon enough, I stopped feeling as though it were my right to be at my own house, and I began to realize that I had no more right than Jane, or Henry. I was part of the Other End. I also stopped hanging around at mealtimes, because they didn't intend to ask me to sit down. As they waved me off, they always hugged me and said how glad they were I was back and what time did I expect to go swimming the next day and would I like to play tennis sometime with Elizabeth. They never once invited me to sleep a night in my room. But there were three women bedded in the nursery, so how could they? And when at last Elizabeth had an hour for tennis, I was nervous and wrought up and played abominably and lost my temper and boasted I could do better with another kind of racket on a better court. John was openly disgusted with my lack of sportsmanship, Elizabeth bored, the guests pitying. Aunt Bettie took me into the kitchen. "You know, dear, you are being a spoilsport. Elizabeth is older, she is stronger, and she is better and you must expect to be beaten by her, and it hasn't to do with your court and your tennis, and your boasting of what you can do when you have your own court. It's unbecoming and your father would be ashamed of you. He'd be very ashamed because he's a fine sportsman and you're just a spoiled little girl. The people around here just feel sorry for you; they say what a pity. Why do you say such unpleasant things?"

I stared. "Miss Dryer *has* whiskers."

"It is true. It's her misfortune. She has a fine mind."

(I didn't think so.)

I had made a very bad mistake in coming East.

"I think maybe you'd better not come this afternoon," Aunt Bettie said.

The forest and I were apart. The Pitmans had their life and went on. Elizabeth was growing up, she didn't need me. The world crowded and I couldn't bear it, the world got on with its business. And I was obnoxious.

Jane talked to me about this on one of our futile walks back.

"You know," she said, "I knew it would be like this. This is the way it is. This is the way it was for me last summer."

And I said, "Did she abandon you too? Did she abandon everybody?"

"No," she said, "just the very young girls, the children, and we're still children. But they're not children and she has her beaux and she doesn't need us."

And I said, "But I came East to see her!"

And Jane's big gray eyes filled and she said, "I thought you came to see us too. We can find everything you want, we can play all the games you love."

And I said, "It isn't the same. It just isn't the same."

Aunt Bettie spread her Southern charm and strove to keep me from the strong and enchanted, and I promised to be thoughtful and considerate, and I promised to realize it was their house, not mine, and the boys' tennis court, not Father's, and Elizabeth's and Aunt Bettie's piano, although I might play my pieces when Elizabeth and Rusty were through, and Aunt Bettie's china, although every piece I remembered and had even unpacked one barrel load from Macy's with Mother. It was all Mother's. I heard her voice. I saw her hands. It was mine. I must pretend it wasn't.

"Why does Elizabeth's young man have so many pimples?" I asked.

I walked in the woods alone.

There remained ballet dancing. I practiced my own forty minutes religiously (all my parents would permit). While I practiced Aunt Marie made the perfect better tones, which I must say were quite excruciating and piercing, with a round mouth. "Dith, oh dith," she screamed.

"Open your mouth, Aunt Marie," I begged, "spread your lips."

"Oh no," she said. "It makes the sound more penetrating."

And indeed it did. And a great deal more unpleasant.

We both persisted. One day I did by myself, in front of the kakemono, four pirouettes on point. I wrote home in triumph. (It is an important fact that I never did this again in my life.) I also organized a daily class for the house mates. We worked on the porch holding onto the railings. I asked Elizabeth if she wouldn't like to see me dance. She was very sweet, but she was occupied and she wouldn't.

Then came Margaret's first letter.

"We're having fun. I hope you're having fun. I take two dance lessons a week. That's not fun! I did two pirouettes yesterday. Mr. Kosloff said they were wasted on me. That's all the dancing news.

"We ran on our new projector Richard Barthelmess in 'Tol'able David,' Tom Meighan in 'Our Leading Citizen,' 'Nice People,' Pop's new picture (excellent), Gloria Swanson in 'Her Gilded Cage' (rotten), 'Nice People' (Pop—excellent), 'The Spider and the Rose' (the worst picture I ever saw), George Melford's 'The Bonded Woman' (Pop said very bad), 'Nice People' (very good). Somerset Maugham came to dinner. I think he's rather stuck up. I have a store-bought dress. Pop gave me the money. Mom was mad. She cried. I brought her some chocolate dolphins. I've saved some for you. Please come back. Charlie Chaplin promised to come to dinner. He didn't. Mother got mad. She'd made Grandma de Mille's southern strawberry float on purpose. Very sincerely, (crossed out). Love."

Father wrote Ed Fisher, the tennis star with the religious fervor. Pop didn't care about pirouettes but Pop cared heavily about forehand drives. I was losing time on all fronts but he was troubled only by the one. In Hollywood I had been drilled by Florence, Ethel, and Violet Sutton (May Sutton, three-time world champion, never turned pro) and by Fred Alexander and was developing some rather surprising back court strokes. Father said the summer must not be wasted. Father said Ed Fisher was to coach me and Father said it must be done on our court. The Pitmans said okay, but only in the early mornings before the boys needed the court. So Ed Fisher came for me every morning at seven-thirty, walking back from Thompson's store at the gate, with his dog Huckleberry, and a large sack of provisions, and we proceeded up the road to our court.

The man was plainly crazy, possibly homicidal. There had been one or two episodes of sudden and irrational losses of temper on the Inn porch, having to do with the possible disparagement of Christ, which had left the neighbors shaken and extremely wary. He made his disputants face the sun open-eyed for purity, with resultant damage to retina; he criticized darling J. I. C. Clarke for obesity and suggested an immediate reduction of the stomach, reinforcing his comments with an unsheathed butcher knife. This caused quite a stir among the morning rockers.

On our walks we were absolutely alone and Ed (being in the ascendant phase of his cycle) talked about God. One day he stopped and murmured, "The only sin Jesus Christ ever committed was on the cross when he dared to question, 'My God, my God, why hast thou forsaken me?' This was wrong of Him. Of course He had to, because He had to show that He was human and suffering, but it was a sin. Yet it was God's will that He do it."

I made a mistake. "If it was God's will, why was it a sin?"

Ed dropped the groceries in the dirt. Huckleberry, sharply conditioned, darted instantly into the bushes. Ed was six foot three and massive. He raised his great arms, capable of such killing strokes. He clenched his fists and he shook them. He threw his head back and roared. "Don't," he was yelling to heaven, "don't you ever question the divinity and righteousness of Christ. You are a wicked girl!" He all but brought his fists down on my face. I was too astonished to move. Besides, he was illogical.

The fist did not come down. It opened. It patted my head. It shoved me forward. "You don't know any better," said Ed. "You didn't mean to do wrong. We've got to work on your backhand."

I told Aunt Bettie in a whisper.

"Yes," she said, "he attacked J.I.C. on the sun porch the other day. I'll write your Father that I've halted the tennis training."

"And the walks," I added.

"Yes, the walks."

Ed retired to Kampski. We could hear him bellowing down there from time to time.

Aunt Bettie had been nervous about the long solitary walks when he came to fetch me, about the sudden operatic denunciations, about his frenzies over the position of my thumb, or the shifting of weight on my feet. Aunt Marie was frantic. He rallied with me of course, but then he spent long sequences talking on my side of the net with my grip in his. It was a very special kind of tennis coaching. But it was on my court with Elizabeth going and coming close by and sometimes she had to play with me before Fred Felter had painted the lines: Father had written.

But Elizabeth had hurt me, so the next time I saw her alone I said, "Why do you wear store-bought clothes? Mother says they're vulgar."

Elizabeth looked at me with icy eyes and went away. Oh, my love! I went off and put my face on a rock.

So Elizabeth didn't play with me and she didn't ask me back. I was never invited again to play a game on my court, with Elizabeth or anyone else.

Aunt Bettie listened to my whining attentively and always got me lemonade or sarsaparilla, quietly keeping me cornered and occupied through the long sweet afternoons.

"She's a completely spoiled and egocentric girl," said Aunt Bettie to Uncle Rich, often within the hearing of the others, and always within my hearing. It was true. I was spoiled rotten. I was impossible. I was a pain in the ass. And at the same time I was the mysterious child, powerful and beautiful. I was the possible lover. When I stood in the woods alone, as I did with increasing frequency, I was capable of passion. I was the age of the great heroines. I knew all sensitivity, all power, all awareness, all terrible blinding curiosity. I was mysterious and shaking. There were moments, always alone, when anything could have happened, anything.

One morning in the swamp, near Old Sixteen where I had been expressly forbidden to go, I found myself again alone.

In stillness, on twisted threadlike stems, chewed naked by the deer, the rhododendrons banked their glossy, massive foliage. The lucent open throats glistened as though with breath, while from their freckled depths thrust out into the air the long tasting stamens. I followed a deer trail. Underfoot the moss was comfortable as sponge, but the horny huckleberry bushes whipped and stung my legs, lacing them in a pleasant fretting. I wandered on among undiscovered hedges, along inhuman spidery paths until my foot trod soft on a furry skeleton. The little white bones lay chipped and broken miserably about, tufts of hair on the brambles, the long skull white in broad daylight. And the blue of the sky grew suddenly more intense and I was aware of the blossoms and the humming stillness and my isolation in the wilderness and the blood trickling on my dear legs. And I pressed my forearm hard against my new chest and opened my mouth to the air and listened. There was no sound but day in the forest. I thought suddenly of Mother, of myself as Mother, her slim beloved body in gracious dresses, waiting in the afternoons, serene and lovely, knowing Father would be there surely for supper, quietly waiting with the foreknowledge of sure happiness. I thought of Mother, myself as Mother, facing Father through the supper candles and the look I had seen on their faces of recognition as of an unexpected meeting between friends, quite apropos of nothing, while Mother fixed the salad dressing in a wooden spoon and Father talked of dialogue and tennis strokes. Their faces grew suddenly unfamiliar. Their dear home faces became like the faces of strangers, young and remote. And I had to turn my eyes away, and I trembled.

I thought of Mother tying up my hair with a ribbon, handing me the prettiest peony, doing small services because she was richer, and more powerful, and had the evening before her, pretending to placate her little girl out of pitying, tender love and as a token of recognition for the girl's own future.

I picked up a skull and tucked it under my arm. It smelled a little high, but that was rather a good thing in this hot land of bloom and bush. I scrubbed it clean by the pool and put it on the top nursery shelf where it disturbed the house guests. Remarkably, I had brought death into the house and tamed it like a pussy-cat.

That night I dreamed again that all the trees had been cut down.

Jane and I tried together to grow up. We used to spend time in front of our mirrors putting our hair up, something we were not going to be permitted to do officially for a good three years. We once surreptitiously tried on Bee's evening dresses, but this was no use because we wore kid's underclothing. I still wore little girls' pantywaists with buttons down the back. John had felt them when he lifted me out of the car on arrival and had been astonished. He felt them whenever, under his Mother's admonishing, he danced with me at the Saturday night parties and his gorge rose. A boy is not used to feeling that sort of thing under a girl's dress.

Jane surveyed our torsos with fourteen-year-old resignation before one Saturday dance. "We look fat, don't we," she said. "I have freckles and you have sunburn and we both have busts. My nipples show and you look swollen and we can't keep them from showing. What'll we do?"

I turned away.

"Don't worry," said Jane. "I expect we'll be able to bear them someday. The older ones do."

But as the summer waxed, I tightened with expectation, rage, and unexpressed passion. Jane saw and was frightened. I practiced dancing frenetically. It was never any good.

What did we talk about in the grass, on the pine needles? We couldn't talk about dress. We didn't have any. We couldn't talk about dates; one sentence disposed of George Braga, who was soppy with love for Little Bea, or Ernie Moody, who was the same. We couldn't talk about schoolwork; that was over until fall. We couldn't talk about careers; that was secret. We talked about husbands and the unmentionable: we talked about menstruation. We were children but we were already trapped. It was dirty, it was annoying, it was shaming. Sometimes it was very painful and it had to be absolutely secret from all boys, of course, but especially from fathers. They were not to know. "Falling Off the Roof" or "The Curse" we called it. It embarrassed and disturbed me. The others talked. Little Bea had a particularly rich physiological life. She was ripe. I imagine we talked more than girls do nowadays because it was troublesome, involving lots of laundry like babies and there were no commercial products to help. It rendered us inferior to men. And it had to be secret, secret. About sex between the sexes we knew absolutely nothing. We guessed and we talked and we felt shamefully inferior. And we wondered about every woman we saw. Was she or wasn't she? And we were ashamed for her.

Where was the wildness gone, the untrammeled freedom? The dear wild possibilities of our youth lost and never to be recovered! We were now tainted by dreadful grown-up involvements. Blood had touched us; we saw it on our clothes.

We were still mostly gawky girls. We were social idiots, but we were in the midst of bodily revolution. I liked things the way they were; I'd show them; I would not be trapped.

Fat Aunt Alice, our spinster cousin, joined in our talks. Aunt Marie never did. She was too busy and she was above all this. Bee George never did either. She was off reading *The Science of Political Economy,* by Henry George. She read one of his books every summer.

"Why do men have mistresses?" Allie would ask rhetorically. "Well, what is a mistress like? A mistress is always clean—absolutely dainty and clean."

"Aren't our mothers clean?" we asked.

"Your mothers are sometimes mussed," she said. "A mistress is never mussed and she is always glad and attentive. For instance, your mother [this was to me] sometimes sews as she listens to your father. It drives men crazy to have women always doing something—like bits of sewing, little bits of knitting. The men want all their wives' attention. Every bit of it. And," said Allie, opening her gray eyes very wide, "they want it all the time."

"But she's doing it for him, she's doing it for us. She's sewing on his buttons."

"It drives your father crazy just the same."

"If I fell in love with a married man and he couldn't get a divorce," I said, "I'd have an affair with him."

"It would be better to die," said Allie and turned sadly away. "Sex isn't so much. Except lying in one another's arms. I've heard there was peace in that."

Little Bea was still very young, and the center of male adoration, but she thought only of Jo, and while she enjoyed having the other boys pay attention, she didn't treat them seriously in any way at all.

We were all ready for something.

That fateful summer Merriewold was swarming with young musicians, most of them Aunt Takamine's protégés. This was before there were musical camps established by summer operas or by big foundations to help young performing artists. The MacDowell colony and Yaddo were the only noteworthy experiments. Caroline Takamine attempted another alone in our wood.

Caroline discovered no geniuses, although she would dearly

have loved to. But the aptness for discovery requires force and discrimination and Caroline was never aggressive. Jokichi Takamine took no part in her experiments, merely indulging her, although the cost of the hobby did "make him nervous," as the chauffeur said.

The prevailing ideas in our woods used to be politics and economics; now it was music. Besides our upright pianos, the woods now had violins, cellos, and voices and in this larger, adventurous sound there was diversion. I could stop thinking of my misery for some minutes. They practiced very good music, not very well, all over the place and we heard bits of violin and bits of piano and bits of vocalizing wherever we walked.

The concert itself was to take place in early August. Toward the end of July, Aunt Caroline Takamine thought she would like to have an audition to see how her hopefuls were progressing.

We were on the shadowy porch, the performers inside the great gold room, with just enough light for the piano. The very little girl, Zepoleto, with the abundant hair, played the first movement of the Max Bruch violin concerto, and then as climax Martha Attwood, of the Metropolitan Opera and La Scala, and Sergei Radamsky, of no opera but of high hopes for an Aeolian Hall concert to be sponsored by Aunt Caroline, sang and when they finished he called her "Lady Caroline," kissed her hand, and sat at her feet. The artists were all hers. She had paid for them. She felt, I guess, like Ludwig II of Bavaria.

Would I dance?

Aunt Takamine leaned toward me out of the great suspended swinging couch where she sat and fanned with the pretty paper fan with the ideographs. Aunt Bettie was going to play my Brahms accompaniment at the concert, but she wasn't there and this night I could use the gramophone, hand-wound. I chose "Le

Nil," sung by Alma Gluck, violin obligato by her husband, Efrem Zimbalist. And this was good performing.

Suddenly I could.

There were the great sentinel pines and their black branches unmoving. And there was the classic night.

And I could. I went through. It was o.k. for me to dance on that wonderful porch in that garden. I was going to know greatness. I could carry the night. I made my mark on the garden right then. Some part of my life was left there. There had been more formal occasions and greater people, but this was mine. I was going to be an artist.

Aunt Takamine knew it and I knew it.

"Very good," she said. "Unusually good. In fact, I'm surprised." We looked at one another dumfounded. This is the first time, I think, she really saw me.

But Radamsky was kissing her hand again and the rest were jabbering. It didn't matter. I knew.

I felt guilty for having known this joy without Elizabeth. I never needed her when I was dancing. But I did feel guilty.

Next day I returned to the life of front porches and underwear.

All summer the tension had grown and then finally the night was come. It was the night of a Saturday dance, which was just as always. The older ones crept around the floor hugging one another. The younger boys sat in all the available chairs with their feet straight out in the way. The younger girls stood in clots waiting for something to happen. Nothing ever happened. They were taken home.

As a matter of fact Elizabeth was always very thoughtful (she was a wonderful popular dancer and swooped deliciously in the "Camel Glide"). She stopped between partners to speak to me and to share a pop bottle. And John always danced with me once. There was a full moon and it was hot. I crept outside alone and let the party take all of the old wooden building.

Outside it was different, in the woods, in the big night, the shadows of laurel leaves moved. The woods lay waiting, the soft and shadow of lunar transparencies dappling the world. I held my breath and listened.

The nerves thrilled up the insides of my legs. My stomach fainted as though I were dropping from heights. Reaching blindly for the porch rail I knew again the old weakness, the summer unknowable, the footfall in the grass. Above me the sky swam with light. When I looked up I grew dizzy and it seemed that I must plunge downward through night, light, and space as vast as seas. The moment of death, I thought, would be like this, or something very like death, a sweet numbness wherein I sank through ecstasy to the fullness and quiet of all-pervasive rest, absorbed as in a tide, with the sensitivity of all things about my head beating and whirring like birds. Four times I had dreamed of sinking into this intoxicated oblivion and wakened just in time. I had lain shaking with happiness and listening to the reassurance of Mag's breathing in the next bed. Was it possible that some skins and brains were susceptible to night as others to plain day and, moon-burned, could not bear the provocation of the monthly climax?

The silly music inside the clubhouse continued. I turned my eyes downward to where the earth smells rose damp and fumey. On the hill a branch snapped.

I longed suddenly, overwhelmingly to go to the deer's running ground, to see those floral groves enduring the night in their princely beauty. I had only once dared to go there since coming back, for down there waited my young mother, young and in love with a beloved husband. But if now I went back, I felt I would find my own life, not my mother's. And if I had a companion I could seal the moment. I was no longer a child. I needed to communicate. I wanted Elizabeth to go with me into the woods.

I found my cousin sitting on the rail by the back porch, sucking pop from a bottle and swinging her long legs rhythmically. Her young man, Jim, was talking low. Now and then they chuckled. The vulgarity of saxophone and piano persisted, and the beat of the drum which seemed to drop into the pit of the stomach. I stood for some time before they noticed me.

"Want some pop?" asked Jim with real generosity. He wished I'd go away and drop dead. They had hidden at the very back of the porch where the shadows were deepest.

"Elizabeth, I must speak to you," I said huskily.

"Excuse me," said Elizabeth, handing her pop with its bent straw to her escort. She drew me back outside the shaded scullery window.

"What's the matter? Need a pin? Button's popped? What is it?"

"Elizabeth, can you come away for a little bit?"

"Are you sick? Land sakes, I'll get Jim to walk you home."

"No, I'm all right. I just want to go down into the woods for a bit."

"Not alone you don't. Not at night. No, sirree."

"I want you to come with me."

"Are you cuckoo? I wouldn't dream of going into the woods now."

"But they're so beautiful!"

"I'll go tomorrow. They'll be beautiful tomorrow or the next day. You can go alone tomorrow in the light if you want to."

"I want to see them in the moonlight. It's full moon. In California there are no trees like this. I can't imagine what it's like with the flowers all out. We'd never forget it. Oh please. We've hardly had a moment alone together this summer."

In my agony I grabbed the organdy frill in Elizabeth's dress. Her presence thickened and blocked.

"I've waited years to see you. Please come with me."

"You know what?" Elizabeth's dear voice grew flat and too loud. Jim would hear. "You just want someone to pay attention to you."

"It's awful here. It's quiet in the woods."

"For the love of Pete, no! I'm having a good time. I'm not going to leave my guest and go rambling off with you. What would he think? If you're bored, go play Ping-Pong with the kids. You've been hanging around my neck all summer and I don't like it. Now let go of my dress, do you understand? I don't like it."

I flattened against the house wall and heard all the sounds of the porch suddenly, the thump-thump of the music, the creak of the rockers, footsteps racing on wood, some boy yelling, "Look out, here I come," the answering, "Oh you big piece of cheese!" a girl saying, "There now, you've spilled a whole bottle." Dishes were being stacked noisily behind the drawn shade. Well, all summer I had known. From the moment I had gotten off the train I had known clearly Elizabeth was through. She'd grown up.

I went down to the lake. I went down to the water and sat in a moored flat-bottomed boat, and slapped and sloshed and just sat. The moon was up and very beautiful, but I looked at nothing. It would, of course, be eventful down in the woods. But that was not for me, none of that. It didn't matter. It was finished. The woods were finished. It was all stale. Mother's young love, her impossible young love, over. The woods were emptied. The wilderness had become cement streets. It was all cement, it was finished.

I grew aware of a tall silent figure on the bank.

"Is that you, Ed?" I asked. He didn't move.

"Do you love Jesus?" he said.

"Yes," I answered.

"How much?"

"Very much."

"All the time?"

"Yes."

"Well, that's all right. That will be all right for tonight."

"Ed, will you see me to the Georges' house, please, Ed."

"As long as you love Him."

"Ed, please."

"All right." He took my hand when I got out of the boat and we walked. He talked without stop. He talked about the love of God and the beauty of Christ. I didn't have to say a word. When I got to the house I said good night and he kissed me on the forehead very sweetly and said I'd be all right as long as I stayed with Jesus, and left, talking, into the woods.

Aunt Marie was appalled.

"You went alone with that man through the forest all the way home?"

I didn't answer.

"Alone? Your father won't like that, I must let your father know."

I went to bed without saying a word to anyone.

That's all there was, there was no more. The end of vernal love, the end of young happiness. The end of my mother's young hope and happiness. The end of my father's goodness.

I put my face against the bark of the trees and prayed: "Let me not grow to hate Elizabeth." But I did. And I have forgot why, but I remember the hate.

Oh, where was Mamie? How was she? Was she all right? Where was Ruth? And Professor Meyerhofer, and John Erskine, and Madame Gerville-Réache, and all those people who thought it was nice, all those people who lent us glory, and loved Mother and Father and thought they were special?

I hated dancing. The future and all interest filled me with distress. I wanted nothing—not food, not event, not association, not converse. I talked to Aunt Bettie over iced tea, kicked my heels against the porch balustrade. Elizabeth was never there. She was never there anymore.

"You're stale," Aunt Bettie said. "You must rest from practicing."

I was dead. I must rest from loving.

There was a hayride scheduled for the next night. One of the old ones, with a ladder and a stuffed wain, and lumbering horses, and Frank Felter stooped and silent at the reins. Only five years and he was stooped and silent, now and then spitting. The children and the young sat bolt upright and rigid, having been warned of the extreme dangers of sex. The young marrieds, having overcome their fears, lolled in the hay with people they were not related to. We children drew tighter and tighter into a cordon sanitaire. The hay filled up with bootleg bottles and our elders.

"Lean on me. It's all right, I won't pet," said a nice boy.

"Don't," said Jane.

I didn't. Mother had warned me. Jane and I remained bolt. Good-bye Mongaup Falls. Good-bye summer roads. We looked at the young marrieds petting.

"Horrid," said Jane.

Entrance to the bedroom suite.

Sho-Foo-Den.

The grown-ups took our hayride over and spoiled it. It was ours, they shouldn't have come.

But they did come. It was the last hayride. Elizabeth didn't come. She had her own projects.

Then came Margaret's second letter.

> We're having great fun with our Sunday picnics at Santa Monica. I hope you are. I take two ballet lessons a week. Mother takes me in and goes shopping at the Robinson's monthly sales while I have the lesson. Mr. Kosloff says you should take four lessons a week. He says your heels have no juice and that you must get your juice in order to be a good dancer. He told Uncle C that you had the best pantomime that he had ever seen outside of Russia. He wouldn't tell you, and Father wouldn't tell you. I'm telling you. Ends has just had worms. Miss Jane Cowell just came to tea. Mother fired the gardener; she said he got fresh with the cook. Our beach umbrella is new. Tommy Meighan is Father's new star. He gave me a bookmark. Father said I couldn't go to the set for two weeks because he'd heard I'd had a crush on the new actor, Rudolph Valentino. I think he's unreasonable.
>
> Yesterday we had the L.A. Tennis Tournament finals, and Pop was one umpire. Fred Alexander was another. Harvey Snodgrass won. Johnny Doeg, Mrs. Violet Sutton Doeg's little boy, won Juniors. Pop says he's going to be a champion. Next week Bill Tilden gives exhibition matches and Pop says he's going to invite him to play on our court. It's the best in Hollywood I've got a new dress. Last Saturday we had Uncle Cecil's yacht. Mother got seasick. Father got cross. I met Ramon Novarro. I like him a lot. I hope Pop doesn't get unreasonable. Love, Maggy Ming.

P.S. If you'll come home I'll give you a new costume book. I've saved up. Love, Miggie.

Who was she? She was a beautiful eleven-year-old child with beaux, with excitements, with interests.

Elizabeth had her interests and young men, but Margaret had Ramon Novarro—and Margaret was rebuked by our parents for indiscretion.

Anything could happen. To me too.

"I want to go home," I said to Aunt Bettie, and for the first time I meant Hollywood.

They found somebody going west.

I arrived in Pasadena at five-thirty in the evening. Mother and Margaret met me.

We were still collecting bags when Margaret gabbled: "We're going to La Jolla on location tomorrow. Wait until you see the new leading man. He's yummy."

"Where's Pop?"

Mother answered laconically, "Shooting, of course."

Margaret suddenly said, "I'm glad you're back—we all are."

Who was this bright-eyed lovely child? My sister. My own sister.

"Mother has let us have silk dresses."

"I don't believe you!"

Mother said, "It's true, it's quite true."

Childhood was over.

Chapter 9

❧ We stayed in California twelve years, seven years after my ill-fated trip back, and Margaret and I grew up. Margaret very quickly grew much older than I. Lots of things happened while we were growing up out West. The aunts wrote and later Jane and Little Bea told me all the details.

Jo married while I was in California and when I came back to visit, Little Bea had been just sixteen and radiantly, bloomingly lovely, with a stillness about her. Since they were first cousins and Jo a grown man, while Bea was still half child no one thought anything about them. Obviously he had to marry someone outside the family. Bea never said anything. She seemed to be waiting.

Jo had married a svelte and seductively pretty Norwegian girl named Hilde. Caroline never learned anything about the bride's family, her antecedents or her past history. They knew from observation she was very slender and definitely sensual. Also that she was straightforward and she had a good heart. Above all, she was observant, which was fortunate. She observed Caroline and she realized she had much to learn from her extraordinary mother-in-law and she immediately set about doing so. Their two children, Jokichi Takamine III and little Caroline, turned out to be flaxen-haired, blue-eyed, white-skinned and long in skeleton—the purest Scandinavian types—and they warmed their grandmother's heart. Little Bea made friends with the Norwegian wife, "the most honest person I ever met." Beth let Bea spend lots of time at Jo's cottage by the lake in the years that followed. Bea was allowed one cocktail, and Beth trusted Hilde to see there were no more. Everybody else had more. Everybody else was drunk the whole weekend. They were always drunk to the extent that Jo couldn't keep the car on the road, was in fact never sober outside of the office. In her own home Caroline could impose certain rules: no drinking. But not in her son's and not in her own when she was absent. Once on leaving Merriewold for a very brief trip she got them to promise on their honor with every reassurance. Elmoore said she had barely driven down the drive before the bottles were opened. That's how it was in the postwar years, in the twenties.

Jane says that Aunt Caroline believed the Japanese could not stand alcohol, that once started they could not stop drinking, as with Jo. That may be so, but there are a great many people not Japanese who cannot handle alcohol; they are called alcoholics.

Bea seemed to be waiting and she grew lovelier each day. George Braga thought so. Once at a picnic at Camp Columbia two of her long, long hairs got wrapped around his roasted marshmallow and he ate them as a kind of sacrament.

Eben, too, got married. He met his wife, Ethel, on a boat. She was traveling with another man, but she was pretty and she was, on occasion, soft-voiced. She quickly discovered his Dun and Bradstreet rating and she judged his appearance, although odd, tolerably acceptable. Japanese he was, certainly; but six feet tall and very jolly. She nailed him.

The parents accepted her. What could they do else? She was pale blond and looked just like Lillian Gish. She was waspish, greedy, mean, and conniving, but she had kittenish tricks and in no time at all she had got around the Doctor. The venerable man, so smart in all other ways, had given her ropes of oriental pearls and the farm adjacent to Merriewold Park. That was to be hers outright, no matter what happened. So she felt freer to behave as she liked, and her inclinations were not attractive. On a less important level, she put on airs. She was snippy to us. She demanded that Bea and Jane suddenly start calling their cousins "Cousin Eben" and "Cousin Jo." Imagine calling good old Jo "Cousin!" She snapped at me when I said she looked like Lillian Gish, whom I really thought very pretty. We loathed her.

"Don't bother about Ethel," said the other children. But the men bothered, including the sage and distinguished Doctor. We children didn't pay her much mind, nor Hilde either. We had our own concerns.

So no one noticed what was happening. The trouble began in usual daily ways, as it nearly always does. When the Doctor arrived back from New York he always went straight to his bedroom and his feet were washed for him, as in Japan. Aunt Takamine had her own personal French maid and also a very pretty young Japanese woman who had worked at the Consul General's as maid to the Consul General's wife, but had left or been dismissed suddenly. The Doctor engaged her and she was a sort of sub-housekeeper at Sho-Foo-Den. Whatever she was doing —mending, pressing, cleaning—she stopped when she heard the car drive up or the Doctor's voice on the open porches. Then she scampered for the bowl of scented water and the towel.

"You're not finished, are you?" asked Aunt Caroline sharply once, as she started to go. Auntie was having tea on her chaise longue with the Brussels lace throw over her feet. (Bea was idling through the *Women's Pictorial,* so she saw it all.)

"The master," mumbled Jun.

"I'll meet him," said Aunt Caroline with some asperity and suddenly standing. "You go on with what you're doing."

But when she led Uncle Jo back to his room, there was Jun bowing with the bowl. Auntie bit her lip and flushed. As she shut the door the soft Japanese started and the light laughter, like the twittering of birds in a cage. Bea was ready to leave when Minnie came in.

"Where's Caroline?" She sat down just as though it were her own room, poured herself some tea and began nibbling. "Is the sacred foot-washing going on?" Bea went red to her hair. The nerve! Then Auntie entered. Minnie took one look at her face and shot her heavy eyebrows up to heaven in a sign to Bea.

Auntie paced up and down several times, her chiffon skirts dragging on the carpet, and then she said, "Do you mind, dears? I have something to talk to Uncle Jo about."

"About time," said Minnie under her breath. "Only she won't." This was outside in the hall as she made her way to her bedroom. "She hasn't in twenty years. Why now?"

I suppose she didn't.

After Uncle Jo had gone down to New York a few days later and the morning post had come, Auntie, on reading a page, suddenly went dead white, folded the sheet and put it in her bosom, then excused herself and hurried away. The rest of the day she was absent from meals, keeping to her room. Minnie was terribly alarmed and quite irritated at being shut out, but she went personally to fetch Marie, who was closeted with Caroline for hours. When Marie came out of the bedroom Minnie accosted her.

"She's perfectly fine. Leave her alone."

Marie then went home, cooked dinner for her own brood, served and ate it. Later that evening she and her Bee walked over with branches of hardhack. Auntie had gone to bed with headache pills. The Doctor was in New York.

The episode of the letters was repeated four different times. Young Jo took to screening the mail. Bea caught his arm in the carriage entrance.

"Who is writing to Auntie to trouble her so?"

"We don't know. The letters aren't signed."

"What do the letters say?"

"Now *that,* Blue Eyes, is none of your business."

"Is it serious?"

He nodded.

"Not you, again?"

"No, darling. Not this time. Not I."

"Who?"

He put an arm around Bea.

"Don't ever ask, Bea. We're in trouble. If you love us, don't ask."

When Uncle Jo came up that weekend he seemed happy and serene. He had tremendous good news about the factory.

No niece ever saw Aunt Takamine cry, but her eyes were red those days, and since she wore no makeup except the slightest touch to her lips, all emotions were betrayed nakedly on her skin. She was pale and there were smudges under her eyes.

"She never complained," as Minnie said—not even at the sad events that were to follow.

Jun suddenly left, without a good-bye. LaRue Kinney took her and her bundles in the Packard to St. Joseph's station.

"Why has she gone?" Bea asked Auntie.

"She displeased me," said Aunt Takamine.

"Why?" Bea asked young Jo.

"Why, goodness, darling," said Jo, "she was pregnant. Didn't you see? She's gone back to Japan." Then he suddenly looked at her hard. "I guess you didn't know. I guess nobody knew. I shouldn't have spoken."

"You?" Bea blurted.

"No, no, Bea," he said. "She's gone to Japan and we'll never see her again."

But Bea interrupted. "Uncle Jo goes to Japan often and he stays there for very long times."

Jo said, "I pray everything will be all right again. You'll help us." And he put a finger on Bea's lips.

Uncle Jokichi offered Caroline a divorce. Aunt Marie told me this when she was in her eighties and Caroline long since dead. (It would have had to be he who offered her a divorce. She could not demand it. She was Japanese.) "She didn't think she'd like a divorce." The house stood. The letter writer was, they believe, the malicious and strange young second wife of old, blind Captain Hitch, who out of spite and jealousy of Caroline wanted to hurt and did, and the contents were common knowledge, it seemed, at least to the grown-ups. Caroline held her head higher and was more gracious than ever.

The Doctor busied himself with international projects. Aunt Caroline collected a coterie, and continued with rather sleazy musicians.

She was lonely. Her friends, her family, were all subordinates, all dependent. And Minnie, the oldest friend of all, was the most dependent, "the first lady of the bed chamber." The boys led secret lives. Their wives were not close.

She was beautiful, powerful, and very rich, and she was lonely. There began, understandably, to be diversions. The Doctor was totally occupied and spending large stretches of the year in Japan. Caroline Takamine sought solace with young men. Eben introduced his friends, many of whom fell directly in love. In all their lives they'd never met anything like Caroline Takamine. One of them played the piano and Auntie sat for hours listening. One of them was a devout Catholic and they had long walks through the woods talking mysticism and the afterlife and other reassuring matters.

"Your mother is a wonderful, wonderful woman," the young man had said to Eben on the train back.

Beth had lots to say about those talks.

"Some of them were in a closed New York taxicab," she said, and she wouldn't be quiet about it. "A closed cab," said Beth, and her eyes danced.

The inevitable happened. Caroline converted.

"It was her love of music and form," Minnie suspected, "rather than inner conviction, that led her to Catholicism." There Caroline's romanticism could flower unchecked, and in a sense she treated it, the Roman Church, as an expression of her personal creativity. She was at times pretty bossy, even with God's priests.

"It was her interest in the young man," said Jane.

"It was her loneliness," said I.

On her knees her poor, proud, isolated spirit found companionship. And now, on Sundays, she could go to St. Joseph's as to her real home, and often to confession, very often. And when vespers sounded, she bowed her head and she knew peace for the first time. The gongs sounded too, of course, but the vesper bells would surely come and they were hers.

The Doctor's activities never slackened. Between Tokyo, Los Angeles, Washington, New York, and Merriewold he hurried back and forth, weighted with honors, dragging protocol along like a great net that bound his life to two countries, clarifying laws, establishing scholarships, promoting schools and industries, presiding at dinners. There may have been gossip and threats of ruin. (Eben had a fling with toothbrushes and lost a real fortune. His father paid up every penny. "The name Takamine will never be dragged through a bankruptcy court," proclaimed the Doctor proudly.) But we didn't know about the disasters; he was proud and kept them from us. And above all, the effort and the struggle was to be for the sons and for their sons, and he was content.

And then one night after a great testimonial banquet tendered him in New York, he was stricken with an old liver complaint. Hurried to the Lenox Hill Hospital, he lay fighting for his life, Caroline at his side. But he weakened steadily and seemed to show fear for the first time. His nurse was a Catholic. "Do you think," he asked piteously, "if I convert to your faith my life will be spared?" She seemed to answer in the affirmative. A priest was sent for and Jokichi Takamine became a Roman Catholic to the gratitude and joy of his wife, to the distress of his friends. He was, however, beyond physical help. He died soon after on July 22, 1922, at the age of sixty-eight. There were those who felt he did not quite know what his conversion was about and that he had yielded to untimely pressure. Maybe this is not so; maybe he found comfort and hope in the new faith. In any case, Aunt Takamine, in a flooding of gratitude for the nurse's spiritual reinforcement, gave her a string of jade worth a thousand dollars.

For two days he lay in state in the Nippon Club which he had founded, on a catafalque heaped with flowers from all the legations, from princes, from barons, from scientists, from educators, from unknowns. Besides the daimyo's ideographs were simple messages, "You saved my life." Flags flew at half-mast in the towns where Takamine lived—in Monticello and Paterson, New Jersey, at the pharmaceutical plants in Tokyo and at his birthplace, Kamazawa. He was buried from St. Patrick's with high pontifical mass.

In his will he had stipulated that his brain be given to the Yale School of Medicine, his body to medical schools; then cremated and the ashes buried in Japan and the United States. But Caroline overruled all this. The Doctor's soft voice was not there to insist and he was interred in a beautiful new family sepulcher in Woodlawn with full Catholic rites. Neither his scientific associates nor his Buddhist relatives approved.

Many of us grieved for the gentle and charming Japanese, the little father, so courtly, so extraordinarily kind to children. Little Bea mourned. The George orphans felt bereft anew ("I shall now be your father," he had said as he gathered them into his arms at Uncle Harry's death) and every time they looked toward the rhododendron hedges they saw their Uncle Jo, white-haired, fresh pink-and-white-skinned, with snapping black eyes, his small, quiet figure moving in and out of the shadows beside the smaller bent gardener. Every time it's spring in Washington there are many people who stop and lift their heads in gratitude. And in his beloved homeland, after the dreadful war which devastated his country, a request was sent to Washington and grafts from the gift trees were shipped back and now bloom gloriously along Tokyo's grand Araca Canal. There are the many scholarships, the international societies, and the legislation which he accomplished for Japanese-American good will. No matter who takes credit for the actual discovery of Adrenalin, it happened and he made this possible. This is a remarkable fact and one we can all acknowledge.

Caroline may not have mourned the Doctor. They had not been happy or close for some time. There were ugly rumors, mainly among the Japanese, of her exultations of freedom at the moment of his death, and it is true she did not grieve as Aunt Marie had with ceaseless midnight tears, or my mother was to learn to grieve forever. But she had kept the home and the Doctor's prestige unblemished. She honored him. She was a Samurai's wife.

Ethel stood by just long enough to benefit by her inheritance, then divorced Eben to marry a man with a yacht. The family, except Eben who loved her, sighed with relief. But there may have been something on her side too. She said to Minnie Dickens "with her hands in the air, 'I'm tired, I'm tired, I'm tired! For ten years I've tried to understand the Japanese!'" As a final gesture, profiting by the family's absence from Sho-Foo-Den, she removed everything portable, including several fine stone figures and the canvas walls of the carriage entrance with all the distinguished guests' poems. These she cut from their casings with a knife. It was a matter of years before the murals were recovered.

After the Doctor's death Caroline's existence was even more empty. A woman of vast wealth, her children grown and married, her purpose in life gradually evolved into that of being a perpetual hostess. She made several pleasure trips, once around the world with Minnie Dickens, and then back, always back.

After the Doctor's death the visitors at Sho-Foo-Den were less distinguished. The daily routine was that of a great English country house. Caroline kept to her room all morning, busy with staff and correspondence. At noon she indulged in a brief and sedate walk in her high white laced boots, in Minnie's garrulous company, then lunch and then for the rest of the day anything the guests wished. On rainy days the bridge games lasted until midnight in front of the fire in her great bedroom. Her life had lost all point and she was bored.

Beth too was bored. Beth stayed every summer with Marie, being waited on, being cozened, being given house room for her enormous wardrobe. She arrived for a three-week visit at her hard-working sister's with two trunks and at least five suitcases. Her clothes filled all the upstairs closet space and she changed her costume at least four times a day. Always fresh and always enticing, she came to her sister's stove-cooked dinner, a little late but exquisite. Marie had only time to mop her brow and push back the straggles of her hair. Beth conversed throughout as though she were dining in a palace and for several weeks she would indeed visit the palace. She was pleased to visit Sho-Foo-Den, because it was famous and grand. But in spite of all the glory she was bored. "Inside of all those temple bells, there's no life," I overheard her say to Aunt Marie. "I've read all the books I've brought and I don't care for Carrie's, and I can't spend every afternoon and evening playing bridge. That's for old ladies. And the guests on weekends are stuffed shirts."

"Why, Beth," said Auntie Marie, "they're the flower of our time."

"In Japanese arrangements," said Beth, roaring with laughter.

So Beth began to frequent the Inn.

Caroline never went to the Inn. She stayed back in her fortress and received on her own terms and she tried vainly to keep Beth with her. Beth struggled. "No life! No life! I'm young and I'm bored."

She wasn't young, but she felt her youth—well, her middle age —well, her time—was being wasted.

"Why is your mother so restless?" Caroline asked Little Bea. "What is the matter with her? She keeps saying she wants to go to New York to see a play. She keeps asking LaRue to drive her to the station. What were those pills the New York doctor gave her for her nerves? Do you know? Minnie says . . ." and then noticing Bea's expression, she hastily caught herself. "I really think what she needs is quiet—at her age—and no more of those pills."

Caroline, Bea gathered, suspected that Beth was taking drugs. Aunt Caroline had also once believed that I had syphilis simply because I had cried on saying "good-bye" to Mother and was gloomy. I learned this later; when Aunt Marie was aged eighty-

three she told me, and at this I was astonished and somewhat
shocked. I was always gloomy at that point. As a matter of fact, I
cried because I had agreed to break off with a boy to whom
Mother was extremely antagonistic.

Beth spent more and more time at the dam in smart white or
bathing suits, or on the Inn porch in chiffon veils and large hats,
at the dances in evening dresses—and the new daring ones without sleeves, sometimes without even straps.

Around her, the siren, the witch, there was always a ring of
enchanted males and she played with them like a cat in heat.
And surrounding these there was always a circle of highly disturbed and watchful wives. And beyond them in the shadows,
the enchantress, the true enchantresses, the daughters, including
Little Bea, a beauty, but shy and muted in her effects.

It was after one of these dances that George Braga's grandmother and Bea's said to him, "You'd better stop mooning about
after Bea. You can't have her. You're her first cousin."

George had never taken this in and was startled. "But," he said
sadly, "I don't think she loves me."

"That's neither here nor there. Your mother and her father are
brother and sister, my own children. Nothing will ever change
that. That's final."

So Bea was forbidden and marked, as the Takamine boys had
been forbidden and marked. In a sense they were outlawed.

George once said to her, "I know you don't care about me."

"Oh, George, for pity's sake! I love you dearly but—"

"But you can't have Jo either. He's your first cousin too."

"I never thought about it. He's married and he's older."

But Bea was very troubled.

Beth continued with her plans. One memorable masquerade
Club party (the Inn was now the Club) Beth came as a cave
woman with her white skin stained brown, which made her

lovely eyes real violet; her hair was down her back in a tangle, and ropes of ground pine hung about her and her legs were bare. She was deadly and she was out to get "El Señor," Bernardo Braga, who had recently been widowed because Maud had succumbed to cancer. Beth pursued him past the rows of little boys in all the good chairs, past the girls waiting around, past the boys with their hip flasks, past the couples in the shadows, past Laura Graves who was dressed in a Spanish shawl and nothing else and showing at last a bit of wear and tear, past Jo Takamine, laughing, past Hilde in a corner of the porch with the young men, and she cornered Braga on the tennis court. "Bernardo," she breathed, and her eyes were simply extraordinary.

"Helen!" he called at the top of his voice, with the voice that made him the terror of the cane fields. "Helen, come get me!"

And Helen got him. She saved him that night, but Beth was back at her exercise the next day.

Bernardo was an attractive and full-blooded Spaniard; he was rich; he had a very young son who needed mothering and there were many applicants, but Beth was the most aggressive.

Beth was dangerous. She was not acceptable to the Braga clan. She had been one of them, loyally and closely, but they could never forget that while she had been married to Will Atkinson she had fallen in love, had divorced Will and married her third husband, Clark of Kansas City. The Atkinsons regarded her conduct as flighty, not fine.

George stepped in to his father's rescue. He felt he must, since his father seemed bewildered and George and his young brother, Ronnie, were the crux of the situation. It was the children then who settled it, little Bea and George in the moonlight down by the lake at Sho-Foo-Den. There on a small, rocky peninsula that juts out in close proximity to the opposite mirroring protuberance (but not quite close enough for a leap and that is the tease, the joke of the garden), there they sat in the warm moonlight and George ended their love. Bea had lived in his home and they were dear to one another and George had adored her, but he told her quietly that he would not see her again, not for years. The situation with her mother had become intolerable and the family was concerned. Beth was lively and amusing and attractive, he admitted, but they did not want her as a mother.

Also, and George did not say this as he sat silently beside Bea while the fireflies threaded the dark, he was very tired. He had been held in thrall, in hopeless adulation all of his youth. He simply had to rest and breathe again.

"Good-bye, dear," said George and walked her up the hill between the rhododendrons to the big house. Bea was tired too, but not entirely with George. Bea went to sleep in Jo's room. Jo was down by the lake in the cottage with Hilde.

Love died for George. It was only calf love, he now says. Still he did not marry for thirty years, nor did he dare to love anyone in all that time. He had committed himself so deeply and been so wasted.

Helen married Bernardo. Very soon.

Eben had gone to Arizona and was staying on a working ranch where he lived in basic simplicity with the owner, the head wrangler, one Charles Beach. He invited his mother to visit them, and she was bored, so she went.

At the end of the visit Charles Beach simply took Caroline in his arms. This had never happened to her before and she was swept off her feet. He was thirty years her junior.

Charles Beach and Caroline Takamine were made man and wife. Beth's eyes snapped when she heard the family news. Thirty years younger? How about her young violinist, age twenty-one? She was only fifty-nine and widowed. How about him?

Beach was a rancher, a cowboy. He had been in love with Caroline, he claimed, since he first saw her picture. After the ceremony they went home to his shack on the mountain. "If it was good enough for her man, it was good enough for her." Caroline cooked his ham and eggs, laid the table with a clean new checked cloth, and dished up the supper on porcelain that had been the gift of the daimyo and the mikado, the father of Hirohito (with the Imperial crest inverted as on all Imperial gifts). She always dressed for the evening meal. The bridegroom was absolutely bewitched. He stared silently at her as though he could not believe his fortune was real. I remember him looking at her as she crossed the room, his face transfigured with love. "She's nice," he said softly. Nothing in Herrick's love lyrics conveyed more.

The Doctor had not talked very much, had said little but "Ah!" but his will stood like the rocks under the earth. Charlie said even less, but he was candid. At the end of her life she had found a man direct, understanding, and plain. What an astonishing revelation that was! At sixty-five she put on her sunglasses and her wide-brimmed hat and drove beside her Charlie in the choking dust whenever he asked her to.

Clouds and rain were the news in Caroline's life now; breeding and calving spelled the seasons' changes. In all that land there was no sound except when a cow tore at a bush too prickly to eat and snuffled softly at her calf. The Rancho de los Oscilitos was all but indistinguishable on the side of the mountain in the wilderness of speckle and dazzle. The horned toads sat unblinking on the bleached rock. Lizards were visible only as speed.

"How could she have stood her Japanese marriage," I once asked her blond grandson, Dr. Jokichi Takamine III, "and the loneliness of her young married years?"

"How could she have stood the cowboy, Charlie Beach?" he countered. Well, how could she? But she did, and happily.

She entered the community activities. She thought perhaps a second Catholic church would be a help. The bishop explained that in view of the extreme poverty, what the people needed chiefly was a hospital and schools and not more stained glass. Caroline was stubborn. The local bishop washed his hands of the matter, but the bishop of Chicago, Caroline's good friend, proved much more understanding and accordingly came West in 1935 and dedicated the Chapel of Santa Rita in the Desert, the gift of Caroline Takamine Beach to the town of Vail, Arizona. The bell, vestments, altar linen, and holy paraphernalia were donated by friends of Dr. Takamine in Europe, the United States, and Japan. When Minnie Dickens heard of this she said to Little Bea, "Caroline has built a church? What a pity! She could have given the money to me," a remark which for simplicity and directness I found hard to better. Golden-hearted Charlie encouraged this project. It apparently never occurred to him to be jealous, then or on any other occasion. The chapel functions today as part of the diocese of Chicago.

Jo was now the host at Sho-Foo-Den. No one who was ever his guest forgot what he offered: renaissance courtliness laced with Yankee wit and Creole sweetness of manner. The style of living was less Japanese than before, less decorous, and as the days passed, certainly less sober, but equally opulent; it was, above all, democratic. Jo let the neighbors and tennis players in, something his mother had never done.

Aunt Takamine came East on one of her semiannual business trips, ostensibly to visit her grandchildren, but also to see how things were.

Things were bad. Hilde had left home once and had threatened to take the children. Jo would not, could not, settle into domesticity. His mother reasoned and warned. He became inaccessible, as his father always had in moments of tension, as Eben had done to Ethel's frustrated rage. He refused to acknowledge a problem. He refused to answer. Hilde grew bitter and desperate and Caroline stern. There was one dreadful interview. No one knows what was said except that Jo declared that he would not be possessed and refused to answer charges or make promises for the future. One thing was clear: Jo was miserable. Little Bea happened by in the aftermath of this and found Auntie's door closed and Hilde gone out. Jo was pacing, a cigarette in his fingers. Bea murmured, "Excuse me."

"Don't go," said Jo sharply. She waited silent and frightened. Suddenly he grabbed her and held her close to him. "You forgive me. You forgive me, darling."

"Always," she whispered.

"I must get out of here." And he was gone.

One day she cornered him.

"Jo, what's the matter?"

"Nothing, darling. It's time you got a serious beau."

"Jo, seriously. Don't joke."

"Seriously, Blue Eyes? Seriously?"

Her eyes filled. "We're all so worried about you."

"You worry?"

"I die for you."

The black eyes went opaque. Suddenly his arms were around her. "Oh, God, Bea. No peace. If only you weren't my cousin."

"Does that matter?"

"Our mothers are sisters. Not here. Not in Japan. And you're so young."

"I die for you."

"No."

He kissed her on the mouth then for the first and only time.

"A pity. A pity."

Soon after that it happened.

It was in New York. One night Jo had been kept late at the office; he called home and found that his mother and Hilde had gone out together. So he went out by himself. Oh, how bitterly Caroline reproached herself for the fact that she and Hilde had not been there for him. How they both later went over the possibilities and the alternatives! But in reality there was no alternative.

Jo was found lying outside a strange hotel window, scrabbling around in the dirt and litter on a lower roof. The occupants heard him trying to crawl and trying to talk. He was broken. The police found the open window above, and a drunk woman inside. Jo couldn't explain because he couldn't speak. The woman was babbling inanities.

Aunt Takamine stood by his bedside in the hospital. It is not certain whether he heard her. Her life lay bleeding away on the pillow before her; yet she must stand in judgment. "Oh, my darling," she said, "you have to face it. You have to answer the questions now. You cannot always run away or fool people. Not always. Not forever. You cannot fool God. You know that now."

Then he died.

All that beauty, that manhood, the gaiety, zest, and fun, the gifts, the great gifts in the dirt and refuse of a hotel roof.

The family gathered from all parts of the States as Jokichi, Jr., was laid at his father's side. Throughout the funeral service the flaxen-haired Hilde stood quietly with her hand on the coffin. That was her answer, and the only one she ever made. She never talked about her marriage again, even to the children. She never mentioned Jo. Not once.

All the businessmen of Clifton and Paterson, New Jersey, the men who had refused to let him dine inside at the golf club with his Norwegian wife, as well as all the staffs of the factories, gave up a whole working day to attend the funeral, as Jokichi Takamine, Jr., was laid at his father's side.

Charles Beach came on to be with his wife. She never broke or lost her nerve but she was haggard. She had grown old. She went often to the cemetery, and often, she said, as she approached the grave, a young unknown woman rose from her knees and withdrew.

Every afternoon in Arizona when Charlie was away on ranch business and safe from bothering, she wept in the arms of María López. She wept the tears of death.

Caroline's faculty of not recognizing what was unbearable saved her reason. Jo had been murdered, she said. There were bootleggers who had never ceased to bribe and threaten for his knowledge of the techniques of making ferments, for the equipment ready at his hand. He had been plagued throughout Prohibition and had resisted all requests. He could have made a separate fortune if he had chosen to do business with criminals. He had been threatened once again, claimed Caroline, cornered and killed and his death rigged to look like an unsavory accident. There was something about his hat, with a hole torn in it, found far from the location of the fall. He had been killed, said Caroline, by gangsters so that he had died a hero. This is what she said publicly and told the children.

No arrests or charges were ever made and neither she nor the state pursued the case, but such was the condition of the police and the power of political domination under Mayor Jimmy

Walker that no inference should be taken from this fact that Caroline was wrong.

Jo was gone, cut off in the flower of his youth, and the family devastated. No matter that the promise was unfulfilled; there was a nobility, a gallantry, quite specifically Jo's, that lent an air to everything he touched. Wherever he passed, adventure was possible, and Jo was virile as legends were virile. "And then he was gifted." Little Bea's face glowed as she said this. He was exciting. The men always laughed as they remembered. He took what he wanted in sheer zest! And when he came to the Club or played tennis or poker or went to the dam for swimming, everything was better and more fun. The most trivial incidents became significant. Life intensified. It pounded as in the big moments.

Merriewold was no longer enchanted to Little Bea. It was just a place to go for dawdling, for Aunt Marie's pie. But the magic, the danger . . . Merriewold was just a pleasant place in a forest. It had been alive and quick with promise and risk. Now it had become female.

Chapter 10

❧ The women took over.

Mother and Father were divorced after twenty-three years.
The last eight years were unrelieved pain, although Mother to the
day of her death never understood why he had stopped loving
her. In brief, she drove him crazy, although she never learned
why. Indeed, she never learned anything about human living.
There was Mother's particular, personal habit of always demanding perfection, without mercy or respite. Nothing less was acceptable in members of the family. She always had to inquire and to
supervise. This can be wearing.

But there was another reason: Father fell in love with someone
else. But why did he fall in love when he had loved so deeply before? Mother was nervous and fussy, but none of these reasons
are enough. Father discovered sex. Mother could have discovered
sex too, but not without help. And there was no help for our
mothers. The ignorance of our fathers was abysmal and rigid;
the ignorance of our mothers, total. What's more, they rather
prided themselves on staying that way, as though it were a virtue,
certainly an enhancement. Whereas it was a deliberate deforma-
tion, rendering them semihelpless, although supposedly flattering
the men as superior. But it also fatigued the men and bored them.

The nineteenth-century man had done what he could; the women had prayed. But the twentieth-century man got out. It was in the early twentieth century that women began to have to meet divorce head on, and their lives broke. Emotionally and sexually crippled, dazed by shame and grief, they set out to make a new world. The biggest revolution we have had in this century, the most profound and altering to human life is not reaching the moon, nor even achieving the atom bomb, nor yet inventing the electric light, but the realization that women are equal and regard themselves as human beings with human needs and appetites and requirements and that they intend to satisfy them. And also that every man and woman intends to be recompensed fairly for labor. All men and all women.

But in my youth wives were faithful and married for life, until death, and spinsters were virgins, real ones. And sometimes as they grew older, they went out of their minds. The most valuable thing a woman had was her "good name." This did not apply to her intelligence, her skill, her charm, her honesty, her reliability, her steadfastness, or her courage, which were essentially male virtues and the basis for male character and reputation. Women's, on the other hand, rested on one fact alone: that no man had been illegally close. And also equally important that no one could say so. And men killed to stop talk.

Mother was smug. In her forties, after the divorce, she boasted, "I know nothing about sex. Of course I know that babies don't come from cabbages. But nothing more." It was as though she were giving superior credentials. She was thoroughbred, an innocent, that is, ignorant—a lady.

Married or single, she was not permitted to know anything of the rough side of life—which meant anything rough that happened outside the home, or in her husband's or son's lives outside the home. In this, they assured her, lay her great good fortune.

The baby might set his hair on fire, the plumbing stop the day of the dinner party; there might be a sudden smell of gas, or the dog die of strychnine in her arms; she might feel extremely queer and frightened because the doctor had warned her about having another child; she might feel puzzled and hurt because her husband hadn't been to bed with her in a year; the priest arrived to see why Maggie, the upstairs girl, would not go back to her drunken husband; Aunt Jane announced an imminent four-month visit. No matter. Her life was sheltered. She knew where her place was; in the shelter. And she was always going to be shielded from getting out of it to see how really ugly things could be.

The more robust troubles, illegitimacy, drunkenness, insanity, adultery, homosexuality, occurred then, as now, and had to be absorbed into the family pattern. But they were to be absorbed quietly with absolutely no talk. There was to be no discussion before children or servants, and only the briefest with a husband behind closed doors, or with a friend of one's bosom. A lady did not gossip. She had no time off either, no trips alone, no change of occupation. She had religion. She had causes. She had headaches.

When driven beyond endurance, she took herself out on her children; it was the children that bore the brunt and showed the scars, and although the shifting of punishment was quite unconscious and altogether against original intent, the result of the passing along of pain was unfortunate, for the ladies were not always able to transfer the valor that made it bearable.

The women took over and they were very different in their homemade dresses and very individual, but all of them, rich or poor, within their spheres were the bosses, uncompromising, undeviating, unadjusting. Never having disciplined themselves to a paid job, they were unrestrained in the home. ("I always used to yield up my kitchen," says the mature Jane, now a mother of a family, "and gave up cooking when Mother visited to save argument.") The boys left, of course, most of them, not all. And not all the girls did and not soon enough.

Our mothers were stubborn. It was clear to them that life was at fault, not the rules they lived by. Their suffering was, as a consequence, dreadful. I stand as witness that the suffering of women like my mother was excruciating and lifelong. It engulfed the men too, and it was quite needless. My mother's generation may have been the last generation to know this particular agony. But they gave not an inch, hardening their hearts with righteousness and becoming under pressure the spirits that without vote changed governments, enacted statutes, altered city ordinances and labor rulings, and formed a background of steel-like resilience from which their men and children recoiled, lashed away, and in the end returned to.

They were the polestar, the focal point, dead center, gravity. The men expected of them what they did not ask of anyone else, certainly not of themselves, not of their President, mayor, teacher, doctor, not even perhaps of their priest: They asked unblemished integrity and idealism. These women gave the generations they served a tonality not matched today—a kind of perfect pitch to which all the members of their society referred.

Were they happy?

Well, happiness is, in the last analysis, always a personal matter and is closely linked with the ability to love. Our mothers knew this. Their generation understood what gallantry meant. In their retiring way they represented what may prove to be the last stand of chivalry.

I must emphasize that not one word of these matters ever passed the lips of my mother and father before or after the separation. Not one word marred the perfect discretion of their privacy, and I fear that they might be offended by my speaking now.

Mother had made mistakes. But Father had loved her—oh, he had. His mouth grimaced with pain when he spoke of it and his eyes misted over, even twenty years later.

Mother and Margaret and I came East to live. I wrote Pop that we had no place for summer weekends. So he threw the Pitmans out and gave Merriewold to me. He should have given it to Mother; it was her heritage, her expectation. But he was unfriendly to Mother and he gave it to me. Nor did he give it to Margaret and me. He believed in primogeniture and he gave it to the elder. Mag, out of deep hurt, said she didn't want it anyway.

For six years we had been losing Father and then we lost him. He wanted to stay close to Margaret and me but that was out of the question. "You don't understand how much I have always loved you." No, I didn't. ("Anne, come blow your child's nose.")

And, golden-haired, quick of body, nimble-witted but not grossly sharp as I had once been, educated, panting, I now played Schubert well enough and Scarlatti exquisitely (it was my touch) and substantial Chopin, and I sat mooning at the untuned keys of the old upright and went out to stare into the woods where— where what? Nothing. I ran away. It was there, the love, the waiting. I couldn't stand it and I ran away.

Margaret ran away too, and got married to a moving-picture producer and returned to Hollywood for some years. (The wedding took place at Aunt Takamine's ranch in Arizona.) I couldn't bear to stay alone with Mother in the house in the woods. Back there, back in Merriewold were Mother and Father walking in the twilight, the early spring, in the violets, in the bluebells of England, in the lupin of the Sierra Madre. Wherever I went, wherever in the world, it was always to be Father I walked with, Mother I walked with. Down by the stone pylon at the Gordons' I dreamed of waiting as a young girl (good God, I was a young girl) waiting for my love to come as Mother had waited. "I am ready," I said, wrapping my arms around the tree trunks, as Mother had been ready when Father came up the road, as her father had walked with his Annie. And now I entered the gray years and they were my twenties.

Of course, I couldn't pay even the very small taxes, so Mother took over. She kept Merriewold beautifully and improved it with electricity and indoor plumbing, against my remonstrances. I wanted nothing changed, as though this would prevent the marks of time and preserve all circumstances of my extreme youth static. Mother had no such taboos.

Nor could I bear to go there except very occasionally and for the briefest weekends. I kept busy, but since I had no jobs, I did not keep busy enough. But I didn't want to be reminded of the promise. I was twenty-one, and this was the time for beginnings. But there was no beginning. There were only memories. At twenty-one!

Mother told me stories about every turn of the road and every change of weather. They were all concerned with the dead or the very old. I didn't want to hear; I found the dead stuffy people in black dresses all related in the end to The Movement. I shut my ears. But the facts were all pure gold. The Takamine story, for instance. She knew lots. She could have told but I wouldn't listen. It was entrapment, and Father could have told but I wasn't seeing him!

There were many new families now, and a new generation of the old ones and they were vigorous and lusty but they did not affect me largely because I was away for long stretches and because I held myself aloof. Margaret knew them. My story concerns the families I knew, the old, fading friends of my childhood.

Now in all our lives it was the women who dominated, the sad, lonely women who walked the paths of Merriewold. The women dominated and made the decisions. The men were either dead or divorced or run away. Some of the women, like Mother and Aunt Marie, were really undivorceable. Marriage was for life, until death, and the men's dying had no effect whatever on this point of view.

I finally fled to England, and after a few years Margaret and her husband came back and lived with Mother, enabling Mother to take charge of the granddaughter. Margaret had a fine time flirting with the Braga nephews, the young wild Antunias. El Señor always had an eye for a beautiful woman.

"She's irresistible," Bernardo Braga said as she teased and toyed. "She's like a Spanish woman. She has eyes that bite."

Aunt Bettie was frequently there with one or both of the girls, but she disapproved of the younger generation. It wasn't healthy, and it wasn't sporting, and it wasn't decent. Aunt Bettie was, of course, man-oriented and was inseparable from her husband. But in a sense she had consumed him, so in deferring to his will, she was pleasing herself, and it was quite frequently at great cost to her daughters. And they all deferred to John, the son, the male. (He was nicknamed by the teenagers, "John, Our God, Pitman.") Aunt Bettie watched over the girls' virginity, their Southern aristocratic ladyhood. As before, little makeup, plain good clothes, absolute strength and honesty. Spinsters. The last of their kind. They came constantly to visit us. Aunt Bettie was of Father's tribe, but she remained devoted to Mother. Louise went off to the North Carolina mountains and devoted her life to the highlanders, to handcrafts and good works. Elizabeth went into the Red Cross. John was courting Edith O'Connor, who lived in the Gordon house. The women watched over his progress like broody hens, because it was their romance, too.

Aunt Marie and Henry spent weeks in the summer alone, Henry with his dog and his medical studies and his articles on the fourth dimension. Bee George got married. The cousins got married. Henry continued with his dog and his metaphysics. Aunt Marie washed floors and cooked. There was now no servant, not even Mrs. Soeles. Aunt Marie drudged for him always, and for Jane and for Bea and her husband, for the visiting girls and their families sometimes.

The Takamine companies were dissolved and the stock was now worthless. They were poor because Henry made only a pittance as a medic and as contributor to magazines.

And then in 1929 Aunt Marie lost all. In 1929, with true family loyalty, she had put all her savings and power of attorney in the hands of a nephew, her older sister Kate's son, Boo. Aunt Caroline had used Boo as stockbroker also, but had withdrawn her money in time. And Caroline did not warn the really dependent Elmoore and Marie. "It would have been disloyal to our nephew and undermining to his confidence as a broker."

"How about your sisters?" cried Jane, aghast.

Minnie Dickens was hurt as well and Minnie hounded Boo for decades. Caroline had lost five thousand only, and she did not offer to help. "They have to face up to their losses. They are grown-up women," she said.

Aunt Marie would not say anything harsh about a nephew but Jane went to see him alone, and Jane was blazing. The young man shrugged. "Fortunes of war," he said.

The money for Henry's medical education was gone.

Caroline offered Marie a position as housekeeper for ten dollars a week and such was Marie's humility that she would have accepted it to help toward the children's education if Jane had not objected. Jane knew that Caroline was at that point contributing toward the support of several musicians. Jane was eloquent. So Marie, who felt it was her fault, her own stupidity, did without the ten dollars and went out to recover what she could. She sold books door to door and that wonderful heart and willing mind thought nothing of a congressman's widow tramping around with a heavy bag of samples to sour-faced women with their hair in curlers and vacuum cleaners in their hands, but rather of the treasure she offered them for their children, the chance to open their children's minds. Her face shone and her eyes blazed.

"But I do get tired," she admitted.

It was for Henry, because he was the male. As before, Henry did not help with the domestic chores. Jane did all the cooking and cleaning and Henry's sense of guilt mounted appreciably year by year. Now and then he asked somebody to marry him. One was Elizabeth Pitman, who was invited to be given the standard Henry treatment: one dance, one operation, and one proposal. Among other things, she was taken aback. There had never been the slightest attraction between them, and their interests were quite different. He was five years her junior.

"What's the matter with me?" demanded Henry.

Aunt Takamine ruled what was left of her family even from across the United States. The nieces and the nephews came to visit her, and the great-nieces, and her rule held like iron, as though these things mattered anymore. No lipstick, no drinking, no shorts, no petting or whatever they called it now, no disloyalty or unkindness to mothers and older women.

The next generation paid not much mind except in her presence, but the sisters still jumped to attention.

I think she would have liked to settle in Merriewold where the remnants of her glory were, but she was still in midstream, as the other younger women were not. Charlie's occupation and his land were located in Vail, Arizona. Eben did not want the responsibility of Sho-Foo-Den. There was nothing to do but to sell it.

Sell Sho-Foo-Den? It was desecration. It was like selling our childhood. Caroline offered it first to the Japanese Embassy, but although they had made good use of it in times past, they wanted none of the responsibility now and declined to buy. So she sold it to a neighbor, John Moody of Moody's Investors Service (whose house I had complacently watched burn), and he presented Sho-Foo-Den to his plump wife to her dumfoundment. "Follow Caroline Takamine into that mansion?" Mrs. Moody was a charming lady with an exaggerated bosom and sentimental pretensions, but she had enough sense to be slightly intimidated by the prospect of maintaining this glorious house. Still, it was to be her home and she chintzed it up and placed comfy wicker chairs about and screened the porch against mosquitoes and set out a Greek stone bench or two by the lake. She took down the Hiroshige and Utamaro prints and put up in their place her son Ernest's watercolors. It was a home in a way, but she did say she thought she was running a summer hotel. She kept up Caroline's tradition of support for second-rate musicians. Her husband, who was a financial expert and not the least bit interested in music or art or any of the finer things, carpentered a lot of miniature houses, and he surprised everyone by becoming a convert to the Catholic Church. And now friends from St. Joseph's made regular visits, and even occasionally a red hat or two moved among the ancient Buddhist lanterns and Shinto gods.

Aunt Takamine came back once during the war to visit Hilde and the grandchildren at the lake cottage and to show Sho-Foo-Den to Charlie. It was a wistful visit for Caroline. Eben was no longer managing the factories. He was still a Japanese citizen, although he had from his first year lived almost continuously in the United States. Japan was now our terrible and dreaded enemy. Eben was not a Nisei and he could have been interned, but he was not and his mother was grateful for this. In the interest of the war effort, however, he voluntarily relinquished control of his own business. "I sometimes wonder," said Caroline Takamine to me, fanning herself with a small Japanese fan and speaking in a voice like wind bells, "I sometimes wonder if Admiral Perry knew what he was about when he sailed into Edo Bay. That way of life is all gone, a better way, gone forever."

I bowed my head. At this point Japan held the majority of the islands in the Pacific, except Hawaii and Samoa. Japan had engulfed Asia and the Pacific.

During this same visit to Merriewold I overheard a conversation between Mother and Aunt Takamine. Mother had been vehemently condemning the wife of a world-famous man whose infidelities were notorious. Mother spoke with passion.

"She should divorce him," said Mother. "She is condoning his conduct. She is making it harder for every married woman. If wives will accept this, then that is what they are going to get. She should not forgive unfaithfulness."

"Oh, no, no," said Aunt Takamine, softly and sadly. "Oh, no. She has made her choice. She is standing by her family and her husband. She may not forgive, but she stands by."

"Then she cannot really care. She has no pride," said Mother, who was fiery and zestful, also inflexible, and who considered her own divorce of seventeen years standing inexplicable. She looked toward the lake shore that she had known for so long. She heard again the thrush, Father's whistle.

"Oh, yes, she cares," said Caroline. "It is her pride that makes her able to endure this. She has never herself taken a young lover, and who would not be pleased to have as mistress such a rich and famous lady, the wife of a world-famous figure. She has never once hurt his name. The depth of suffering and humiliation she has endured no one will ever know. She has been down to hell and back many times. Of this I am sure. But her conduct is unblemished. This is another kind of love. Don't you think her husband recognizes that?" She rose and stood, looking through the porch screen toward the pines.

Mother said softly and with iron, "She lets down the code."

"Oh, the code. That," said Caroline.

"Yes, that."

My wicked and curious instinct pricked me to believe that Caroline was speaking of herself. The infinite quiet sadness in her voice, the exhaustion, the absence of hopeful energy all revealed personal grief. This attitude, whether recognized or not, was Japanese and feudal. No Samurai's wife ever spoke more traditionally. This was not what her mother, Mary Beatrice, had taught her. This Caroline had found out for herself.

I walked home with Mother past the Cohens', now the chemist's, Hugh Darbey's, past the Gordons', now the O'Connors', whose daughter was waiting for her bridegroom, John Pitman, to come back from the South Pacific (he didn't come back), past the Clarkes', whose beautiful grandson married Fred Alexander's daughter and was shortly to be killed in France. We walked to where the road led to the old golf course. She stopped and her old blue eyes filmed over and she shook her head. I spoke very softly.

"Aunt Takamine has a new life, Mother."

But Mother had pride.

"Come along home."

Since the spring day she had walked out of the Hollywood home, Mother had never spoken to Father, not one single time.

The thrush called again the three notes of Father's whistle.

On March 20, 1973, by virtue of the McCarren-Walter Immigration Act, Ebenezer Takashi Takamine became a citizen of the United States, the first Japanese in Bergen County, New Jersey, to be naturalized. Five months later, on August 28, six days after his sixty-fourth birthday, he dropped dead of a heart attack.

The doctors kept Eben's death from Caroline, who was dying herself in Arizona, but she guessed. "Eben's gone to God. I know it. Eben's with Jo, my darling's ahead of me." She drifted into senile babbling.

Caroline's final illness was long and her husband waited on her with unceasing and tender devotion. She died in his arms. The Bishop of Tucson officiated at her funeral. Her body was brought East by Charles to be buried beside the Doctor and Jo, Jr., and beside Eben. They lie together just as though Charlie hadn't existed. Charles made no plans to be buried with her. "I think he would have felt like an interloper," said Little Bea. Caroline was really Takamine-san to the end.

Aunt Nan Moody got tired of "hotel-keeping." Her grandchildren were grown and she longed for a simpler life. Sho-Foo-Den was once more put up for sale.

John Moody had loved Merriewold very much and he had cherished Sho-Foo-Den, although I think he didn't understand it at all. But he was a kind of godfather to the Club and he shouldered their annual debts, which were invariably offered to him to shoulder; with great good nature he paid off. When he finally went away the Club members had to face reality.

Strangely enough, John Moody did not offer Sho-Foo-Den to

the then surviving son, Ebenezer, nor even mention the sale to him, nor to Jo's children. He offered it to another neighbor, George Abbott, the director, but Abbott was advised against buying by his real estate consultant. The palace was on the way down, he was told. (Abbott now has a very pretty cottage made out of the Takamine boathouse.) Sho-Foo-Den was then offered to the Merriewold Club—buildings, forty acres of land, gardens, carvings, stone figures, farm, and all—for $25,000. The governing board of the Club did not think it worth $25,000. It was sold at a somewhat higher figure to a real estate operator in Monticello who claimed he wanted it for his family.

The new owner turned it into a motel. More buildings were added, a plastic swimming pool and manifold arched red bridges. A good part of the trees were sold for timber. In the interest of sprightliness the six-hundred-year-old wood carvings were painted over in cheerful colors. "Desecration," said the plain-spoken Jane George to the pleased, proud, and complacent landlord. Several of the smaller ancient garden figures have disappeared—likely stolen. The gardens are gone. In our youth the rhododendrons were just head-high and glossy. Now, naked and scraggly, they look like rows of ostriches, all secrets revealed through their scrawny legs. The cornfield opposite the Georges' is gone, replaced by a golf course, the greens of which take all the water. No more dragon fountain, no more moss-padded sluiceways or spitting bronze frogs. The little lake is now a mud puddle.

The cars rush by at the Two Ends. There are no Ends. No one walks to anyone's house—not even to the next-door neighbor. The cars rush by all the time.

Bea never recovered from Jo's death. After a while she married a man who broke her heart. Love had little to do with it. I think her golden time had been here in the woods with her foolish and fascinating mother, who married and unmarried with quicksilver caprice. The last one, the violinist, thirty-one years her junior, unfortunately reverted to his own generation and Beth had to go questing again, but Bea never did. Bea was faithful. I saw her face on the hospital pillow, transfigured as she remembered, as her poor, misshapen hands, twisted with rheumatoid arthritis, tried to clutch the mountain laurel I brought her. "He was so greatly gifted," she said, her deep blue eyes under their heavy brows misting over, "and he was—well, Jo. We all knew what Jo was—like nobility."

The countryside has changed in forty years. Our beautiful Neversink has become polluted. ("Running garbage," says a local paper.) Mongaup Falls, which was the best landmark in our part of the state, is in a metal container and provides the electric power for all of Sullivan County. The beautiful pouring column of water, the Indian wilderness is gone. Now, among cement ramparts and pipelines, it is impossible to find. Where it had been, it just isn't. But our bathrooms are lighted and we have TV.

Monticello has become the summer haven particularly for taxi-drivers from New York. Between Decoration and Labor days the one-room, rented cottages clustering like mushrooms provide privileges to a communal plastic pool and a view of Route 42, down which roar at eighty miles an hour day and night cars bound for supermarkets and the new race track. These cottages rent for one thousand dollars a month.

Monticello is bustling with touts, pimps, drug pushers, and muggers. Monticello is dangerous.

The pleasure complexes known as Grossinger's, Concord, The Laurels, bring delights that none of us ever knew.

The terrain itself has changed.

What has disappeared from our forest are open fields—the forest encroaches—wild cats, whip-poor-wills (one summer suddenly there just were no more), snakes of all kinds (rattlers, grass, garter, and king), fireweed, red wood lilies, wild orchids, lunar moths, puffball mushrooms, chestnut trees (in 1911 there were a chestnut blight that killed every adult tree in North America—no sapling has grown to maturity since), silence.

Also the people. They've disappeared—the permanents—or moved, all the old proud pioneers, the Kings, the Felters, the Moors, the McCormacks, the Mapes, the Kinneys, the Soeles, and the Kleins.

They're remembered by their kin. When Mrs. King or Mrs. Soeles got old and something sagged on her or stretched or broke too far for repair, what happened to her? Did they throw her away? Did her children look after her when she couldn't work for them, when she couldn't work for two dollars a day? What happened to her? The weeds cover the ruins of her house. The land, of which they owned a lot and which afforded them no sustenance except wild berries three months a year, did, as Henry George promised, get valuable, and now the children and grandchildren live better; carpeted and heated houses, TVs and cars. They're educated and they have their teeth. I don't know about the drinking. It's not rotgut behind the woodpile at any rate. But the pride and the unconquerable honesty. That, of course, is different too.

For years old white-haired, sad, beautiful-eyed Fred Felter could be found hanging about the country bars. He had no occupation. He never married, for naturally no girl could trust him. Then he got old and ailing and whining—a ruin. Then he too disappeared. Mae McCormack became rich. She was extraordinarily shrewd, intrepidly stingy, and lucky. The telephone had come to the wilderness and she played the stock market.

What has grown scarce are red salamanders, trillium, pink moccasin flowers, foxes, bears, bats, and the white deadly amanita or "destroying angel," snapping turtles, domestic help.

What has become abundant are the day lilies, tawny hemerocallis, banks of them, by the open fields, unknown in my youth or rare, since naturalized.

What has become overabundant are mosquitoes, red deer, cottages, trailer camps with their inhabitants and refuse, and gypsy moths; the forest is fighting for its life against the gypsy moth.

What endures are the trees, self-replenishing, zestful, the young ever-renewing growth.

And the immutable rocks.

In the spring of 1950 there had been a hurricane and many pine trees went over. Mae McCormack said it sounded like a barrage of artillery. The pines have very shallow roots and they cracked as they fell. The then-president of our Club decided it would be profitable to sell the lot. But the lumberer wanted not the fallen trees but the standing ones, nearly two hundred years old, and he took them for three thousand dollars. He ran out of money and defaulted on all payments and all the trees were left, a wasteland, lying where they had been felled. And there was daylight and rubbishy weeds where there had been silence and mystery. Our Pine Grove was destroyed and we not a penny the richer. This is the way the leaders of the Club acted in those days.

Now and then I go up past the wasteland of the Pine Grove to the old golf course. The trees grow tall on the links. One can only see glimpses of St. Joseph's dormitories and the small ridge of Pennsylvania mountains. In the rank meadow grass the huckleberry bushes stand head-high. One steps over deer droppings and the spoor of bear who come for the berries. The bees hum daylong. It is sunny in this place and quite quiet. Vandals have been at the teahouse; the weather first, of course, but the house was cunningly wrought and for fifty years resisted the terrible cold and wind. But it could not withstand the boys from the nearby summer camps. They smashed the glass first, then broke the roof. The rains and snows did the rest. Not one stick rests on another—all is open and rotted away. I pick up hand-forged nails quite rusted through and the pretty bronze rosettes that studded the rafter joists, and in the grass and clover I find the long, beautiful roof beams; hand-hewn, the cuts of the adze still upon them and marked with a carpenter's brush in black ideographs, and beside these I see quite clearly stenciled in American ink, "St. Louis —1904."

Epilogue

❧ Somehow we all knew it was to be the last, that glorious autumn of 1914. "This is the most beautiful time of the whole year," Mother said as she looked around in a kind of wonder at the yellowing ferns. "The air is like wine and the rotting ferns—" The sky was high blue and absolutely flat—flat as enamel—the gold trees cut out against it as though with scissors. Not a leaf stirred. In the reflected green and gold light of the deep afternoon there was a sudden green rush of fern, untouched yet by frost, still verdant, still sweet-smelling, and puffs—cushions of moss, green as Imperial satin. On this the rosy little mushrooms bloomed. Occasionally an acorn dropped, and silently, all through the windless air, the yellow leaves drifted down, golden, golden, falling forever. They made a sound like a pricking, a sort of tinkling. It was the sound of time.

I walked the three miles to the station with the boys. You can be sure I did—I wasn't going to ride with the women. Mother carried my best hat. Margaret wore hers, of course, very jauntily, and Margaret rode. She rode with all the grown-ups in the wagon with Fred Felter driving. We were the last of the summer visitors to leave.

We waited in between lives at St. Joseph's station for the down-the-track whistle. How many springs this little "toot" had heralded! How many beginnings, how many new ways, new leaves, new air untried, feet on the rocks, feet learning, young legs. How many!

The station was small and important then; now it's domestic, with geraniums, a cute little house, impotent. They ripped the tracks up one summer and threw away the Ontario & Western. The roadbed is a blind way now, off to nowhere from nowhere, rather pretty and very wild. But then it was taut, then it was challenging, with soot and effort, focused on the prospect of summer ahead or acrid with autumn and the prospect of city winter, the sad time. But no matter which, still strenuous.

It was always baroque autumn when we went away. There was blood in it. The going away seemed a mystery, a going away from the enchanted land, a sealing off. There is a photograph of us all at the station on that day, Mother quite smart in a city suit. I remember she had washed the long moiré bows of her little hat in milk to make them stiff—she had a slightly dairy odor which she countered with violet water. Aunt Bettie wore an outrageous hat, all askew, the round hatpin jabbed among the hatpin holes; but she looked very bright and expectant, very birdlike. Darling Mamie in her Sunday black net meringue, and Allie, practical, alert, bustling, pulled in, pulled up, girt. All the young wore the listless, impatient, nonplused expression children acquire when told to pose, with only Baby Margaret, smart and pretty and absolutely in the middle of the moment and absolutely in front of the camera. Elizabeth is there and I am there but grimacing, my hat for once on straight.

"Do you remember California in September?"

The blue sky behind the golden trees, the last morning, and all the children squinting in the sun. And there was going to come at any moment the prophetic toot. (Oh, how I've lain in bed at night and heard the crying of the trains in the wilderness, that sound that has now gone from our countryside.) It was going to come, never fear. We were going to be for it.

What was going to come?

It.

Well, why not? What then?

Mother is gone, Aunt Bettie, Mamie, Allie, and young John, young John on an atoll in the Pacific.

I would never again be able to find the secret spots of Merriewold that I knew so well in my dreams; where I danced the lost dances; where I died.

> In wreathed dust my hair lay quiet,
> My hair lay thin, the thin dust by it,
> But the top of the forest was flat with wind.

There were landmarks of the underlife, true to all periods of my life, but located in the Merriewold woods. As was the fear, the knowledge that it would end, the fear of the cutting down of the trees, of paved streets, wilderness gone, secrecy gone, freedom, the unknown, the unexpected, gone. Death.

Well, why not?

And was it?

> Oh green in the wild-wood laurel trees grow
> And thick they nod by the paths and slow
> And the night will lie big in the bosky lane.

I always was most alive in the woods. My hair got redder. I moved directly, like an animal. I was quiet, I listened. I knew about waiting. I liked waiting. I relished it. I understood about

Mrs. King, Mrs. Soeles, the Felters. I became permanent like them. I was there.

But the reminders were there too, the real statement, the beauty remained. Unmade, unformed, the use of my life was to be unmade; I dared not stand in those woods. I dared not lie in the night and hear the forest or look up to the sky. (Mother used to walk with Father holding hands and there would be nothing to guide their steps but the strip of sky between the treetops. That was in the dark of the moon. When the moon came out, my God, you could see color!) But I couldn't bear it. I couldn't stand the waste.

> I woke in the night
> And my breath came hot,
> I touched the wall beside my cot,
> I touched my linen counterpane.
> I woke in the day
> And my breath came short,
> The gardener was rolling the tennis court
> And the nursery floor was all wet with rain.

Young womanhood passed, virginity passed, the passionate years, all wasted. I had lovers, bonny boys and ardent, but there was never peace. Flitting back and forth, Mother settled in with me, just as I had dreamed when I went home in the gray dreams. We were a twosome, Mother and I, although I didn't live with her. I didn't dare to. I came back to Merriewold briefly, but only to flee again—London, Paris, Copenhagen, Los Angeles, New York. You couldn't say my life wasn't full. At the heart was the listening for the train crying at night, listening for the lonely loon, listening, alone.

Sing, sing, sing it away.

I got married, but there was a war and I was again alone. During that whole time I went up to Merriewold, I think, only four weekends. But during this time I committed two acts of vandalism to try to get rid of the doom-hold of the past, the drugging of the ferns. I had my grandfather's roll-top desk, on which he'd written his successful but poor plays, taken out into the forest and lost. Father later asked me about the desk several times, and I always lied. I served the upright piano in the same way. The mice had lived in it for generations. It was toothless, and its scale was outside of music. But to throw away a piano! Like a living thing, like a member of the family. Good-bye, Mr. Meyerhofer, and Aunt Bettie with her long, delicate fingers and her birdlike glances, and Elizabeth who still in her forties took piano lessons (it filled in the time), and Mother singing Mozart and Father singing Debussy:

> Les donneurs de sérénades
> Et les belles écouteuses

Good-bye to the music of my childhood.

I absented myself from the house at Merriewold that day when they took the piano away. And when I got back the room seemed much bigger and better.

And then the war was over and my husband came home and we had a baby. That was in the spring.

Very early that summer I took my bridegroom to Merriewold. We'd been married three years, but he'd not been able to come to my woods because of the war.

We arrived in the deep evening. The slamming doors of the car sounded very loud. We stepped out and then the smells assailed us: young fern, pine, penetrating rotten wood, damp with the azaleas wild and sweet, the searching smell of fresh roots, of earth, damp; it could be death; it was also life. A whip-poor-will called. Down there, down there, the presence waited. Bats flickered across the slate-colored sky.

We staggered up the path under our bundles, bending the low overgrown branches from our faces. Then we stamped through last October's leaves on the hollow porch (something rustled underneath), turned the old, old skinny key and went in. Damp, damp, forgotten and forlorn. Field mice had been there, the shrews, possibly something worse. We turned on a light. Everything was in a jumble. But then the gentle night air came in and the smell of the acres of ferns and flowering ash. A friend scampered over the roof. And we shut the door. But the fragrance had got inside.

We lay in Mother's bed, in the big brass bed, in Father's bed. The window curtains stirred. The night voices occurred, the whole nocturnal, secret industrious adventure.

His breathing came slow and regular. Mother and Father were young again. Margaret and I had the whole of the world, the whole of the summer, tomorrow morning in front of us.

It was beginning. ⫸